About the Author

Mr. Wannall is a native of Washington, D.C. After receiving his law degree from Columbus School of Law, now part of Catholic University of America, in 1942, he was admitted to the D.C. Bar the same year and entered the FBI as a Special Agent, from which he retired in 1976. All but five of his years in the Bureau were spent at FBI Headquarters in the Intelligence Division, which was responsible for all FBI operations regarding intelligence, counterintelligence, counter-terrorism, security, espionage and related matters. His last position was head of the Division as an Assistant Director of the FBI, and in this capacity he served as the Bureau's representative on the United States Intelligence Board, as well as one of its spokesmen before Congressional committees, civic and other groups.

(continued on back flap)

The Real
J. Edgar Hoover
For The Record

Ray
Wannall

TURNER PUBLISHING COMPANY
Paducah, Kentucky

TURNER PUBLISHING COMPANY

Copyright © 2000 Ray Wannall
Publishing Rights: Turner Publishing Company
All Rights Reserved.

Bill Schiller, Editor
Herbert C. Banks II, Designer

Library of Congress Catalog Number: 00-101690
ISBN 978-1-68162-330-6

This book or any part thereof may not be reproduced without the written
consent of the author and publisher.

This publication was produced using available material. The publisher regrets
it cannot assume liability for errors or omissions.

Additional copies may be purchased directly from the publisher.

Dedicated to my wife, Trudie,
whose support and forbearance
during my service as an FBI agent
made my career possible and enjoyable,
and whose counsel and assistance
helped give life to this book.

Ray Wannall

TABLE OF CONTENTS

ACKNOWLEDGMENTS

This book was undertaken at the suggestion of renowned author William B. Breuer. In 1996 when Bill and his wife, Vivien, were gathering material for his 29th book, *Vendetta!*, at his request I sent him a lecture I had given, from which he was able to draw a bit of information. In commenting on this, Bill paid me a high compliment. He said, "Ray, why don't you tell the story about the real J. Edgar Hoover? You don't write like a lawyer." (I do have a legal background.)

In January 1997, I began to follow his suggestion and this book is the result. I cannot justifiably record all the extensive and much needed help Bill volunteered. If this recitation of my view of Director Hoover accomplishes its purpose--to depict the real man as we who served under him remember him--it will be due in large part to the advice and guidance of my good friend and mentor Bill Breuer.

I appreciate the valued assistance of Patricia G. Solley, Unit Chief, Office of Public and Congressional Affairs, FBI, in working through the pre-publication review process.

To record individual contributions of hundreds of friends in the Society of former Special Agents of the Federal Bureau of Investigation would take several pages. Through association with them since joining the society in 1976, I have been exposed to their comments and observations about the Director which have guided my journey through several chapter. Numerous ex-FBI friends have responded to my specific request assistance. Among them, Leonard Viner has been most generous in his contributions. My special thanks also to Tom Smith, Mark Felt, Deke DeLoach, Val and Don Stewart, Ben Fulton, Art Cammarota, Jack Grady, Jim Nolan, Dick Fletcher and Bernie Wells.

I am grateful to Dave Turner, President of Turner Publishing Company, who agreed to publish this book while other publishers speculated that there had been a surfeit of books on J. Edgar Hoover. He could not have assigned as my editor anyone more helpful and cooperative than Bill Schiller. His expert guidance and counsel in bringing my manuscript to fruition were all I could have asked for, and more. And, you have in your hands evidence of the superiority of Herb Banks of Turner Publishing as a book designer.

AUTHOR'S NOTE

Two months before his death at age 77, J. Edgar Hoover testified before the House Appropriations Subcommittee. Chairman John Rooney stated, "I would like to say to Mr. Hoover that he seems to thrive... on the barbs of those foul balls that have been trying to lay a glove on him." The Director, as he preferred to be called within the Federal Bureau of Investigation, replied, "Mr. Chairman, I have a philosophy that you are honored by your friends and you are distinguished by your enemies. I have been very distinguished."

J. Edgar Hoover was not just the <u>head</u> of the FBI, he <u>was</u> the FBI. One of the most powerful men in Washington, he directed the Bureau for 48 years on appointment by eight successive presidents, Republican and Democratic.

Was Hoover a homosexual, a cross-dresser, a blackmailer as claimed by radicals at both ends of the political spectrum, law violators, anti-anti-communists, and sleazy authors grubbing for financial gain and media attention? How did this feisty, petty, egotistical, formidable, domineering man — as described by one of his lieutenants — manage to stay in office for nearly a half-century? Why would many thousands of his hard working and highly trained special agents over the years tolerate this staunch disciplinarian?

This book faces up to these hard questions about this enigmatic personality. The answers, thoroughly documented, no doubt will be a surprising revelation to those not yet born when Hoover passed away in 1972, or those too young to have a personal recollection of him.

But the men and women of Hoover's generation, patriotic and law-abiding citizens who followed the career of the head of the fabled G-Men, will nod a knowing, "I told you so!"

For 33 years until retiring in 1976, I served in the FBI, first as a special agent, then as an assistant director assigned to headquarters, where I worked directly under Hoover. Over the years, I became aware of how the man thought, reasoned, and acted. This knowledge was cumulative, derived from submitting ideas and recommendations for his approval, reviewing and responding to his instructions and comments, and reacting to his demands for answers to questions and for results.

I conferred with the Director in his office or by phone. On occasion, I attended business and social receptions where he was also a guest, and had the opportunity to talk with him about non-business matters.

I was not a close personal friend of Hoover's. Mainly because of the demanding task that was his — directing the security of this nation against foreign and domestic enemies — he had few cronies. But I was a close observer of him for a quarter century, and in the years following his death, I have talked with scores of former special agents and officials about him, reminiscing and exchanging anecdotes.

Convinced that my views reflect those of nearly all of the thousands of members of the Society of Former Special Agents of the Federal Bureau of Investigation, I have written this book to help set the record straight about the <u>real</u> J. Edgar Hoover.

DISCIPLINARIAN AT THE HELM

In March of 1924, President Calvin Coolidge nominated Harlan Fiske Stone to be his attorney general. Coolige had been nicknamed *Silent Cal* because he used the very minimum of words when he spoke. However, on the occasion, he sent a loud, clear mandate for Stone to clean up the scandal-ridden Department of Justice. As vice-president, Coolidge, a former classmate of Stone's at Amherst College, had succeeded to the presidency via the death of President Warren Harding. He inherited a Justice Department that reeked with problems.

Harding, formerly a small town newspaper editor and politician in Ohio, had been the first Republican to capture the White House in eight years. Following his March 4, 1921 inauguration, he began drawing from men who had been his poker-playing pals and his political board of strategy. One of these men, Harry M. Daugherty, was named as his attorney general. Under Daugherty, the Bureau of Investigation (early name of the Federal Bureau of Investigation) was almost wrecked. The Department of Justice was referred to as the "Department of Easy Virtue."

One of Daugherty's early acts was to fire William J. Flynn, director of the Bureau of Investigation, and appoint William J. Burns in his place. Burns was the President of the William J. Burns International Detective Agency. In the Daugherty shake-up of the department, J. Edgar Hoover (an employee since 1917) found himself transferred from his post as special assistant to the attorney general to the position of assistant director of the Bureau of Investigation on August 22, 1921, his first direct connection with the Bureau.

Burns was no friend of labor. A Canadian newspaper expose charged that his Canada-based detective agency had solicited to spy on manufacturers' workers in their plants or union conventions and report "when, where and how labor trouble will break out." His agents were accused of deliberately fomenting labor discord.

Once Burns assumed his position as head of the Bureau, the strong political influences at work in the Harding administration were soon evident in the agency's files. Burns received a memorandum from a senator which gave a break-down of the party affiliations of the Bureau's agents in the Chicago office. Republicans were listed without comment but the names of democrats had appended comments such as: "Son-in-law of Democratic State Senator;" "Placed by Congressman A, Democrat;" "Democrat and active as such."

A shady figure named Gaston B. Means was appointed by Burns as a Bureau agent two months after Hoover became assistant director and soon became Burns' favorite investigator and close friend. Means and Hoover clashed almost immediately. Hoover asked Burns to order Means to stay out of his office. He didn't like the man's spending habits or morals.

Means was charged by the New York *Sun* of having been an agent of Germany in 1916, and the accused murderer of a wealthy widow. Following his acquittal of the murder, he filed a forged will which would have put her estate practically at his disposal.

Senate hearings disclosed that Bureau agents working under Burns sneaked into senators' private offices in the capitol, opened their mail, and searched their files in an effort to obtain damaging information that could be used to blackmail legislators into halting a Senate probe of Attorney General Daugherty. Means gave shocking testimony, never settled whether true or false, dovetailing with the general pattern of Harding administration corruption splashed across the front pages in America.[1]

In the wake of the blockbuster disclosures against the Department of Justice, Calvin Coolidge fired Daugherty March 28, 1924, and his nominee to succeed him, Harlan Fiske Stone, soon confirmed overwhelmingly by the Senate, began the momentous challenge of returning an aura of integrity to the Department of Justice, and especially to the critically tarnished Bureau of Investigation.

Little wonder, considering the atmosphere in the Department of Justice and the storm warnings it had generated, that Assistant Director J. Edgar Hoover responded to a summons to Stone's office with some feelings of apprehension. They were not allayed when he stood in front of Stone, described as "a large, imposing figure who was seated behind his desk, scowling." Later, all in the Bureau would realize that scowling was a Harlan Stone trademark.

Stone came to the point quickly; he wanted Hoover to be Acting Director of the Bureau. Since Hoover was not yet 30 years old and had only limited investigative experience, the young man was stunned. Nevertheless he had reservations.

"Sir," he said, "I'll take the job, but only on certain conditions. The Bureau must be totally divorced from politics, not a catch-all for political hacks. Appointments and promotions must be based on merit and proved ability."

With a lifted, quizzical eyebrow Stone asked, "Is that all?"

"Just one thing more, Mr. Stone. The Bureau will be responsible only to the attorney general."

"I wouldn't give it to you under any other conditions. That's all, Hoover. Good day."

Noted author William B. Breuer painted a graphic picture of the situation into which the 29-year-old had been launched and how he set about renovating the sullied image of the Bureau:

"No one had ever accused John Edgar Hoover of being a shrinking violet. Within 24 hours, the new acting director began throwing his weight around in an all-out crusade to reconstruct the Bureau from the shambles he had inherited. Hoover knew things were bad, but they were even worse than he had suspected.

Carefully studying the personnel file of each agent, the acting director confirmed what he had long suspected: the Bureau was saturated with hacks who had been given jobs as agents because members of Congress and the executive branch had used the Bureau as a dumping ground to reward the political faithful. Numerous agents had close ties to the underworld, Hoover found, and some were ex-convicts. A few were alcoholics who seldom had bothered to show up for work.

[Attorney General Harry M.] Daugherty's Department of Jus-

tice, Hoover discovered to his dismay, had handed one man an agent's badge because of his expertise in furnishing friendly chorus girls to a top government official. Another agent had received his job because of his skill in singing risqué ditties in front of the Department of Justice Building for the entertainment of federal employees during lunch hours.

Within the first few months as head of the Bureau, J. Edgar Hoover fired more than 100 agents, about two-thirds of the total force. Once he had swept out the flotsam, Hoover set about elevating the standards for the appointment of Bureau agents.[2]

Upon taking over the reins of the Bureau and finding these deplorable conditions, Hoover's somewhat late-Victorian morals orientation shifted into high gear. An early chronicler of Hoover's FBI, Don Whitehead, commented, "There can be no understanding of the modern FBI without an understanding of Hoover's view on discipline."

In May 1925, at the end of his first year as Director, Hoover sent a communication to the ranking official in each Bureau field office, known as the special agent in charge (SAC), to explain why he felt so strongly about agents' conducting themselves with circumspection:

I want to bring to your personal attention certain conditions existing in the Bureau in the past which I do not intend shall continue in the future.... I do know that some years past the forces of the Bureau of Investigation did not enjoy the best reputation... I am strongly of the opinion that the only way whereby we can again gain public respect and support is through proper conduct on our part.... .

I do believe that when a man becomes a part of this Bureau he must so conduct himself, both officially and unofficially, as to eliminate the slightest possibility of criticism as to his conduct or actions.... .

This Bureau cannot afford to have a public scandal visited upon it in view of the all too numerous attacks made... during the past few years. I do not want this Bureau to be referred to in terms I have frequently heard used against other government agencies.... .

What I am trying to do is to protect the force of the Bureau of Investigation from outside criticism and from bringing the Bureau of Investigation into disrepute because of isolated circumstances of misconduct upon the part of employees who are too strongly addicted to their own personal desires and tastes to properly keep in mind at all times and upon all occasions the honor and integrity of the service of which they are a part.[3]

This was a theme to which Hoover was dedicated throughout his long years of service in the FBI. In 1956 he declared:

No one person has built the FBI to the organization it is today. It was built by the loyal, sacrificial efforts of the thousands of men and women who have served in its ranks over the years. I tell my associates repeatedly that one man did not build the reputation of the FBI — but one man can pull it down.

To carry the credentials of the FBI is a trust. It always has been and it must remain so through all the years to come The FBI must always be conscious of its trust. A part of that trust is confidence. Without confidence we cannot possibly fulfill our responsibilities.[4]

By the time I became an FBI agent in July 1942, Hoover's reputation as a strong disciplinarian was well established. He kept us on our toes. We seemed continuously to be going up to the plate against a pitcher noted for his hard, straight fastball who could surprise occasionally with an unexpected curve. Recognizing that the head of a law enforcement and intelligence agency must demand order in the ranks, just about all who served under him accepted this. There were a few agents who caved in and opted out over disciplinary matters. Over the years they have been the source of some of the more disparaging things said about the Director.

Alan H. Belmont made an astute comment about these quitters. If ever there was a legend in his time in the FBI, it was Al. He was admired and respected by agents who worked with him or under his leadership. He became a special agent in 1936 and, after serving in six field offices, being SAC of two of them, he was transferred to Bureau headquarters in 1950 to head its intelligence operations. In 1961 Hoover selected him as assistant to the director, the No. 3 position in the FBI, in charge of all investigations. He dealt with the Director personally on an almost daily basis and knew him well enough to joke with him.

Belmont's observations about dissident former FBI agents is apropos:

Occasionally an employee will turn sour in the FBI and voice his complaints, real and fancied, to the public. He does this, it seems to me, for one or more of several reasons: (1) He wants to write a book and needs controversial material to make the book sell; (2) He can't take the pressure, discipline, and hard work of the FBI and wants to justify his departure to himself and others; (3) By attacking a highly regarded organization or its leader he gains the perverse sort of satisfaction that comes to all who seek to destroy something bigger than they are. At any rate, these misfits seldom adhere to the truth. They build up fantastic stories from gossip and rumor and relay them as fact. An examination of the records of the authors of these so-called inside stories shows they have left the Bureau as a result of some disciplinary action. Some have tried desperately to rejoin the FBI and, failing, have loosed their venom on the Bureau. At any rate, I have no use for these persons. They have failed to measure up to the motto of the FBI — Fidelity, Bravery and Integrity.[5]

Although he was strong on discipline and demanded perfection from himself as well as his subordinates, Hoover was known to have a soft spot. An agent found to have committed a grievous error might receive a letter transferring him from the office to which he was assigned to a less desirable office, possibly one in a distant state. If he could meet with the Director, often the transfer would be canceled. This was particularly so if the agent had an acceptable reason for not making the move, such as a health or other personal problem involving his wife, or children, or parents.

Further, Hoover was not vindictive. Neither did he hold a grudge. There were very few FBI officials, either at headquarters or in the 59 field offices, who had not been disciplined somewhere along their career paths for failing to measure up to the high standards set by him. Once an agent had served a sentence meted out and an appropriate time had elapsed, his slate was cleansed. Those agents who held the most responsible positions were frequently the ones who, in Bureau parlance, had broken their picks most often.

The Director was as quick to commend as he was to condemn. Hundreds of personnel files contained a fair sprinkling of letters of appreciation and evidences of meritorious raises or bonuses for outstanding service.

In the Hoover FBI there was no such thing as rank having its privileges. I was told that, in no uncertain terms, when I had a half-hour conversation with the Director in March 1962. At the time, I was within three months of celebrating my twentieth anniversary as a special agent, but this was my first one-on-one meeting with him.

I had requested an appointment to thank him for his promoting me from assistant chief to chief of the section to which I was assigned in the Intelligence Division at FBI headquarters. When I arrived in his outer office, a receptionist conducted me through a large conference room which had a desk at the far end. This was where Hoover posed for pictures with employees celebrating service anniversaries in the Bureau and with visitors. We moved past that desk to a smaller office in which the Director had his work desk and where he was awaiting my visit. He was quite imposing in appearance, having a military bearing and strong facial features. When he rose to greet me and shake hands, I noted that he was about my height, a fraction under 5 feet 10 inches tall. I had heard he was quite short, but I have considered my own height about average — and that's what I judged him to be. As he welcomed me, he looked me squarely in the eyes, and during our conversation, he continued the eye contact.

After expressing my appreciation for the promotion, I asked whether he had any instructions concerning my new job. It would not be completely truthful to say we talked about this. Whenever he met with any of his personnel, he dominated the conversation, and agents were expected to take copious notes. It took me all of three minutes to speak my piece then sit back prepared to take copious notes. He spent the rest of the 30 minutes talking principally about a problem caused by a top official, and made it clear to me how I was expected to conduct myself as I advanced in the hierarchy.

"Don't get executivitis," he said. "Don't get the idea that you'll sit behind a big desk and tell other people what to do. I expect you to be a leader, to supervise by example, to lead, not simply order others to do the hard jobs. I will hold you personally responsible for the operations under you. If one of your men makes an error, you as well as he will be accountable."

He cited a specific example to emphasize what he meant: "Recently

I was being driven in a snow storm in Pennsylvania to a meeting where I was to give a talk and receive an award. The car had a flat tire. When the agent driving opened the trunk to get the spare, he found that it, too, was flat. Someone had failed to check it. When I returned to my office, I called the assistant director in charge of the division responsible for maintenance of our cars and other equipment. He told me that a clerk thirty-second down the line was responsible. While I didn't expect the assistant director personally to inflate the spare tire, I expected him to assure that it was properly done. I held him responsible and censured him."

The Director didn't say any more. He didn't have to. I got the drift of his expectations, and resolved not to have any flat tires in the ranks.

Early Environment

J. Edgar Hoover, born January 1, 1895, in Washington DC, entered duty in the Department of Justice as a file reviewer in 1917, after receiving degrees of bachelor of laws and master of laws from George Washington University. Two years after that he was promoted to the position of special assistant to Attorney General A. Mitchell Palmer before becoming assistant director then director of the Bureau of Investigation.[1]

The greatest influence in the life of Hoover was his mother, Annie Hoover. She was the cornerstone of the family, a model homemaker, staunch Presbyterian, and a woman with strong ideals. Patriotic sentiment was vigorously spoken around the home and there was constant emphasis on high moral standards, regular church attendance, and strict sobriety.[2]

While the place of Hoover's birth carried the sophisticated name City of Washington, it was, during his early years and certainly at the time of his appointment to head the Bureau of Investigation, simply a series of small neighborhood villages. Often these little villages had identifying names: Foggy Bottom, Georgetown, Swampoodle, Eckington. Brightwood, Petworth, Woodridge. Many of them have clung to these names to the present time. Some areas had no such separate designations. But whether glorified by a name of its own or referred to merely as The Neighborhood, each village usually had its own "Main Street" where life centered, where villagers met, bantered, bartered, bargained, and formed lasting friendships.

In Georgetown (which, indeed, began as a separate city, not just as a village of the Washington it pre-dated) "Main Street" was Wisconsin Avenue, centered on M Street. A few blocks north of M Street on the Avenue there was a "plowpit" beneath the streetcar tracks where each electrically operated car was converted from plow-power to trolley-power before entering the sparsely settled area beyond the village on its stentorian junket to a distant suburban terminal. There were similar plowpits strategically located along the perimeter of the more urban villages.

Families arrived in early 20th-century automobiles to do the weekly Saturday grocery shopping at the Arcade Market located at Park Road on 14th Street, Northwest, which served as "Main Street" for Petworth and several other neighborhoods. That ultra modern market edifice was so advanced in design as to have a parking area on its one-story-high roof for those of the newly popular automobiles and trucks boasting enough horsepower to climb the steep, zigzagging ramp that originated in an alley off Park Road. To test the climbing ability of the family car beforehand, the man of the house would surely have driven it up the city's toughest incline, 13th Street NW from Florida Avenue to Clifton Street, beside the tract which years later became Central High School.

Central, at its former locale at 9th Street and Rhode Island Avenue, NW, was Edgar Hoover's high school alma mater. He was on its debating team, which won 12 decisions in 12 meets, and he went on to become valedictorian of his graduation class.[3]

This was the Washington of villages that nurtured young Hoover. It fostered a much simpler and less sophisticated sort of existence.

However, the bitterness and hostility which the Civil War had generated was still rampant throughout the country, and this was especially true in the nation's capital. Despite the fact that it was the seat of the Union Government during the war, the sympathies of a large segment of the city's population had been with the South, and its defeat certainly did nothing to alleviate a potentially incendiary situation. At the time of Hoover's birth, some people reacted to the conflict, then three decades removed, as many of today's Americans now view the disastrous debacle in Vietnam.

Many former slaves had earlier found their way to Washington expecting to find peace and support in their new freedom. The unspoken rancor toward them, which seemed to emanate principally from the former rooters for the South, colored their thinking and influenced their demeanor. Some of them did not experience all the rights and benefits they felt had been assured by their emancipation, and they looked upon themselves as subservient; in what they considered to be a world still dominated by their former oppressors,

Hoover with debate team at Central High. (Charles Summer School Museum and Archives)

they often acted as such. This deplorable condition carried over well into the next century. It was 80 years after the Civil War before the U.S. Navy on October 19, 1944, permitted the first black woman, Bessie Garrett, to enter the WAVES (Women Accepted for Volunteer Emergency Service).[4]

Other branches of the military services also practiced segregation in their forces during World War II, and public schools were still segregated in the early 1950s.

Particularly during his formative years, this was the atmosphere in which Hoover attended school, in which he was raised. This may well have given rise to some charges of racism leveled against him later in life, charges which were alleged but never proven. His close friendship with and reliance upon a Black special agent bodyguard, James E. Crawford, and a Jewish refugee from Russia, Harry Viner, certainly give the lie to such allegations.

He also was blessed, or cursed — depending upon one's point of view — by the strict moral code of the late-Victorian age which prevailed when he first saw the light of day. For example: a man and woman living together without benefit of marriage would, in his view, be intolerable; he would not condone R-rated motion pictures belching forth filthy language from movie screens across the country; neither would he have had any appreciation whatsoever for high-decibel hard rock music, such as composer Richard Berry's "Louie, Louie," which became a rock anthem, especially at fraternity parties. If asked to name his favorite rock group, chances are Hoover would have said something like, "Mt. Rushmore." In the minds of many of today's generation he'd probably be considered a "square."

This was Hoover's Washington, the environment which contributed to his progress through boyhood and into the man he was when he was called upon to head what was then a scandal-racked law enforcement entity, one he proceeded to make into the most respected agency of its type in the entire world. This was the foundation for his lifetime devotion to a campaign against crime, communism, and any "ism" other than Americanism.

ESCALATING RESPONSIBILITIES

Attorney General Charles J. Bonaparte on instructions of President Theodore Roosevelt issued orders on July 26, 1908, creating an investigative agency within the Department of Justice — the beginning of today's FBI. The early jurisdiction of the agency, known as the Bureau of Investigation, was limited to a few violations involving interstate crimes.[1]

With the outbreak of hostilities in Europe in 1914, and this nation's participation in 1917, a flood of new responsibilities faced the 300 or so agents who were then employed by the Bureau. After its creation, there had been a gradual build-up in the number of criminal violations referred to it for investigation: crimes on Government lands, bank and bankruptcy frauds, forgery matters, and kindred offenses. With the coming of war, concern over potential sabotage activities and alien propaganda grew within the nation, and the Bureau was assigned a new role. No longer were the Bureau's interests limited to the traditional areas of criminal investigation but were now broadened to encompass matters concerning internal security and national defense. In 1917, congress enacted the Selective Service and Training Act, the Espionage Act, and the Trading with the Enemy Act, followed in 1918 by the Sabotage and Deportation Acts. Enforcement responsibilities for the most part fell on the Bureau of Investigation.

To meet the added burdens, the Bureau agent complement was increased to approximately 400. The additional work generated by this build-up resulted in a corresponding increase in the work in that part of the Department of Justice handling wartime matters. It soon became so heavy that a special assistant to the attorney general for war work was hired in 1917. He added many aides to his staff, including J. Edgar Hoover, whom he hired on July 26, 1917, coincidentally, the ninth anniversary of the creation of the Bureau of Investigation.[2]

The increase in the number of agents proved to be insufficient to respond to the spiraling problems. In an effort to solve them, Attorney General Thomas W. Gregory and Bureau Chief A. Bruce Bielaski conceived a plan they felt might suffice to alleviate them. The American Protective League (APL), composed of well-meaning private individuals, was formed as a citizens' auxiliary to "assist" the Bureau of Investigation. In addition to the authorized auxiliary, ad hoc groups took it upon themselves to "investigate" what they felt were un-American activities. Although the intentions of both groups were undoubtedly patriotic and in some instances beneficial, the overall result was the denial of constitutional safeguards and administrative confusion. To see the problem, one need only consider the mass deprivation of rights incident to deserter and selective service raids in New York and New Jersey in 1918. Thirty-five Bureau agents assisted by 2,000 APL operatives, 2,350 military personnel, and several hundred police officers rounded up and arrested some 50,000 individuals; approximately 1,500 were inducted into the military service and 15,000 were referred to draft boards.

It became clear that using citizen auxiliary personnel was not the answer to national defense manpower problems.[3]

The lesson learned from this experience served well at the outbreak of World War II. As soon as the United States began to feel the effects of the conflict which started in Europe in September 1939, President Franklin D. Roosevelt issued a directive vesting in the FBI responsibility for investigating violations of wartime crimes and subversive activities, and calling on law enforcement officers throughout the country to refer any such matters coming to their attention to the FBI for handling.

When Attorney General Harlan Fiske Stone named Hoover head of the FBI in 1924, there was a clear understanding between the two men that the Bureau would function solely as a fact-gathering organization, and its activities would be limited strictly to the investigation of violations of federal laws. Both were determined to prevent any future situation comparable to the so-called Palmer Red Raids.

A controversial post-World War I development was action instituted by then-Attorney General A. Mitchell Palmer whereby hundreds of aliens suspected of advocating the overthrow of the U. S. Government were rounded up and considered for deportation.

This great "red-radical scare" followed closely on the heels of World War I, apparently the social reaction to the aftermath of the war and the Russian Revolution of 1917. The violence and anarchism associated with the activities of such radicals were of concern to the government and the public alike.[4]

Bombs were mailed to government officials in May 1919. The next month a bomb tossed at the home of Attorney General Palmer shattered the library, cracked the ceiling, broke windows, and knocked pictures from the wall. It was so powerful it blew out the windows of the residence across the street of Assistant Secretary of the Navy Franklin Roosevelt, damaged the house next door, shattered windows in the home of Senator Claude A. Swanson, two doors from the Roosevelts, and damaged houses two blocks away. The following year, on September 16, a dynamite bomb in a horse-drawn wagon exploded on Broad Street in New York City killing 30 in the immediate vicinity and injuring 300. The blast also killed an employee in a nearby business office and severely damaged surrounding financial houses.[5]

In an effort to counter the radicals and anarchists, the Department of Justice and the Bureau of Investigation, in conjunction with the Department of Labor, which had primary jurisdiction over immigration matters, used the provisions of the Deportation Statute as an answer.

The following excerpts are from a confidential letter to all special agents and employees of the Bureau from Director W. J. Flynn, dated August 12, 1919:

> The Bureau requires a vigorous and comprehensive investigation of Anarchistic and similar classes, Bolshevism, and kindred agitations advocating change in the present form of Government by force or violence, the promotion of sedition and

revolution, bomb throwing, and similar activities. In the present state of the federal law this investigation should be particularly directed to persons not citizens of the United States, with a view of obtaining deportation cases... .

While you are required to investigate particularly with regard to aliens, you should also make full investigation of similar activities of citizens of the United States with a view to securing evidence which may be of use in prosecutions under the present existing state or federal laws or under legislation of that nature which may hereinafter be enacted... .

These investigations resulted in the much-criticized Palmer Red Raids.[6]

In 1919 Hoover was not yet a part of the Bureau of Investigation which conducted the foregoing investigations. As a Department of Justice attorney he was placed in charge of the General Intelligence Division that had the responsibility of correlating information for the purpose of preparing material for deportation proceedings in court. This included not just information developed by the Bureau but also that arising as a result of deportation hearings conducted by the Department of Labor, in which Hoover had no part. There was widespread criticism of the manner in which the investigations and subsequent deportation hearings were handled. Hoover's later appointment to the FBI position was a clear exoneration of him from any responsibility for the controversial Palmer Red Raids.

For ten years after becoming Bureau director, Hoover adhered without deviation to his commitment that the organization would only gather facts and investigate law violations, eschewing a course of engaging in general domestic security intelligence operations. He held to this despite calls from others that the Bureau become involved. The communist-anarchist problem was ever present and of great concern to the public, Executive Branch officials, and members of Congress. Further, the "red radicals" and anarchists were no longer alone in the field. In the early 1930s National Socialism, the ideology of the Nazi Party of Adolph Hitler, flourished in Germany, resulting in anti-Semitic and anti-racial propaganda being peddled in the United States by Nazi operatives, aliens, and pro-German Americans.[7]

Various elements of Congress were anxious for Hoover to undertake domestic intelligence investigations against both communist radicals and the Nazi movement. Commencing in 1930, Congressman Hamilton Fish, Jr., then Chairman of a House committee investigating communist and radical activities, corresponded with both the Bureau and the Department of Justice regarding proposed legislation which would authorize and empower the Bureau "to investigate the revolutionary propaganda and activities of communists in the United States, and of all entities, groups or individuals who teach or advocate the overthrow by force and violence the republican form of government." [8]

The Bureau's position and response to all such inquiries and requests during this period can be summarized in Hoover's comments on January 19, 1931, when he advised Congressman Fish that he "thought it better not to expand the power of the [FBI], since the Bureau has never been established by legislation, but operates solely on an appropriation bill" and further, that "it would be better to make it a crime to participate in such activities.... . If the Bureau is given special power to investigate [activities not subject to the penal law] it would be in the position of having a mass of material with which nothing could be done, because there is no legislation to take care of it."[9]

Events soon transpired which caused a departure from the policy of restricting investigations to potential violations of laws relating to domestic security. Direct instructions from President Franklin Roosevelt formed the basis for a limited intelligence-type investigation of the Nazi movement in 1934, and, beginning in 1936, for broader investigations of subversive activities in the United States, particularly fascism and communism.[10]

Hoover at the Department of Justice. (National Photo Co./Library of Congress)

By that time, Japan had invaded Korea and Manchuria; the fascist regimes of Hitler and Mussolini were in control in Germany and Italy, respectively; the communist government of Joseph Stalin held the USSR in an iron grip and was exporting communism to the United States and other western nations; and the fascists and communists were vying for superiority in Spain.

On May 8, 1934, Hoover attended a conference with President Roosevelt at the White House at which the attorney general, secretary of state, secretary of the treasury, secretary of labor, and chief of the Secret Service were also present. The topic of concern was the Nazi movement in the country. As ordered by FDR, Hoover two days later instructed all field offices to conduct an intensive investigation of the movement, with particular reference to anti-racial and anti-American activities having any possible connection to official representatives of the German Government in the United States. The investigation was not expanded into any other areas and was closed as soon as the instructions of the President were met. [11]

As of July 13, 1936, correspondence with various parties revealed that the Bureau was not conducting any general intelligence investigations concerning communism and radicals. [12]

During two White House conferences the following month, FDR told the FBI Director that with regard to subversive activities in the United States, "particularly fascism and communism," he was interested in a "broad picture" of their effect on the economic and political life of the country as a whole. Hoover told the President that there was no governmental organization which was obtaining "general intelligence information" upon this subject. FDR, indicating his desire that he be provided with such intelligence, asked what suggestions Hoover might offer.

The Director told him that the congressional appropriation of the Federal Bureau of Investigation contained a provision that it might investigate any matters referred to it by the Department of State; that if the State Department requested such an investigation as desired by the President, the Bureau could handle it under authority it already had through the appropriation grant. FDR expressed his reluctance to have a formal request come through the Department of State "because of the many leaks therein." He said he would put a handwritten memorandum of his own in his safe at the White House and have Secretary of State Cordell Hull orally request this, which he did. FDR instructed that the matter be handled quite confidentially, with only the President, Secretary Hull, and Hoover being aware of it. Upon the conclusion of the two conferences at the White House, Hoover discussed the President's orders with his superior official, the attorney general, and was given his concurrence. [13]

This resulted in the Bureau's becoming the principal intelligence-gathering agency of the Executive Branch of the government as well as its principal criminal investigative and fact-gathering arm.

On October 20, 1938, Attorney General Homer S. Cummings sent a letter to FDR enclosing a lengthy communication addressed to the President by Hoover in which the latter explained what arrangements had been made to provide Roosevelt with the information he had requested during the August 1936 conferences. Hoover reported that he had established within the FBI a General Intelligence Section to collect through investigative activity, and correlate, subversive and "so-called intelligence type" information. He then wrote:

> In order that there may be a clearer view of the detailed information covered, there is set forth the following break-up of the various subjects that appear in the files of the Intelligence Section: Maritime; government; industry (steel, automobile, coal mining and miscellaneous); general strike; armed forces; educational institutions; Fascisti; Nazi; organized labor; Negroes; youth; strikes; newspaper field; and miscellaneous... . Indicative of the present size of this index, there are approximately 2500 names now in the index of the various types of individuals engaged in activities of Communism, Nazism, and various types of foreign espionage.

At the request of FDR, Hoover met him on the presidential special train when it arrived in Pennsylvania Station, New York City, on November 2, 1938. Roosevelt told the Director that he had approved Hoover's communication addressed to him and forwarded as an enclosure to the attorney general's letter of October 20, 1938.[14]

Between the 1936 White House conferences and Hitler's invasion of Poland on September 1, 1939, there was no public disclosure of the fact that the FBI had been instructed to undertake action to gather intelligence on subversive activities. There were thereafter four directives regarding this presidential action, issued publicly, the first on September 6, 1939, just five days after the invasion. It declared that the attorney general had been requested to instruct the FBI "to take charge of investigative work in matters relating to espionage, sabotage, and violations of the neutrality regulations." It concluded:

> To this end I request all police officers, sheriffs, and all other law enforcement officers in the United States promptly to turn over to the nearest representative of the Federal Bureau of Investigation any information obtained by them relating to espionage, counterespionage, sabotage, subversive activities and violations of the neutrality laws.[15]

Once this FBI responsibility was revealed publicly by the President, Hoover was completely forthright in acknowledging the Bureau's intelligence role. In congressional testimony on November 30, 1939, he explained that, in accordance with the President's orders, he had established the new section at FBI Headquarters, and outlined its functions. He said that extensive indices had been established of individuals, groups, and organizations engaged in subversive activities, espionage, or "any activities that are possibly detrimental to the United States." Congress and the American people as a whole were quite concerned about those elements in the country who advocated the violent overthrow of the U.S. Government.

When testifying before a House subcommittee on appropriations on January 5, 1940, Hoover explained how the Bureau had been organized to discharge its responsibilities under the September 6, 1939, Presidential Directive. In his public testimony, he told the Subcommittee that special investigations had been initiated of persons reported to be engaged in subversive activities or in movements detrimental to the internal security. One point he made was: "(I)n the event of any greater emergency coming to our country we will be able to locate immediately these various persons who may need to be the subject of further investigation."

This testimony was given when the Soviet Union and Hitler's Germany were allies in the war against the west, they having signed a non-aggression pact during the night of August 23-24, 1939, a mere eight days before the German invasion of Poland. Communists in the United States took immediate umbrage over Hoover's plans to locate persons for further investigative attention in the event of an emergency threatening the country. At a February 6, 1940, meeting of communist leaders in Washington, plans were made for a campaign having two principal phases: "... one an attack upon the Bureau as violating civil liberties and secondly a personal attack upon the Director." That same day, the campaign got under way when Bureau agents arrested a dozen people who were either admitted Communist Party members, members of known communist front organizations, or openly communist sympathizers.[16]

Mimeographed resolutions flooded trade unions and other organizations charging, "There is every evidence to believe that J. Edgar Hoover is preparing for a repetition of the shameful Palmer raids, in which he participated, with the object of attacking and destroying the various unions." Hoover was defended and supported by the attorney general, a prominent columnist, a prominent member of Congress, and even an attorney who had defended aliens rounded up in the Palmer raids for deportation. The latter in a letter to Hoover recalled that the Director had nothing to do with any irregularities during the raids or harsh treatment of aliens suspected of being communists. He acknowledged that he was present at a hearing when Hoover deplored "as sincerely as we did the incident attending the circumstances connected with arrests of aliens in New England, and I recalled how genuinely I was impressed with your sincerity as well as with your thoroughness in presenting your argument... ." He wrote that he felt it his duty to "say a word in defense of a man unjustly accused of wrongdoing."

During early 1940 the attacks on Hoover snowballed, even finding supporters for them on Capitol Hill, but the support for him as outlined above caused them gradually to subside. They were finally put to rest at a White House correspondents' dinner March 16, 1940, attended by both FDR and Hoover. The President asked, "Edgar, what are they trying to do to you on the Hill?" Hoover replied, "I don't know, Mr. President." Roosevelt grinned, turned his thumbs down, and said, "That's for them." Word soon spread around the city that Roosevelt had turned thumbs down on the attackers of both Hoover and the FBI.[17]

When Germany breached the August 1939 non-aggression pact with the USSR and invaded that country on June 22, 1941, concern echoed throughout the government. President Roosevelt had given a radio address to the nation two weeks before in which he stated that the United States would not wait until Hitler invaded the country to strike back. He proclaimed, "We in America will decide for ourselves whether and when and where our American interests are attacked and our security threatened." The concern was highlighted when, following the German invasion of the Soviet Union, Senator Josh Lee of Oklahoma reminded the Senate, "If Hitler conquers Russia, he will be within shouting distance of Alaska."

Word went out to J. Edgar Hoover to reap the benefits of those special investigations he had described in his January 5, 1940, testimony before the House Subcommittee on Appropriations. On June 29, 1941, what he referred to as "the greatest spy roundup in U. S. history" took place. Thirty-three persons snared in an FBI dragnet were charged with conspiracy to violate espionage laws while acting on behalf of the Nazi government. All were found guilty on assorted accounts.[18]

In 1956, looking back over his 32 years as FBI Director, Hoover made a statement which seemed to portray how he approached the challenges faced when increasing responsibilities resulted in the Bureau's having to add intelligence jurisdiction to its law enforcement duties: "From its earliest days the FBI has reflected the tempo of the times. Its work when carefully observed is like a barometer foretelling the stormy and bright days which lie immediately ahead." [19]

The man seemed to have a certain amount of clairvoyance in his makeup. He appeared to have his finger on the public pulse, to understand what the people wanted and expected of the country's principal federal investigative agency. I discussed this with former Special Agent Richard (Dick) Fletcher of San Mateo, California, who served under Hoover 37 years and had many conversations with him.

"Ray," Dick said, "I remember one of the boss' favorite expressions, 'Only dead fish flow with the tide.' He just seemed to keep several steps ahead of everybody else."[20]

He also recognized that Americans did not want excessive power lodged in the federal government, and he resisted all efforts and talk about making the FBI a national police organization:

> I wish to state emphatically that the FBI is not and never can be a national police organization as long as its development continues to be on cooperative lines. The most lasting contributions made by the FBI have been those which encourage cooperation with local, county and state law enforcement agencies. [21]

And, speaking in the vernacular, Hoover put his money where his mouth was. In 1935 he established the FBI National Academy.

On May 2, 1997, 250 members and friends of the Society of Former Special Agents of the FBI attended a series of events, including a grave side service, to commemorate the twenty-fifth anniversary of the death of Hoover. The official program of events carried a tribute to the deceased Director which conveyed eloquently the value of the National Academy and its contributions to cooperative law enforcement on both a national and international basis. The tribute was submitted by President J. Robert Hamrick of the FBI National Academy Associates:

J. Edgar Hoover understood how important it is for society to have a highly trained, educated, and respected state and local law enforcement, which led to the establishment of the FBI National Academy. His willingness to commit FBI resources to provide needed training and to share the FBI's expertise, to develop a higher level of professionalism within the ranks, and to foster cooperation among all levels of law enforcement truly operationalized the FBI's motto: Fidelity - Bravery - Integrity. Since the inception of the National Academy in 1935, the FBI has ensured that it has continued as "the institution" to provide that which Mr. Hoover initiated. Today, over 30,000 officers, world-wide, have graduated from the program. The 17,000 active members of the FBI National Academy Associates serve as testimony to the National Academy motto: Knowledge - Courage - Integrity. Mr. Hoover was confident that the National Academy would be an important step in modernizing and professionalizing law enforcement, and his thinking was correct. The National Academy is the model for the true spirit of law enforcement academic excellence, cooperation, and partnership. Mr. Hoover is the father of modern law enforcement and his influence remains with us today.

We are grateful for his vision and law enforcement leadership.

The Academy which he established to train law enforcement officers, as anticipated by Hoover, fostered a spirit of cooperation between state and local police agencies on one hand and the FBI on the other. This worked much to the nation's advantage when, in 1939, FDR called upon "all police officers, sheriffs, and all other law enforcement officers" to report any information obtained regarding subversion and crimes affecting the nation's security to the Bureau.

A large percentage of the police officers trained in the Academy returned to their respective agencies and advanced through the ranks to head their departments. Bureau agents attended law enforcement training schools on a local basis throughout the United States and conducted nationwide law enforcement conferences. These efforts contributed measurably toward assisting in raising the work of police across the nation to a professional level and engendered the spirit of cooperation needed to meet the challenges of threats to the nation during World War II.

Pro-fascist and pro-communist activities were intensified in the United States with the ascension to power of Adolph Hitler and our diplomatic recognition of the Soviet Union in 1933. Within two years after President Roosevelt ordered the FBI Director to undertake investigation of these activities and provided the authority for him to do so, the FBI had developed a broad picture of these subversive movements. It was two to four years after the Bureau launched its intelligence efforts that Congress, expressing the will of the American people, was able to complete the cumbersome legislative processes and pass statutes directed against these movements, such as the Foreign Agents Registration Act of 1938, the Voorhis Act, and the Internal Security Act of 1940 (Smith Act).

In the years following World War II, as the wartime alliance with the Soviet Union cooled down, the country saw the cold war develop. If anyone today believes the Soviet threat at that time was imagined or created for the sake of lending impetus to the anti-communist legislation generated in the early 1950s, he has only to refer to developments documented by history. Among them:

• By 1948, Estonia, Latvia, and Lithuania had been absorbed by the USSR, and Romania, Bulgaria, Hungary, and Poland had already been reduced to Soviet satellite status.

• In 1948, Czechoslovakia was subverted, drawing what British Prime Minister Winston Churchill described as an "iron curtain" across the face of Europe.

• In the same year, in an effort to force the United States and Great Britain to leave West Berlin to which their forces had access under an agreement with the Soviets, the USSR halted all surface traffic into that area. Troops of the two allied powers launched an airlift, moving more than 2,343,000 tons of food and coal into that portion of the beleaguered city between April 1, 1948, and September 30, 1949. By that time the blockade had been lifted and the Soviet attempt had been defeated, but it had "heated up" the cold war and led to the formation of the North American Treaty Organization (NATO).[22]

• In the summer of 1948 in Washington, Elizabeth Terrill Bentley, a secretary in an import house, and Whittaker Chambers, a writer for Time and Life magazines, testified separately before the House Committee on Un-American Activities (HCUA). Both were defected Soviet intelligence service couriers. During their testimony, they named highly placed U.S. government officials as Soviet spies. More than two dozen of these Americans were named by Bentley, and the list was increased in length by revelations of Hede Massing, divorced wife of Soviet spy Gerhart Eisler. Here are but a few of these home-grown traitors:

Alger Hiss, an adviser to President Roosevelt at the 1945 disastrous Yalta conference where FDR and Winston Churchill obtained nothing more substantial from Stalin than a declaration prescribing support for "democratic elements" and "free elections" to produce "governments responsive to the will of the people." Based on this, Stalin was able to establish a virtual fiefdom of Eastern Europe. In return for intervention in the war against Japan (within three months of the expected German surrender), it was agreed he would have control over two Japanese islands and certain facilities in Southeast Asia plus membership in the to-be-organized United Nations. Following his advisory duty at Yalta, Hiss, three months later, became the guiding secretary general at the San Francisco conference that adopted the United Nations charter. Consider the advantage the Soviets attained through Hiss as a result of the strategic positions he occupied in influencing both U.S. policy at Yalta and U.N. policy at San Francisco.[23]

Harry Dexter White, chief assistant to Secretary of the Treasury Henry Morganthau, Jr. The latter was known for having formulated the so-called Morganthau Plan, which aimed at crippling the industrial potential of the Soviet's bitterest enemy, Germany, after World War II, for all practical purposes turning it into an agricultural nation. The influence of the USSR on this proposal through Morganthau's chief assistant is readily apparent. The plan was never put into effect.

Laurence Dugan, a colleague of Hiss' at the Department of State. Ten days after he was publicly revealed to have been a Soviet spy, he apparently committed suicide in New York City by jumping from a Manhattan hotel window.

Nathan Gregory Silvermaster, Russian-born official of the Farm Security Administration. He with his wife and many associates in government formed one of the networks which spied for the Soviets.

Lauchlin Currie, administrative assistant to FDR. Currie was described by Whittaker Chambers as a "fellow traveler." Elizabeth Bentley, testifying under oath, said that in his position at the White House he had inside information on government policy, such as the U. S. attitude toward China and other nations, and once relayed to the Soviets information to the effect that the American government was on the verge of breaking their code.

• To cap the climax, on September 23, 1949, the people were shocked when President Harry Truman announced that the Soviets had exploded an atomic device.

The Berlin blockade tested America's mettle but resulted in victory in the confrontation with the communist empire. However, even before it was over, Americans faced the startling revelations of Chambers and Bentley ... proof that the highest levels of the federal government's Executive Branch were penetrated by Soviet spies and/or sympathizers. The Truman Administration reacted by trying to discredit the two defected Soviet intelligence service couriers or, in the alternative, throw a blanket over the mess.

White House staffer George M. Elsey on August 16, 1948, after consultation with Department of Justice officials, reported to Presidential Advisor Clark M. Clifford that the consensus was, "The President should not at this time make a statement regarding the 'spies'." It was concluded that the Justice Department should make every effort to ascertain if Whittaker Chambers was guilty of perjury, and "Investigation of Chambers' confinement in mental institution" should be conducted.

As for Bentley, Elsey's report stated:

The Attorney General will furnish the White House with a description of the data Miss Bentley claims to have obtained for Soviet agents during the war, and the White House should endeavor to determine how much of this information was freely available to the Soviet Government through routine official liaison between the U.S. and the U.S.S.R. The purpose of this would be to make it clear that Miss Bentley was not successful in transmitting secret material to the Russians that they did not already have.

This leaves one wondering whether the White House, having had someone as sympathetic to the Soviets as Lauchlin Currie on board, was as interested in a cover- up to protect the Soviets as it was to protect the Administration.

Whatever the objectives of these efforts, the concern over the permeation of the U.S. Government by Soviet spies did not abate among the American electorate. Five months after the Chambers and Bentley revelations, President Truman cast about for a reason to vent his spleen on what he called "the do-nothing Congress" because of its failure to give him full support. Referring to the House Committee on Un-American Activities (HCUA) as the "House Un-American Activities Committee" (HUAC) to convey the thought that it was the Committee's own activities which were un-American (a ploy often adopted by Committee opponents), he sent this memorandum to the attorney general on December 16, 1948:

I wonder if we could not get a statement of facts from the FBI about the meddling of the House Un-American Activities Committee and how they dried up sources of information which would have been accessible in the prosecution of spies and communists.

Their meddling efforts were in fact a "red herring" to detract attention not only from the shortcomings of the 80th Congress but also contributed to the escape of certain communists who should have been indicted.

I'll appreciate it if you will look into this a little bit and we will talk it over in the Cabinet meeting tomorrow.[24]

The outcome of the Cabinet discussion is not known; but it is known that the FBI had been discreetly investigating the matters revealed by the former Soviet intelligence service couriers for more than three years — since an interview with Bentley November 7, 1945, when she named 27 persons still employed in the U.S. government. This information was furnished to the White House and attorney general at that time. Disclosure of the subjects' identities to the public, thus alerting them to the fact that they had been compromised, did not take place until nearly three years later. The chances of sources being dried up and communists fleeing to escape indictments were remote.[25]

Thirteen months after Americans learned of the success of the Soviets in penetrating the government in Washington, President Truman had to make the announcement on September 23, 1949, that they also had the A-bomb. This shook the foundations to which America's feelings of security had been tethered. Prior to this, the U.S. alone had the expertise necessary to make an atomic bomb and was in a position to discourage a sneak attack by a nation that had called the United States "the main enemy." This deterrent advantage was now lost.

This, then, was the background for that period following World War II which today's apologists for communism in the United States derisively refer to as the "red scare."

During that era, Hoover was deep into the investigation of the turncoats who worked clandestinely for the USSR and against their own country: It was 1950 before Congress was able to process and pass the Internal Security Act of that year (the McCarran-Walter Act). It was four more years before Congress reacted with the Communist Control Act of 1954. These statutes in effect supported and underpinned the investigative authority conferred upon Hoover by Roosevelt in 1936 and later confirmed by future presidents.

In the late 1950s and early 1960s, Ku Klux Klan-inspired violence began to increase. Lacking statutory jurisdiction to investigate local acts of violence, Hoover first offered cooperative assistance to local authorities having primary responsibilities (laboratory and fingerprint examinations and coverage of out-of-state leads). Later, through authority issued by the attorney general under whose jurisdiction the FBI operated (and still does), Hoover was able to expand his assistance to local authorities. This included close checks on the activities of Klan members, physical surveillances, and interviews calculated to let Klan leaders know that their "secret" organization was not secret from federal authorities.

This increased assistance was possible after Department of Justice officials became concerned in mid-1964 about the spread of KKK activity and violence in the deep South. Attorney General Robert F. Kennedy advised President Lyndon B. Johnson that because of the "unique difficulty" presented by the situation where "lawless activities" had the "sanction of local law enforcement agencies," the FBI should apply to the Klan the same "techniques" used previously "in the infiltration of communist groups." He was referring to the Counterintelligence Program (COINTELPRO) which eventually pulled the teeth of the Communist Party.[26]

By 1964 Congress was able to guide through the legislative processes a strengthened Civil Rights Act, and another such act in 1968, demonstrating the strong determination of the nation to oppose the type of discrimination the Klan practiced in its most violent form.

As a matter of historical interest, the type of interviews conducted with Klan leaders did much to discourage the types of discriminatory activities Congress found sufficiently abhorrent to outlaw by federal statute. They were also, be it noted, precisely the COINTELPRO-type interviews and other counterintelligence actions looked upon with manifestations of horror by the Senate Select Committee to Study Governmental Operations With Respect to Intelligence Activities, chaired by Senator Frank Church of Idaho and usually referred to as the Church Committee. The televised, highly politicized committee hearings in 1975 wreaked heavy damage upon the Federal Bureau of Investigation and other members of the United States intelligence community.

Six of the eleven Senators who comprised the membership of the committee had their sights set on the White House: Frank Church, Walter Mondale, Gary Hart, Charles Mathias, Howard Baker, and Richard Schweiker. The staff director, William G. Miller, took note of the fact that problems arising within the committee derived from the "natural clash of egos and ambitions," especially as a result of the "large group of aggressive litigators who are seeking in part glory and are prone to the phototropism of televised hearings." According to Miller, Senator Church was "too abuse oriented;" some believed he was "dazzled by the klieg lights" and was going for whatever would attract the cameras which were recording the hearings for media outlets.[27]

The House of Representatives counterpart of the Senate Church Committee was chaired by Representative Otis G. Pike (New York). Known as the House Select Committee on Intelligence, it conducted a public hearing November 18, 1975, on "FBI Domestic Intelligence Programs," most of which had been undertaken during Hoover's lifetime. The hearing had all the earmarks of a three-ring circus. Seven witnesses hostile to the Bureau (including officials of the Socialist Workers Party and the Institute for Policy Studies, both organizations plaintiffs in multi-million dollar law suits against the FBI) were permitted to testify at length regarding serious allegations against the Bureau, many unsupported and unchallenged. Bureau officials were then called upon to respond to these allegations cold, never before having been advised what to expect at the hearing. Congressman Robert McClory (Illinois) performed yeoman service to the nation's overall intelligence operations. He strongly defended the Bureau's domestic ones, but his efforts might have been compared to trying to sweep back the tide with a broom.

In the Senate, the Church Committee did an in-depth study of FBI intelligence and counterintelligence operations, concentrating on those conducted by the Bureau during Mr. Hoover's stewardship. Ignoring the tenor of the times and the threats posed to the nation's security, the Church Committee held televised hearings on COINTELPRO activities, some of which, presented out of context of the violent times and official demands for action, painted Hoover as a bureaucrat who operated without regard for people's civil rights and, at times, even outside the law. Its final report became the public starting point for much of the subsequent vilification of Hoover and the FBI.

Aleksandr I. Solzhenitsyn, novelist, historian, and indictor of the "evil empire" in the name of the Soviet people and Russian history, gave a speech at Harvard University in June 1978. One wonders if he had in mind the Church Committee's accusing Hoover of disregarding people's civil rights when he said, "When a government earnestly undertakes to root out terrorism, public opinion immediately accuses it of violating the terrorists' civil rights."[28]

The 1960s brought new threats to the nation's free society. In the last half of that decade members of Marxist-Leninist groups generally referred to as the New Left, and members and supporters of other violence-prone organizations (for example: Black Panther Party, Revolutionary Union, Armed Forces of National Liberation, Black Liberation Army, and the Weatherman, later known as the Weather Underground Organization), participated in protest activities which at times took the form of rioting, looting, bombing, and firebombing. Such activities were met with intelligence investigations which, on occasion, included a limited number of COINTELPRO actions of the types which had frustrated the Ku Klux Klan.

During that decade and reaching into the '70s, there were dissidents who talked of kidnapping Henry Kissinger and visiting heads of state. There were plans to paralyze the nation's Capital by widespread sabotage and an actual bombing inside the Capitol building. Policemen were being ambushed and murdered across the country. Heroin and LSD were being pandered to youngsters. Hundreds of bombs were exploding in the nation. Some of the terrorists responsible openly bragged of their communist beliefs, their ties to or support of unfriendly foreign countries, and their intention to bring down the government by force and violence.[29]

In a frustrating effort to place the activities in a proper perspective, then FBI Director Clarence M. Kelley gave testimony before the Church Committee on December 10, 1975, portraying this violently disruptive period as follows:

> Bomb explosions rocked public and private offices and buildings; rioters led by revolutionary extremists laid siege to military, industrial, and educational facilities; and killings, maimings, and other atrocities accompanied such acts of violence from New England to California.
>
> The victims of these acts were human beings, men, women, and children. As is the case in time of peril, whether real or perceived, they looked to their Government, their elected and appointed leadership, and to the FBI and other law enforcement agencies to protect their lives, their property, and their rights.
>
> There were many calls for action from Members of Congress and others, but few guidelines were furnished. The FBI and other law enforcement agencies were besieged by demands, impatient demands, for immediate action. [30]

Indicative of the seriousness of the problems were figures compiled by the Associated Press showing that, during the first nine months of 1967, racial violence in 67 cities cost 85 lives, injured 3,200 Americans, and resulted in property damage of over one-hundred million dollars.

President Johnson recounted these problems in a television address to the nation on July 24, 1967. In an effort to forestall further urban violence, he described events that led to his sending troops to Detroit during that city's riots. He said, "We will not tolerate lawlessness. We will not endure violence. It matters not by whom it is done, or under what slogan or banner. It will not be tolerated." He called upon "all of our people in all of our cities" to "show by word and by deed that rioting, looting, and public disorder will just not be tolerated."

In a second address to the nation just three days later, the President said that the country had "endured a week such that no nation should live through: a time of violence and tragedy." He declared, "(T)he looting and arson and plunder and pillage which have occurred are not part of a civil rights protest. It is no American right," Johnson said, to loot or burn or "fire rifles from the rooftops." The President then told the American people that those having public responsibilities had "an immediate obligation to end disorder by using every means at our command." He issued a warning to public officials: "(I)f your response to these tragic events is only business-as-usual, you invite not only disaster but dishonor... violence must be stopped — quickly, finally and permanently" and pledged, "we will stop it." [31]

He announced that the FBI would "continue to exercise its full authority to investigate these riots, in accordance with my standing instructions, and continue to search for evidence of conspiracy." [32]

He attracted the attention of Capitol Hill. After conferring with the President, House Speaker John W. McCormick said on July 24 that Johnson had told leaders of the Democratic Party that "public order is the first business of government." The next day, Senator Robert C. Byrd advocated "brutal force" to contain urban rioting and said that adult looters should be "shot on the spot."

The President's television appeals and dire warnings seemed to have little effect. On January 12, 1968, Attorney General Ramsey Clark reported to President Johnson that extremist activity to foment "rebellion in urban ghettos" had put a severe strain on the FBI and other Justice Department resources. Clark called this "the most difficult intelligence problem" in the Justice Department. The following month, President Johnson announced that he expected further turmoil in the cities and "several bad summers" before the nation's urban problems were solved.

Ire over the mounting violence spread on Capitol Hill. On April 12, 1968, Representative Clarence D. Long of Maryland urged J. Edgar Hoover, in a letter and in a public statement, to infiltrate extremist groups to head off future riots, and said that FBI agents "could take people like Negro militants Stokely Carmichael and H. Rap Brown out of circulation."

Meanwhile, during these troubled times in our cities while urban agitators were calling for rebellion, college campuses also experienced a "rising tide of intimidation and violence" in the words of University of Wisconsin faculty members.

The St. Louis Globe-Democrat in a February 14, 1969, editorial titled "Throw the Book at Campus Rioters," described campus disorders then sweeping the nation as "a threat to the entire university educational system." The newspaper called on the attorney general to:

> move now to stop these anti-American anarchists and communist stooges in their tracks. He should hit them with every weapon at his command. The American people are fed up with such bearded, anarchist creeps and would applaud a strong drive against them. They have been coddled and given a license to run roughshod over the rights of the majority of col-

lege students for too long. It is time to hit them with every-thing in the book.

Violence causing damage at U.S. universities quickly escalated. During the period January 1 to August 31, 1969, losses specifically traced to campus disorders amounted to $8,946,972.[33]

Traced to all sources, between January 1969 and May 1970 there were 40,000 bomb threats, 3,000 bombings, $21 million worth of damage to property, and 43 deaths attributable to political violence.[34]

The problems were exacerbated by the fact that most of the violent activity involved state and local crimes over which the federal government had no jurisdiction. To wrap at least some of these local criminal acts within the terms of the interstate commerce, civil rights, or other clauses of the Constitution, the wheels of Congress began to grind when Johnson made his "first-order-of business" pitch in mid-1967; but as noted before, those wheels turn ever so slowly.

The principal avenue open to the government, meanwhile, was the intelligence jurisdiction and responsibilities conferred upon J. Edgar Hoover and the FBI by FDR some three decades before and confirmed by presidents since then. Herbert Brownell, U.S. attorney general from January 1953 to November 1957, defined this jurisdiction and these responsibilities during testimony on June 2, 1981, in a civil action brought against the U.S. government by the Socialist Workers Party. He explained that the FBI performed two functions, one intelligence and the other investigation of cases being prepared for court presentation. The intelligence function was delegated by President Roosevelt, who did not specify the means the FBI was to use in discharging this responsibility. When FDR issued his first directive to the FBI, and in subsequent orders from Truman and Eisenhower, there was no definition of the methods to be used in carrying out the directives. Methods were left to the discretion of the FBI. Accordingly, the Bureau was following presidential orders when conducting intelligence investigations.[35]

In compliance with the presidential directives, the Bureau moved into what was, by almost any definition, a combat arena, to gather intelligence and attempt to prevent deaths, injuries, and the loss of millions of dollars in property damages. The FBI conducted campaigns of an intelligence and counterintelligence nature in a concerted effort to help control and to try to eliminate as far as possible the criminal acts until such time as Congress could outlaw them through legislation. The bombing statutes and the Civil Rights Act, both passed in 1968, took a major step in that direction.

Hoover supported legislation such as the federal bombing statutes. They carefully defined areas in which activities would be deemed crimes against the United States as distinguished from crimes the definition and enforcement of which should remain within the prerogative of the various states. As early as 1956, he had made the following observation:

> *In the United States, the subversive is a lawbreaker when he violates the law of the land, not because he disagrees with the party in power. And anyone who violates the law commits a criminal act even if the motives of the lawbreaker are self-servingly claimed to be political. If we ever permit political*

motives to justify lawbreaking, we shall develop political tyrannies in this country as similar instances have developed tyrannies in other countries.[36]

The FBI endeavor during the riotous days of the sizzling sixties is a prime illustration of J. Edgar Hoover's apparent touch of clairvoyance in understanding what the American people wanted and expected of the nation's principal federal investigative agency. Through it all, nevertheless, he kept his focus on the necessity for law enforcement to operate within the framework of the laws of the land, and primarily through state and local law enforcement authorities.

As frequently as he spoke out against subversives and lawbreakers, he also made it known on many occasions that he supported state's rights and opposed a national police force. During an interview with U.S. News and World Report, published in the December 21, 1964, issue, Hoover said, "I recently made the statement that I am inclined toward being a States' righter in matters involving law enforcement. That is, I fully respect the sovereignty of State and local authorities. I consider the local police officer to be our first line of defense against crime, and I am opposed to a national police force... . The need is for effective local action, and this should begin with whole-hearted support of honest, efficient, local law enforcement." *

The legacy he bequeathed to his successors and their contemporaries who are charged with maintaining law and order was published in the FBI Law Enforcement Bulletin issue of May 1, 1972, the day before he died:

Extremists of all stripes in our society ceaselessly attempt to discredit the rule of law as being biased and oppressive... . To permit such attempts to damage the reputation of our Government by law is, of course, a necessary condition of democracy. While it must tolerate the lawfully expressed views of extremists, its citizens cannot through their own ignorance be entrapped with sympathy for bankrupt doctrines that would lay waste to the foundations of their Nation... . (O)ur Nation's history has been a chronicle of change. But the process of change in a democracy requires discipline and responsibility that will not unleash unrestrained forces that would rip the fabric of our freedoms. That fabric derives its strength through the warp and woof of laws that orderly guide the process of change by defining our individual and corporate duties. Change in our society would otherwise simply result from those who could impose their will on others without regard for the validity of their arguments or the rights of those who do not share their views.[37]

---

* Copyright, Dec. 21, 1964, U.S. News and World Report.

Hoover, Wiretaps, and Bugs

There were two types of electronic surveillances utilized by law enforcement agencies during the years Hoover headed the FBI: wiretaps and microphone surveillances, commonly referred to as "bugs." The former seemed to have inherent characteristics of spying and illegality. The latter did not seem to have acquired as despicable a reputation, probably because its coverage was confined to a limited, prescribed area, while a wiretap revealed conversations between its targeted subject, indeed between anyone using his telephone, and any telephone caller or person being called in the entire outside world.

Investigative agencies had little need, and normally no capacity, to intercept radio communications. And, of course, cellular telephones had not yet come on the scene where, today, with a commercially available monitor altered for the purpose, an eavesdropper can intercept a private conversation when at least one participant is utilizing a cellular phone.

During the 48 years of Hoover's stewardship of the FBI, some who sought to besmirch his reputation or hinder the efficiency of the Bureau in fighting crime and investigating subversion accused him of maintaining a vast network of wiretaps.

When Hoover testified before congressional committees to justify the appropriation being requested each year to maintain the Bureau and its operations, he often cited the number of wiretaps then in operation, usually well under 100. During the Church Committee hearings in 1975, staff members were so convinced that these figures were arrived at by reducing the number of taps just prior to the Director's testimony, that they set out to prove their theory. They demanded a count of wiretaps in effect one month before and one month after Hoover's testimony for a period of several years. Satisfying this demand required the removal of personnel from productive work and their assignment to the project. The results proved that the Committee's suspicions were completely groundless, but this will not be found in its final report.

Throughout his entire career, Hoover's reluctance to use wiretaps was a matter of public record, which revealed how he viewed them. While realistically recognizing the necessity of utilizing them in certain cases affecting the national security and in kidnapping and other serious criminal activities, the fact that he disliked wiretapping was never concealed.

In 1928 the Supreme Court upheld the use of wiretapping and ruled that evidence secured through the use of that technique was admissible during trial testimony. By a 5 to 4 vote, the court found that conversations were not protected by the Fourth Amendment and that no invasion of the defendant's house was involved in the wiretapping. When this decision was rendered, among the regulations which were already in effect in the FBI was one providing, "Wiretapping... will not be tolerated by the Bureau." This strict prohibition continued until 1931.[1]

At that time, the Prohibition Bureau, jurisdiction over which had been transferred in the interim from the Treasury Department to the Justice Department, permitted wiretapping. The attorney general, William D. Mitchell, was called before the House Committee on Expenditures in the Executive Departments to explain the inconsistent regulations of two Bureaus in the Department of Justice. He told the Committee that in January of that same year, 1931, he had noted this inconsistency and determined that the same regulations must apply to all. Upon completing his testimony, he ordered Hoover to change his regulation to read: "Telephone or telegraph wires shall not be tapped unless prior authorization of the Director of the Bureau has been secured."[2]

In placing this change into effect, Hoover instructed his headquarters officials not to authorize any wiretap until it had been approved not only by him but also by the assistant attorney general in charge of the case in the Department of Justice, and to get that approval in writing. [3]

When the Supreme Court held in 1937 that evidence obtained by wiretapping in the enforcement of the law could not be used in court, the Department of Justice ruled that the decision had no effect on the FBI's use of this technique since it was utilized for lead purposes only.[4]

Hoover on March 29, 1939, in response to a Department of Justice request, took a strong stand against legislation which would make evidence secured from wiretaps admissible in federal courts. In a memorandum he advised the Department:

> I believe, frankly, that the Department will subject itself to justifiable criticism and potential embarrassment if it approves or endorses any proposed legislation designed to legalize the placing of wiretaps and the utilization of evidence obtained from these taps in Federal Courts... .

> If it appears essential to the Department to draft some legislation legalizing the provisions of the Federal Communications Act with reference to the prohibition against wire tapping, I would suggest that several of the more outstanding lawyers of the United States who are generally considered to be of liberal characteristics be called in for the purpose of drafting the suggested legislation... . [5]

The Director's advice to the Department proved to be on firm ground. A further Supreme Court decision rendered within nine months (December 11, 1939) banned the admissibility even of evidence developed as a result of leads secured from a wiretap, which was known as the "fruit of the poisonous tree" principle. The attorney general issued Departmental Order 3343 on March 15, 1940, prohibiting FBI wiretapping activity. [6]

The smear campaign launched against Director Hoover by the communist leaders on February 6, 1940, was for the obvious purpose of rendering the FBI ineffective in carrying out the internal security responsibilities imposed by President Roosevelt in August 1936. Among charges picked up by the press were: (1) the FBI had indiscriminately tapped the telephones of members of Congress; (2) wiretapping had been used in violation of existing laws; and (3) it had also been used indiscriminately and in violation of fundamental civil rights. On March 13, 1940, the Department of

Justice released a statement by Hoover in which he denied outright that any such practices had been engaged in "since I have been Director of the Bureau."[7]

Since there seemed to be some question about utilizing wiretaps when discharging responsibilities imposed by Roosevelt's directive, Hoover wanted to make clear his stand and took up the matter with Attorney General Robert H. Jackson. On March 18, 1940, Jackson issued a statement to the press which, after stating, "Upon the recommendation of Director J. Edgar Hoover of the Federal Bureau of Investigation," announced that the Bureau would revert to its pre-1931 regulations prohibiting wiretapping. [8]

Hoover utilized graduation ceremonies of the National Academy to convey his philosophy of law enforcement to police officers who were taking the FBI message back to their various agencies across the country. The ceremonies for the 13th session of the Academy were held March 30, 1940, less than two weeks after the press release about the Bureau's discontinuance of the use of wiretaps. He spoke on this occasion of wiretapping and other practices "which could very easily degenerate into the rankest of unethical activities" and declared:

> The records will show that years ago I listed indiscriminate or habitual wiretapping as a thoroughly unethical practice — and I still so list it. No law enforcement officer is deserving of the name if he must resort to the violation of fundamental civil rights... . [9]

It was soon obvious that the discontinuance of wiretapping made it all but impossible to give coverage to known and suspected espionage and sabotage agents. The Nazi war machine was stepping up its tempo, and fifth-column elements — German agents and sympathizers operating in neutral countries — began to manifest themselves. Norway, Denmark, the Netherlands, Belgium, and Luxembourg had become targets of assault. The fall of France was imminent.

The menace from within to the United States was recognized by FDR and he overruled the attorney general and Hoover. On May 21, 1940, he sent a memorandum classified "Confidential" to Attorney General Robert H. Jackson. Referring to fifth columns in other countries "in preparation for sabotage, as well as in actual sabotage," the President wrote:

> It is too late to do anything about it after sabotage, assassinations and "fifth column" activities are completed.
>
> You are, therefore, authorized and directed in such cases as you may approve, after investigation of the need in each case, to authorize the necessary investigating agents that they are at liberty to secure information by listening devices direct to the conversation or other communications of persons suspected of subversive activities against the Government of the United States, including suspected spies. You are requested furthermore to limit these investigations so conducted to a minimum and to limit them insofar as possible to aliens.[10]

President Roosevelt's views concerning the use of "listening devices" were enlarged upon in a letter he wrote to Congressman

Thomas H. Eliot of Massachusetts on February 21, 1941. At the time, a bill to authorize wiretapping by federal agencies was being considered in Congress. The President's letter, which was given wide circulation, stated in part:

> The use of wiretapping to aid law enforcement officers raises squarely the most delicate problem in the field of democratic statesmanship. It is more than desirable, it is necessary that criminals be detected and prosecuted vigilantly as possible. It is more necessary that the citizens of a democracy be protected in their rights of privacy from unwarranted snooping... .
>
> I have no compunction in saying that wiretapping should be used against those persons, not citizens of the United States, and those few citizens who are traitors to their country, who today are engaged in espionage or sabotage against the United States... .
>
> There is only one domestic crime which ought possibly to be included; that is kidnapping. It is a heinous crime for which never is there any justification. Further, wire tapping is a peculiarly effective instrument in the detection of such offenders because of the nature of the crime and the subsequent negotiations surrounding it. This includes extortion.[11]

Noting that the President in his May 21, 1940, memorandum to the attorney general specified that the latter authorize the use of listening devices "in such cases as you may approve," Hoover insisted that if the practice were to be resumed, wiretaps would be used only on the specific authority of the attorney general in each individual case. Thereafter, if it was felt that in the interest of national security or protecting life in a kidnapping case a wiretap would assist in securing vital information, not evidence, then the facts were called to the attention of the attorney general and he either approved or disapproved use of the technique.[12]

With the termination of the second world war, Attorney General Tom C. Clark presented to President Truman a letter dated July 17, 1946, upon which Truman noted his concurrence with the policy then in effect on wiretapping. In the letter Clark indicated that in view of the troubled period in international affairs which then existed, accompanied by an increase in subversive activities, the procedure was deemed as necessary in 1946 as it was in 1940.[13]

During the 15-year period from 1940 to 1955, the propriety of wiretapping as practiced by the FBI had the backing of some of the finest legal minds in the country. This included three presidents and six attorneys general, three of whom later became Supreme Court justices. Experts in their fields publicly addressed the questions of use of wiretaps in national security matters and in serious criminal cases. Particular attention was given to a provision in Section 605 of the Federal Communications Act of 1934. It declared that no person without authorization of the sender should intercept any communication and divulge or publish its existence, contents or substance to any person.

Attorney General Francis Biddle, after serving as solicitor general and as a judge on the Circuit Court of Appeals, on October 8, 1941, gave his first press conference after assuming office as attorney general and commented on this:

> I think that if you don't tap wires your espionage work goes out of the window... .
>
> The question is what is meant by "divulge and (sic) publish." I cannot think that by these words Congress intended to prevent an agent tapping wires in an espionage case and reporting to his superiors. I think in a kidnapping case that I would not hesitate to tap wires between the kidnapper and the parents of the child.[14]

In a ruling submitted to the attorney general on October 6, 1941, Circuit Court of Appeals Judge Charles Fahy, who also had served as solicitor general, concluded:

> It is my opinion that the Commander in Chief as such may lawfully have divulged to him or to someone on his behalf intercepted information relative to the security of the nation... . I conclude that divulgence to or in behalf of the Commander in Chief with respect to matters relating to the military security of the nation is not illegal.[15]

Over the years, there were recurring questions about the interpretation which had been placed on the <u>intercept and divulge</u> provision of Section 605 of the Federal Communications Act. This was addressed in a March 31, 1949, press release by Attorney General Tom C. Clark. He said that there was no justification for criticism made earlier that day by certain officials of the Americans for Democratic Action and the American Civil Liberties Union concerning the policies and practices of the Department of Justice with respect to wiretapping. He denied that the Department had violated this provision, pointing out that the same policy had been followed for many years and had been established " by the highest authorities in the Executive Branch of the Government." He continued:

> "The statutes and the decisions of the courts, including the Supreme Court, concerning wiretapping do not prohibit the tapping of wires, but rather the divulging or publishing of information and use of it as evidence when obtained by wiretapping." [16]

In an appearance before a subcommittee of the House Appropriations Committee on January 13, 1950, Hoover referred to a recent increase in the circulation of inaccurate information and half-truths on wiretapping, and said, "We in the FBI do not make policy. We follow it." He drew a rather convincing example:

> I dare say that the most violent critic of the FBI would urge the use of wiretapping technique if his child was kidnapped, and held in custody. Certainly there is as great a need to utilize this technique to protect our country from those who would enslave us and are engaged in treason, espionage, and subversion and who, if successful, would destroy our institutions and democracy.[17]

In the mid-1950's when Congress was considering legislation on wiretapping, Hoover clearly defined his feelings and philosophy on the subject of wiretaps:

Wiretaps are rarely used [by the FBI] in other than cases involving internal security.... But they can be of great value in kidnapping cases.

As much as I dislike the use of this technique both in and out of the Bureau, there are certain fundamental facts. Responsibility does have a final resting place. Insofar as the FBI is concerned, I want to be certain that regardless of the outcome that we do not evade our responsibility; and if a wiretap will prevent possible disaster or save a life, it is our duty to use it. If, as a result, prosecution cannot succeed, then that responsibility is elsewhere ... . I feel that I have fulfilled my duty by pointing out the need.[18]

On November 2, 1950, Attorney General J. Howard McGrath informed the Director that, in view of his extended absences from the city at times, he did not desire to hold up authorizations for technical surveillances. He said that the Director should approve the same and then take them up with him, McGrath, upon his return to the city so he could give his approval. Hoover told him that he would adhere to these instructions, but that he desired to keep to an absolute minimum authorizations upon his part and would utilize such authority only in extreme emergencies.[19]

Hoover never felt comfortable with this arrangement. He was concerned, as always, about staying within the boundary of his authority and responsibility, and soon had the arrangements altered so the deputy attorney general in his capacity of acting attorney general in the absence of his immediate superior could issue the necessary authority.[20]

During 1951, the Department of Justice was deeply involved in the prosecution of functionaries of the Communist Party, USA, on charges under the Smith Act of 1940 involving overthrow of the United States Government. Defense attorneys began making a series of allegations about FBI electronic surveillances. Hoover, on October 6, 1951, in a letter to Attorney General McGrath reviewed Bureau policy on conducting both wiretap and microphone surveillances. He pointed out that with respect to the latter, in a number of instances it had not been possible to install microphones without trespass. He requested to be advised whether the FBI should continue to utilize these techniques for the purpose of producing intelligence information or discontinue them entirely.

The attorney general delayed answering until February 26, 1952, when he pointed to pending legislation before Congress he had recommended which, if approved, would permit wiretapping under appropriate safeguards and make evidence thus obtained admissible in court. Responding to the specific questions Hoover had raised, he wrote:

I do not intend to alter the existing policy that wire tapping surveillance should be used under the present highly restrictive basis and when specifically authorized by me.

The use of microphone surveillance which does not involve trespass would seem to be permissible under the present state of the law, United States v Goldstein, 316 U.S. 129... .

I cannot authorize the installation of a microphone involving a trespass under existing law... . [21]

On May 27,1952, J. P. McGranery became attorney general of the United States. Whenever a new attorney general took office, Director Hoover followed the practice of briefing him on the work of the FBI, especially important and sensitive matters. He so briefed McGranery on June 6, 1952, and spent some time explaining how wiretap surveillances were handled after obtaining the approval of the sitting attorney general. McGranery said that he approved the procedure followed.[22]

A compilation of statistics in mid-March 1955 revealed that an average of 269 wiretap authorizations had been granted each year since President Franklin D. Roosevelt's May 21, 1940, memorandum. That requests for authorizations submitted by Hoover during the 15-year period were based on substance was attested by the fact that only 69 were not approved. No requests whatsoever were denied after June 2, 1945, as a very strict policy on seeking authorizations was adopted as soon as World War II drew to a close.[23]

Robert F. Kennedy became attorney general January 20, 1961. Three months later, in reply to a request from the Department of Justice, Hoover on April 21 sent a letter to Deputy Attorney General Byron R. White containing his views on Senate Bill 1495 (87th Congress). The legislation provided that the attorney general might authorize any federal law enforcement officer to intercept wire communications in certain specified types of cases. Hoover's reply included this opinion:

I feel the use of wiretapping remains highly unpalatable to the general public and any effort to extend its use to obtain information in cases such as bribery, gambling and racketeering will inevitably result in the defeat of the bill. It would be more desirable to restrict wiretapping to the present areas of espionage, subversive activities and major criminal cases where lives are at stake. [24]

During his tenure as attorney general from 1961 to 1964, Robert F. Kennedy was a staunch advocate of the use of wiretaps. For example, on July 16, 1963, he told an assistant director of the FBI that in view of the possible communist influence in the racial situation, he desired that consideration be given to placing a wiretap on Martin Luther King, Jr., as well as on a New York attorney closely associated with King. He said he thought it advisable to have complete coverage and that he was not concerned with repercussions if it should ever become known that such wiretaps had been put into effect.[25]

Upon the recommendation of Attorney General Nicholas deB. Katzenbach, on June 30, 1965, President Johnson issued a memorandum for the heads of executive departments and agencies which directed that no federal personnel could intercept telephone conversations without the consent of one of the parties except in connection with investigations related to the national security. The memorandum further provided that no interception should be undertaken or continued without first obtaining the approval of the attorney general.[26]

When its provisions were taken up with Attorney General Katzenbach, he told Director Hoover that he would "continue to approve all such requests in the future as I have in the past." He saw "no need to curtail any such activities in the national security field." [27]

Hoover's reaction to President Johnson's June 30, 1965, directive seemed at the time most unusual. He told W. Mark Felt, who was then chief inspector, that he desired a "substantial" cutback in the number of wiretaps being conducted. When Al Belmont, who shouldered the responsibility for all FBI investigative operations, was advised of this by Felt, he opposed any retrenchment. This technique was utilized only in the most important and sensitive cases, and then only after the specific written approval of the attorney general was received in each case. Eliminating the wiretaps in these cases could adversely affect the successful culmination of the investigations. Belmont's area of responsibility included not only investigations in the national security field but also crimes where human life might be in jeopardy, in the investigation of which electronic surveillances had been authorized in the past. The cutbacks proposed by Felt in carrying out the Director's desires were opposed by all members of the Bureau's executive conference, consisting of the top officials at headquarters who considered problem matters and made recommendations to Hoover on their solutions. In each of the first three cases presented, Hoover adopted Felt's recommendation that the wiretap be eliminated. Belmont, recognizing that Hoover with his finger on the pulse of things must have a valid reason for the retrenchment, ultimately cooperated with Felt in accomplishing a thankless task. The total number of wiretaps in operation was reduced from 78 to 38. [28]

Upon completion of the cutback, Hoover sent Attorney General Katzenbach a communication on September 14, 1965, which gives insight to the Director's understanding of where responsibilities rested. Not too subtly it suggested that the attorney general consider living up to his:

> In accordance with the wishes you have expressed during various recent conversations with me, in which you also advised of the concern of the President, the Federal Bureau of Investigation has severely restricted and, in many cases, eliminated the use of special investigative techniques in carrying out our investigative work... .
>
> As a consequence, and at your request, we have discontinued completely the use of microphones... . I have further cut down on wiretaps and I am not requesting authority for any additional wiretaps. I have further refused to authorize any mail covers, trash covers, or use of the polygraph in our cases...
>
> It is axiomatic that we can produce results in direct ratio to our ability to secure information... . To the extent that our knowledge is reduced, to that extent our productiveness is reduced... .
>
> With particular reference to the use of wiretaps and micro-

*phones, I think you are well aware that the selective and re-
strained use of these techniques has made it possible for the
FBI to produce highly significant intelligence information to
assist our makers of international policy, as well as to hold in
check subversive elements within the country. Likewise the use
of microphones in the field of organized crime has produced
extremely valuable intelligence data.*

*I am extremely concerned about this situation because the
heavy responsibilities entrusted to this Bureau in the fields of
internal security and organized crime are in no way abated,
yet many of the tools by which we are able to produce the
results expected of us in these admittedly complex and difficult fields are being taken away from us. On the one hand the
people of this country are crying out for protection against
subversion and the rising crime rate, and on the other hand
the very tools, the restrained and judicious use of which per-
mits us to carry out our mandate, are no longer available to
us.*

*In view of your position, both as head of the President's Na-
tional Commission on Crime and as Attorney General, with a
deep responsibility in both the fields of crime and internal
security, I thought I should make my views known to you.*[29]

By this communication, the FBI Director was conveying his reaction
to the recommendation Katzenbach made to President Johnson which
resulted in the June 30, 1965, directive forbidding the use of an
intrusive investigative technique, wiretapping, "except in conjunction
with investigations related to national security," and reminding him
there were other investigative techniques which could be criticized
on the grounds of intrusion. In effect, Hoover told his boss that it
was up to the attorney general, the principal law enforcement officer
in the country, to make policy which the head of the principal
investigative agency, the FBI, was to follow. As in the case of wiretaps,
microphone surveillances were utilized during Hoover's tenure on
a limited and tightly controlled basis.[30]

When the Director on June 6, 1952, briefed Attorney General
McGranery on wiretap surveillances and how they were handled,
he took the occasion to call his attention to the fact that his
predecessor had, a few months previously, ruled that approval could
not be given to installation of any microphone surveillance where
trespass was involved. He explained that such installations had been
utilized on a very limited basis and only in cases which directly
affected the internal security of the United States, wherein
information could be obtained which would enable the FBI to take
precautionary measures. He told the new attorney general that
following this ruling, Hoover had discontinued the use of microphone
installations where to install them would require technical trespass.
McGranery stated that he thought that it was entirely proper for
such installations to be made in any case where elements were at
work against the security of the United States. He told Hoover that
in instances where he felt there was a need to install microphones,
even though trespass might be committed, he, the attorney general,
would leave it to Hoover's judgment as to the steps to take. Hoover

told him that this authority would only be used in extreme cases, and only in cases involving the internal security of the country.[31]

The next question raised about the FBI's use of microphone surveillances was in a letter to the Director dated May 20, 1954, from Herbert Brownell, Jr., who had succeeded McGranery as attorney general the previous year. Considering that he was the nation's chief law enforcement officer and Hoover's immediate superior, his analysis and opinions were particularly significant and afforded direction in this controversial area. Brownell advised Hoover that a recent decision of the Supreme Court (Irvine v California, 347 U.S. 128), denouncing the use of microphone surveillances by the Police Department of Irvine, California, in a gambling case, made appropriate a reappraisal of the use which might be made in the future by the FBI of microphone surveillances in connection with matters relating to the internal security of the country. The pertinent portions of Brownell's letter follow:

It is clear that in some instances the use of microphone surveillance is the only possible way of uncovering the activities of espionage agents, possible saboteurs, and subversive persons. In such instances I am of the opinion that the national interest requires that microphone surveillance be utilized by the Federal Bureau of Investigation. This use need not be limited to the development of evidence for prosecution. The FBI has an intelligence function in connection with internal security matters equally as important as the duty of developing evidence for presentation to the courts and the national security requires that the FBI be able to use microphone surveillance for the proper discharge of both of such functions. The Department of Justice approves the use of microphone surveillance by the FBI under these circumstances and for these purposes.

I do not consider that the decision of the Supreme Court in Irvine *v.* California, supra, *requires a different course. That case is readily distinguishable on its facts. The language of the Court, however, indicates certain uses of microphones which it would be well to avoid, if possible, even in internal security investigations. It is quite clear that in the* Irvine *case the Justices of the Supreme Court were outraged by what they regarded as the indecency of installing a microphone in a bedroom. They denounced the utilization of such methods of investigation in a gambling case as shocking. The Court's action is a clear indication of the need for discretion and intelligent restraint in the use of microphones by the FBI in all cases, including internal security matters. Obviously, the installation of a microphone in a bedroom or in some comparably intimate location should be avoided wherever possible. It may appear, however, that important intelligence or evidence relating to matters connected with the national security can only be obtained by the installation of a microphone in such a location. It is my opinion that under such circumstances the installation is proper and is not prohibited by the Supreme Court's decision in the* Irvine *case.*

In concluding his letter, Brownell addressed the question of trespass arising in connection with the installation of a microphone. He supported the use of this investigative tool on the grounds that for the FBI to fulfill its important intelligence function, considerations of internal security and the "national safety" were paramount and, therefore, might compel the unrestricted use of this technique in the national interest. The term "national safety" was interpreted to include criminal cases.[32]

The contents of Brownell's letter have been set forth in some detail to highlight not only the broad reach of his opinion but also the fact that the Irvine decision was in a local gambling case investigated by the Police Department of Irvine, California, and in which the FBI had no involvement whatsoever.

Citing Brownell's letter about the case, the Church Committee made this finding:

> *Until 1965, microphone surveillance by intelligence agencies was wholly unregulated in certain classes of cases. Within weeks after a 1954 Supreme Court decision denouncing the* <u>*FBI's installation*</u> *of a microphone in a defendant's bedroom, the Attorney General informed the Bureau that he did not believe the decision applied to national security cases and permitted the FBI to continue to install microphones subject only to its own "intelligent restraint." (Emphasis added.)[33]*

This false statement was fairly typical of misstatements, omissions, and slanted reporting of the Church Committee which did more damage to the U.S. intelligence community than the Soviet intelligence services had been able to inflict in some 40 years of concentrated effort, and, not just incidentally, to besmirch the name and reputation of J. Edgar Hoover almost beyond restoration.

On May 4, 1961, Hoover's views on the use of microphone surveillances in FBI cases were set forth in a letter addressed to Deputy Attorney General Byron R. White, who later became a Supreme Court justice. They were conveyed to White in connection with Attorney General Kennedy's contemplated appearance before the Senate Subcommittee on Constitutional Rights. White was informed that in keeping with the May 20, 1954, advice of Attorney General Brownell, such surveillances were utilized, even though trespass was necessary, in internal security and major criminal matters.[34]

While Attorney General Kennedy did not sanction each microphone surveillance on an individual basis, he did approve and support the FBI's use of this investigative technique.[35]

Kennedy resigned as attorney general in September 1964. His successor, Nicholas Katzenbach, had served as deputy attorney general under him. On March 30, 1965, Katzenbach instructed that his personal authorization be obtained for each microphone installed, thereby putting into effect a suggestion Hoover had discussed with the Department of Justice many years before.[36]

During the spring and early summer of 1965, Katzenbach personally approved a total of 99 such installations in organized crime and security cases. Some of these were new installations, others had been installed under Robert Kennedy's administration and it was their continuance which was approved. Then on July 12, Katzenbach instructed that the FBI discontinue all microphone coverage, which occasioned Hoover's letter to him on September 14 advising that this had been done and that all other special investigative techniques had been discontinued.

Subsequently, the same month, Katzenbach advised that he would consider, on an individual basis, requests for his authority to install microphones for intelligence-gathering purposes in matters involving the national security.[37]

In late December that year, Hoover expressed his views on the use of microphone surveillances in affording coverage to organized crime. He referred to valuable intelligence information gained through microphone sources regarding the operations of this "cancer in our society," and said:

> It is true that in most of our microphone installations in the field of organized crime, the element of trespass has been present. However, the idea that the FBI is irresponsibly invading the privacy of many of our citizens is completely fallacious. In this regard, it may be said that in using this technique, we were 'invading the privacy' of the murderous leaders of organized crime whose very purpose is to terrorize various segments of our society and place large numbers of our citizenry in such fear that they are forced to pay extortionate tribute to this element. Therefore, in effect, not only are we *not* invading the privacy of the average citizen but, on the contrary, through this technique, are attempting to protect and preserve his rights from the onslaught of organized crime. These leading gangsters whose 'privacy' is being invaded, are the very individuals who seek to subvert many phases of government, both local and Federal, through bribery and public corruption. [38]

During the period 1960 through May 1966, the FBI operated a total of 738 microphone surveillances. Only a fraction of these sources was in operation on any given date. Numerous of them were of very temporary duration, covering meetings or subjects in travel status.[39]

When Hoover accepted his appointment by Attorney General Stone to head the Bureau in 1924, both men agreed that the FBI would function solely as a fact-finding organization and limit its activities to the investigation of violations of federal laws.

In issuing a manual of rules and regulations to which his investigative personnel were held, Hoover included the following provision:

> UNETHICAL TACTICS: Wiretapping, entrapment, or the use of any other improper, illegal, or unethical tactics in procuring information in connection with investigative activity will not be tolerated by the Bureau.[40]

Hoover held the Bureau to the commitment to engage only in fact-finding and investigating law violations until he was ordered twice by the President to expand into another area. This first occurred in 1934 when, following a White House conference, Hoover ordered what he termed a "so-called intelligence investigation" of the Nazi movement, concentrating on its possible connection to official representatives of the German government in the United States.

The second expansion was also into this area of so-called intelligence investigations when, during the two White House conferences in August 1936, Roosevelt added to the Bureau's responsibilities, requiring intelligence-gathering in the national security field as well as fact-gathering.

There was another agreement between Attorney General Stone and Hoover in May 1924. The activities of the Bureau were to be under the direction of the attorney general "or under the direction of an Assistant Attorney General regularly conducting the work of the Department of Justice."[41]

Hoover's commitment to this dated back to his early days as Director. When in January 1931 Attorney General William D. Mitchell told him that as Director of the Bureau he could authorize wiretapping, Hoover insisted that his officials also get the written approval of the assistant attorney general in charge of the case in the Department of Justice before utilizing this technique. His adherence to this commitment also carried over to his utilizing electronic surveillance techniques to discharge the Bureau's added responsibilities for intelligence-gathering, techniques which he did not like. As he told the House Appropriations subcommittee on January 13, 1950, when discussing widespread criticism of wiretapping, "We in the FBI don't make policy. We follow it."

The types of operations required of the FBI to discharge responsibilities levied by law, the Attorney General, and the President over the 48 years Hoover headed the organization engendered jealousies and hatreds, particularly on the part of criminal and subversive elements, which came to rest squarely on his shoulders. It is hoped that this study of this very complex man will help allay some of the more vicious charges made against him.

HUMOR AND PRACTICAL JOKES

A special bond exists among FBI special agents who served under J. Edgar Hoover. This developed during the first dozen or so years of his directorship. It was preserved when a small group of ex-agents founded the Society of Former Special Agents of the Federal Bureau of Investigation in New York City in 1937. They wanted to "preserve the substantial friendships which were so characteristic of special agents during the tenure of their service" based upon "a mutuality of interests of the agents, the memories of pleasures enjoyed, and adversities shared." The Society grew by leaps and bounds in the ensuing years and still attracts hundreds of new members annually.[1]

The esprit de corps which developed in the Bureau made for devoted service and for mutual trust, not just for one another among the agents, but also for Hoover himself. He demanded much of them. He gave them much: self respect, self confidence, an enviable reputation which opened doors when they conducted investigations, and opened opportunities when second careers were sought following Bureau service. An employer seeking a reliable and trustworthy employee looked no further when the applicant had carried a special agent's badge and credentials.

The demands on agents were hardly greater than those on their wives and families. A husband and father could say good-bye one morning and end up in a gunfight before nightfall. He might be called upon to engage in an extended physical surveillance of a criminal or suspected spy, requiring travel to a distant city before he could telephone to assure the family he was safe despite his failure to arrive home when expected. Whoever said, "They also serve who only stand and wait," must have had agents' wives in mind.

Assignments such as these developed close associations among agents. In dangerous situations they relied upon one another not only for support but, at times, for the very protection of their lives.

Cartha D. "Deke" DeLoach, one of Hoover's most trusted deputies

Assistant Director C.D. De Loach, F.B.I., U.S. Dept. of Justice. (FBI).

before retiring in 1970 has observed, "In Washington we often forgot that to the rest of the country Hoover was larger than life, a folk hero as awesome as a movie star or a president." [2]

The agent complement in the Bureau included a cross section of America, men who arrived in Washington to work for a folk hero. While that impression of the man did not fade, they soon found time to poke a little fun at their boss, as most employees do. Hoover's expectation that his words of wisdom would be preserved in copious notes, as well as the ever-present possibility of disciplinary action, led to all sorts of humorous stories, often based on a smattering of facts that were somewhat enhanced for audience consumption.

One which may or may not have had any basis in fact but which, nonetheless, was fairly typical, was about a supposed special agent in charge (SAC) of one of the 59 FBI field offices. He had been summoned to headquarters for a special training session, and requested a conference with the Director. A conference of this type, where an SAC might be called upon to answer for the sins of his entire office or commended for its outstanding work, could affect a man's entire future career in the Bureau. To say the least, it could be somewhat awe inspiring.

At the conclusion of the conference, the SAC in question rose from his chair and, instead of leaving Hoover's office, opened the wrong door and ended up in a closet. Now there is a choice of endings to this story. One is, he left the closet, said, "Mr. Hoover you certainly have a mighty fine closet," and departed by the proper door. The other version is that he stayed in the closet until Hoover departed for the day, too embarrassed to come out. Either way, it made for a good story.

Some of the accounts were given an exaggerated twist. Roy Wood, an exceptionally outstanding agent with whom I first worked in St. Louis during World War II, was one of the most inherently funny people I have ever known. He told me about an experience he had when going through the new agents' training course in 1942.

By way of background, early that year the Bureau hired 50 men each week and subjected them to twelve weeks of intensive training to meet the demands made of the FBI following the Pearl Harbor attack on December 7, 1941. The course included indoctrination in federal criminal law, firearms training, investigative procedures, testifying in a moot court, rules and regulations, and many other subjects, all designed to develop a new recruit into a polished FBI agent. Training sessions ran from 9:00 A.M. to 9:00 P.M. Monday through Friday (with an hour for lunch and an hour for dinner), 9:00 A.M. to 5:00 P.M. on Saturday, and 1:00 P.M. to 6:00 P.M. Sunday. Considerable out-of-school studying was required, and along the way, written examinations were afforded covering three separate manuals, the contents of which had to be digested. A passing grade was 85%. A grade less than that required a re-examination. If that was flunked, the new agent was washed out. A personal note: my class of 50 lost 12 men by the end of the twelfth week, not an unusual occurrence. It was a tough regimen.

Hoover would personally address each new class promptly at 11 o'clock on a Friday morning. When he talked to the class which preceded the one Roy was in, three of the recruits failed to take notes. The Director noticed this and told the class counselor that they seemed to have little interest in what he had to say. That same day all three became ex-agents.

This story spread like wild fire throughout the training school. The counselor of Roy's class was like the proverbial hen on a hot griddle all week long, anticipating the Director's upcoming Friday visit. He briefed and rebriefed his charges on their responsibility to be in place well before Hoover's 11 o'clock appearance, properly attired and attentive. And by all means, "Take copious notes."

Came the fateful day. Roy and all of his classmates were seated a full five minutes before Hoover's scheduled appearance, all eyes glued to a clock on the wall. As the second hand reached the top of the dial, marking 11 o'clock, the Director strode through the door, proceeded to the lectern, glanced over the entire class, and said, "Good Morning."

"And," Roy concluded his story, "everybody wrote it down."

A bone of contention developed when the Director back in the 1950s had a weight problem and, for the sake of his health, had to go on a rather strict diet. Noting that life insurance weight charts listed three categories of weight allowances based on height and build — minimum, desirable and maximum — Hoover decided that all his agents should be desirable. This created problems for some of the men. One, a former quarterback for the Maryland football team whose right arm was well developed as a result of his ability to throw long passes quite successfully, complained that his arm alone exceeded his weight allowance.

If during a required annual physical examination an agent's weight was found to be above the desirable standard, he had to weigh in every three months until he brought it down. I recall one of the men arriving at the nurses office at FBIHQ for his three-month weigh-in wearing just an outer layer of light weight clothing with his trousers held up with a rubber band rather than a belt, to save every possible ounce.

Continued failure to meet a desirable weight had its down side; it could result in an agent's being placed on "limited duty." This meant he could not participate in dangerous assignments or strenuous physical exertion and, thus, would not qualify for promotions and salary increases.

Annual physicals were conducted usually at military installations, and the doctors there became somewhat sympathetic toward those men with overdeveloped arms, or imagined other parts of their anatomy. When one examining physician at the Naval hospital in Bethesda greeted an agent with a pleasant "How are you?" he got a quick response, "OK for a man 7 feet 11 inches tall."

As was normal, agents found some fun in Hoover's demand that everyone be desirable. And like Roy Wood's exaggerated story about note-taking, there were exaggerated ones about how to remain desirable and beat the battle of the bulge.

The suggestion circulated to be sure to ask for a particularly sympathetic doctor at the hospital in Bethesda when taking an annual physical. This doctor was said to have weighed an agent minus his shoes, found him to be two pounds over his limit, made him weigh again, this time with his shoes on, which put him up two pounds more, then deducted four pounds for the weight of the shoes.

Regardless of such fun-poking, Hoover was held in the highest regard by nearly all those who served under him and there was ever a long waiting list of applicants for FBI positions. There were many examples of several members of the same family who became agents or became part of the support staff, second or third generations of investigators following in a father's and/or grandfather's footsteps, brother or sister combinations who served as secretaries or in other support capacities.

Somewhat typical were the Southers sisters, Alta., Nancy, Mary, and Donna Gail, talented and dedicated young ladies whose home was in Holden, West Virginia. Each was devoted to the FBI, had looked forward to serving under J. Edgar Hoover, and, as she was ready to try her wings away from home, applied for and received an appointment to a position in Bureau headquarters in Washington. All four developed into outstanding employees with the highest regard for the Director. They were steady in attendance, discreet in handling Bureau information, and could be counted on in demanding situations, which, on occasion, involved working late into the evening or reporting long before regular office hours or on weekends or holidays to meet an emergency.

In 1971, Alta Southers was my administrative assistant when I headed a counterintelligence section which was responsible for the investigation of the famous Pentagon Papers case that involved the unauthorized disclosure of classified information to the press. It

Author dictating to secretary, Alta Southers.

Nationalities Intelligence Section Personnel. Jim Wagner (light suit) had ticket on Pentagon Papers case.

was an investigation which the Director followed very closely. He put a requirement on us to have a memorandum on his desk at 9:00 o'clock each workday morning summarizing the developments during the previous 24 hours or weekend. In addition, any particularly significant developments were called to his attention separately by memoranda which went up the line and across the desk of William C. (Bill) Sullivan, the Number 3 man on the Bureau totem pole.

Sullivan frequently put handwritten notations on our memos in which we included recommendations for investigative steps, voicing his opinion and, in some instances, his objections. By this time the Director was revealing a loss of confidence in, or at least a lack of reliance on, Bill. He was regularly demonstrating an approval of the manner in which the case was being handled by "OK H"-ing our recommendations and routing the memos directly back to me, by-passing Sullivan on their return course to our section. While he could have routed such communications back through Bill by merely checking his name listed in a routing block printed on the Bureau's in-house memorandum stationery, he had to go to the trouble of writing my name below the routing block — as a section chief my position on the totem pole was not sufficiently lofty to warrant my printed name in the routing block.

The first memo that came back via the by-pass route had my surname, prominent in blue ink, carefully written, but spelled Wann<u>ell</u>, rather than <u>all</u>, a not unusual occurrence — it happens all the time. As it hit Alta's desk, she grabbed it, came charging into my office, and, with a twinkle in her eye, said, "Mr. Wannall, look how the Director spelled your name. But don't get alarmed. I've called the Ad-ministrative Division and had your name officially changed.

Everyone knew that the Director didn't make mistakes.

Since Hoover knew pretty well everything which was going on within his domain, it would

Agent E.H. Mossburg with legendary Al Belmont, as Agent Don Stewart looks on.

be to his discredit to think that he had not heard about such bits of fun poked at him. And, no doubt, he got a kick out of them. He even played some of them back on his agents. In 1971 he was honored at a banquet by the Washington, DC, chapter of the society of former agents and was called upon to make a few remarks. Taking note somewhat obliquely of his weight program, he looked over the audience of ex-agents no longer burdened by the program and said, "I recognize the faces but the bodies are not familiar."

He had an off-beat sense of humor, liked playing practical jokes on friends, and enjoyed telling stories at his own expense. Deke DeLoach recalled several of these episodes:

Hoover once told about flying to rural Minnesota in sub-zero weather to assist in searching for a kidnap victim and the victim's abductor. Since he soon learned that the clothing he had brought along was not heavy enough to protect him against the cold, he stopped at a small general store to make a few purchases. A group of locals was huddled around a pot-bellied stove shooting the breeze. Greeting them, Hoover introduced himself by name only, chatted a bit about the hard winter, and mentioned that he was in their neck of the woods trying to help solve the kidnapping case. Shortly after the subsequent capture of the kidnapper and the recovery of the victim, Hoover received a letter from the store proprietor, who told him that the boys around the stove agreed that Hoover wasn't much of a president, but he seemed to be a pretty good policeman.

In another instance, when former Supreme Court Justice Frank Murphy was attorney general, both he and Hoover attended an American Bar Association meeting in El Paso. It is just across the border from Juarez, Mexico, which was then little more than a cluster of night spots and brothels catering to American tourists. One of the FBI's best informants was a madam who ran one of the more notorious establishments. So

Hoover, with Associate Director Clyde Tolson accompanying him, arrived a day early and drove over to Juarez to find out if the woman had any new information about the mob. The prostitutes all saw Hoover enter the establishment, and some must even have recognized him.

The next night, after Murphy had arrived and given a speech, he mentioned that he would like to see the scandalous red light district. So, Hoover hired a driver to take him and the attorney general, a renowned prude, on a brief tour of the joints. When they arrived at the same brothel, one of the girls ran up to the car, peered in, saw Hoover, and said, "Hey, you back again tonight?"

The blue-nosed Murphy turned to Hoover in righteous indignation, and Hoover swore that for a few moments his job was in real jeopardy.[3]

Deputy Associate Director Mark Felt worked most closely with Hoover during the last 10 months of the Director's life. This was a period when Associate Director Clyde Tolson was in such poor health that Hoover needed someone else upon whom he could rely and with whom he could discuss problems, many of which were created by his previous Number 3 man, Bill Sullivan. Felt soon recognized that his boss was not the humorless bureaucrat that some believed him to be and took delight in telling stories about himself in which he was the butt. One of the best of these was his account of a visit to Alcatraz prison during which he bought a canary from the renowned prisoner known as the Bird Man as a present for his mother. It turned out to be a sparrow dyed yellow — and Hoover always laughed the heartiest when retelling the story.

In May of 1971, at the invitation of Martha Mitchell, he made one of his rare public appearances at the American Newspaperwomen's Club. In introducing him, she paid tribute to his many years of service by quipping, "When you've seen one FBI Director, you have seen them all." Hoover, whose caricature had just appeared on the cover of *Life* magazine as a Roman emperor, replied, "I know that those of you who regularly subscribe to an alleged national magazine may have had some difficulty recognizing me in the conventional clothes I am wearing this evening. But like ordinary people we 'emperors' do have our problems, and I regret to say that my toga did not get back from the cleaners on time." [4]

Even Bill Sullivan, who turned against Hoover during the last couple of years of the Director's life and became a bitter enemy, considered him engaging, very interesting and clever in his responses, every once in a while getting quite witty.

On one occasion when sending Sullivan out to speak in the Midwest, Hoover reminded him that the Bureau had been under attack for tapping telephones, and said, "When you are called upon to speak at this conference, I want you to be extremely careful not to say anything that's going to cause us any trouble in the press." Tongue in cheek, Sullivan said, "Mr. Hoover, the only thing I'll talk about if I'm called upon is the weather, the weather conditions." He looked at Sullivan and said, "Oh no, no, no, don't talk about the weather conditions. They'll accuse us of having a tap on the Weather Bureau." [5]

The construction of the J. Edgar Hoover FBI Building was started well before the Director's death but was unfinished when he passed away. In 1971 a newspaper man compared this long period of construction to the building of the Great Pyramid. Hoover disagreed with that observation and quipped that he was convinced the ancient Egyptians took less time to complete their project.[6]

Hoover was not beyond having his nose tweaked in a humorous vein. Al Belmont recalled a prime example of this. When Hoover left town, he never let go of the reins of the FBI. Wherever he was, he would call in on the telephone, usually twice a day, and talk to his secretary and key officials, including Belmont. Now, Hoover was a man of ready temper and not one to brook disagreement with his decisions. This is not to say he would not change his mind if you gave him facts which altered the picture. But during this process of change there could be periods of disagreement and, if he felt a loss of confidence in you, he was quite capable of bypassing you and dealing only with your subordinates, as witness the "Wann_ell_" incident.

Periodically, Belmont would get in this situation for failure to measure up to the Director's expectations or because of opposition to a policy. Yet it was very clear that Hoover did not want to be surrounded by "yes men". He was far too smart for that, realizing the value of different opinions on the same subject. However, in one instance, when Belmont took exception to a particular policy, Hoover would talk regarding matters affecting Al's division only with Belmont's chief assistant, and this went on for weeks.

Finally, Hoover took a trip to Miami and, as Belmont was substituting for the assistant to the director in charge of all investigations, he necessarily handled the telephone when the Director called from Miami on some investigative matter. Al had noticed in the newspapers just before this particular call that on the previous night Vice President Richard M. Nixon and his daughter had gone to Miami. A convention was being held there and Nixon and his daughter were forced to sleep in the lobby of a hotel because no rooms were available. Nixon was a good friend of the FBI's, and the agent in charge of the office in a city like Miami was supposed to have sufficient contacts to assist friends in need. So, Belmont opened the telephone conversation with Hoover by mentioning the newspaper story and the Bureau's insistence that its agents in charge have proper contacts. He then pointed out that as Director, Hoover superseded the agent in charge and it would appear that he had failed to take care of his good friend, Nixon. Under the circumstances, Al pointed out, the normal procedure called for the official in charge to submit a memorandum of explanation to the Bureau.

There was a dead silence at the other end of the line for a few seconds, then Hoover snorted and laughed. He commented on the convention going on and the ice was thus broken. They discussed the FBI business in a normal fashion and Belmont came out of the doghouse.[7]

Like the story of the SAC who tried to depart from Hoover's office by way of a closet, there's one about Senator Joseph R. McCarthy of "McCarthyism" fame, which I haven't been able to document but which obviously had basis in fact. Senator Joe was no friend of Hoover's. Deke DeLoach recalled that the Director didn't like McCarthy, in part because of his failure to speak authoritatively on the threat to the country's internal security, in part because the senator had supplanted the FBI Director as the nation's chief enemy of communism. Hoover couldn't ignore McCarthy, but kept him at arm's length.[8]

Deke's sizing up of the relationship between the two men gives credence to a story told by Lawrence J. (Larry) Heim, one of the stalwarts of the Society of Former Special Agents of the FBI and former editor of its in-house publication *The Grapevine.* Larry spoke of a situation where McCarthy was to visit Hoover at the latter's home. On the appointed evening, the senator approached the front door and found himself excluded by a "Quarantined" sign prominently posted. It was but one of many practical jokes in which Hoover took delight.

Leonard Viner was a former FBI agent, the son of Harry and Rae Viner. Leonard had many recollections about Hoover since the Viner home in the 3500 block of Massachusetts Avenue in Washington was where Hoover spent many Wednesday evenings when Leonard was a young man. Hoover called Mrs. Viner "Aunt Rae" and, in Leonard's words, "fell in love with her and loved her home cooking." Hoover called Harry Viner, a close friend and confidant, "Head G-Man," and addressed him as "HGM."

During the Wednesday night sessions, the two men discussed international affairs and on occasion Hoover would vent his wrath over some media incident or complain about people "looking over his shoulder." Consequently, Harry gave the Director a 4 X 6 inch plaque which he kept on his desk. It contained a statement to the effect that one is better judged by his enemies rather than his friends. This seems to have been the basis for Hoover's remark when, in an appearance before the House Appropriations Subcommittee just two months before he passed away, he commented about being honored by friends but distinguished by enemies.

Leonard said that Hoover called his father very frequently and on one occasion said to Leonard, "I get better advice from your father than anyone else. I know

Tolson and Hoover with the Viner family.

high-level officials, but whenever I want a real, down-to-earth, common-sense answer, I always come back to Harry Viner."

Hoover and Harry Viner were introduced to each other in the mid-thirties by Julius Lulley, proprietor of Harveys Restaurant located next to the Mayflower Hotel on Connecticut Avenue in Washington, an establishment they both frequented. Lulley was a raconteur and

Rae and Harry Viner (Leonard's parents).

bon vivant who would walk around his restaurant, glad-hand his customers, and confidentially whisper to selected ones the latest Washington story going the rounds. It was just natural and ordained that he would introduce Hoover and Viner to each other. As their friendship developed they discovered that they had a mutual interest in Gold Vasser (Gold Water), an alcoholic drink containing little flecks of gold. Lulley provided them with a small, locked container in his restaurant, and a key to it for each, in which they kept two bottles of Gold Vasser, one labeled with Hoover's name and the other marked "HGM."

Harry was born in Russia but escaped because, as a Jew, he had suffered intense discrimination. After arriving in the U.S., he first opened a tailoring firm on Florida Avenue in Washington, then went into the laundry business, processing everything having to do with the care and rejuvenation of textiles of all kinds. Despite the fact that he had little formal education in the United States, he was a shrewd man from a common sense point of view and a highly successful businessman. It was his practical approach to and solution of everyday problems that Hoover found so helpful.

After Harry had known Hoover for some time he asked the Director why he had not purchased a house of his own. Hoover admitted to being no businessman and speculated that he would be taken advantage of if he tried to buy one. Harry had a ready solution for this. He got his lawyer, Leo Schlossberg, to act as straw man and purchase (for Hoover) a house in a beautiful residential section of the nation's capital.

Leonard described his father as a great listener. He said Harry Viner talked like the comedian Jimmy Durante, and Hoover, ever one for a good laugh, got many listening to Harry's colorful expressions, such as:

• Speaking of Switzerland: "Take away the Alps and what have you got?"

• "An oral contract isn't worth the paper it's written on."

• "Include me out."

Leonard noted that the last expression was one usually associated with Hollywood producer Sam Goldwyn but was actually first used by his father.

On holidays, Leonard said, Hoover would send the Viners turkeys and smoked hams. "And," Leonard commented, "even though we were Jewish we ate the hams and enjoyed them."

This evoked a volunteered comment by Leonard who, with his wife Storme, later named a daughter JayE (no punctuation) in honor of J. Edgar Hoover. "All the time I knew the man," he said, "I never once had any indication of anti-Semitism or racism on his part, for which I had great admiration for both Mr. Hoover and his politics." As an illustration of this, Leonard told of a situation which developed when Hoover was serving as an honorary trustee of George Washington University. It was brought to his attention that a young man who applied for admittance to the university's medical school was turned down because he was Jewish. Hoover confronted the university's board of directors with this account and said that if it were true, he was resigning as honorary trustee. As a result, the young man was admitted and in the future there were fewer cases of discrimination.

Hoover some years later was honored as Man of the Year by the Washington Hebrew Congregation, a ceremony in which Leonard played a prominent role. Hoover gave a speech when accepting the honor and was presented with a scroll and a little light which had special significance in the Hebrew Faith.

Harry Viner was a target of one of Hoover's practical jokes. When headed for the Viner residence one evening during a World War II blackout, Hoover saw Harry and Rae Viner just ahead of him. Walking up quietly behind them, he stuck a finger in Harry's back and said, "This is a holdup. Keep walking. Don't try anything funny." He walked them to their home on Massachusetts Avenue, had them open the door, still unaware of who he was, and then all three entered the reception hall. When he had

Hoover with Leonard, Muriel and little namesake, JayE Viner.

them turn on the lights, they discovered who their holdup man was, and Hoover thought it was a great joke. Harry wasn't so convinced and said, "That would have been some big joke if I had had a gun and turned around and shot you." At the moment, neither Harry nor Rae found much humor in the experience, but thought it much funnier weeks later. In fact, it became a favorite story of theirs.

The nature of the close friendship which developed between Harry Viner and Edgar Hoover was attested by the fact that when Harry passed away, Hoover learned that he had been named both executor and trustee of Viner's estate. He served in both capacities.[9]

The practical joke played on the Viner couple was concocted on the spur of the moment as Hoover walked down the street and a window of opportunity opened. But some of these jokes required planning and finesse in execution.

One acquaintance, whom Hoover considered to be somewhat supercilious, was the brunt of one of these. The Director arranged through a friend in Chicago to acquire a large photograph of the Chicago stock yards in which literally hundreds of steers were milling around, many facing squarely in the direction away from the photographer. The Director had a mug shot of his acquaintance superimposed on the south end of a north-bound steer and distributed copies of the resulting picture rather freely among mutual friends. A college- or perhaps even a high school-type prank, but certainly evidence of an inborn strain of humor.[10]

His very favorite practical joke target was Harvey Restaurant proprietor Julius Lulley. Enlisting the cooperation of his long-time Administrative Assistant Helen Gandy, he executed an elaborate one with Lulley as the brunt of it.

Whenever Hoover visited Los Angeles, he stayed in the Ambassador Hotel. That is where Lulley stayed, also, during visits to that city. Upon learning that Julie planned a trip there, Hoover indicated to him, but did not make a definite commitment, that he and Clyde Tolson, the FBI associate director, might also be in Los Angeles.

As soon as Lulley had checked into his Ambassador room, he called the switchboard and asked to be connected to Hoover's room. The operator told him that the hotel had no guest registered under that name. Lulley fumed, but could get nowhere. He decided that for security reasons the operator would not acknowledge the presence of the head of the FBI. He put in a call to Hoover's office in Washington and told Helen Gandy about not being able to reach Hoover's room at the Ambassador. She told him that she would have Hoover call him.

When Hoover did so, Julie complained a bit about the lack of cooperation on the part of the hotel operator, then explained that he was planning a big brunch spread in his room for the next morning and wanted Hoover and Tolson to join him. Among items on the menu would be some of Hoover's favorites: sausages, eggs, Nova Scotia salmon, and bagels.

"Everything you like, Edgar. Will you and Clyde Tolson join me?"

"Yes, of course," he was assured.

Julius made all the arrangements and began waiting the next morning for his guests. And he waited, and waited, and waited. Finally, he called the switchboard and insisted that he be connected with Hoover's room. Again he was told that there was no guest by that name registered. He insisted that there had to be, saying he had talked to him the previous day, but had just failed to ask him for his room number. In desperation, he hung up and again called Hoover's office at FBI Headquarters. He recited his tale of woe to Miss Gandy, who, very accommodatingly, promised to have her boss return his call immediately, which he did.

Hoover said, "I understand you are trying to reach me, Julie."

"I have that brunch all ready. How soon are you and Tolson going to get here?"

"That's impossible," Hoover responded.

"What do you mean, impossible?"

"You are in Los Angeles and we are on the beach in Atlantic City." And they were...end of conversation...end of practical joke.[11]

Hoover became acquainted with many Hollywood personalities, one of whom was Sophie Tucker, an entertainer who was billed as "the last of the red hot mamas." They became good friends.

During one visit by Hoover and Clyde Tolson to Los Angeles in the World War II years, they registered at the same hotel where Leonard Viner and his parents were staying. Being a somewhat inveterate amateur photographer, Hoover took numerous snapshots of his friends, both posed and candid. Upon learning that Sophie Tucker was entertaining at the Florentine Gardens, nothing would suffice but that Hoover, Tolson, and the Viners take in the show together.

When chatting with Sophie, Hoover learned that she was in the process of writing her autobiography. She informed him that she would call it "The Last of the Red Hot Mamas." Hoover liked good jokes, clever jokes, and thought Sophie might be trying to pull one on him.

He asked, "Sophie, are you going to tell the truth, the whole truth, and nothing but the truth?" When she assured him that she was, he continued, "Are you going to tell about all your love affairs?"

"Of course, Edgar," she replied. "That will help sell the book."

Playing along with what he thought might be an effort to pull his leg, he then said, "If you plan to tell the whole truth, I suggest that you have the book bound in asbestos, otherwise it will sizzle the cover right off."

Sophie allowed as how that was a good idea, and said she would speak to her publisher about it. The next time she saw Hoover she told him that her publisher was unable to do this. Because of the shortages in the supply of asbestos, and its requirement for defense purposes, the government had put it under control. "Like Lucky Strike green," Sophie told Hoover, "asbestos has gone to war." This was a reference to the much-repeated slogan, "Lucky Strike green has gone to war," used by the makers of this brand of cigarettes during World War II to account for the switching of the principal color of the packs containing the cigarettes from green to white. May it be noted that the green color was a war casualty, it never returned from the battlefields. But Hoover thoroughly enjoyed Sophie's joke and never tired of telling it to others.[12]

COMPASSION

There was another side to J. Edgar Hoover little known to the general public. His compassion when agents suffered hardships or experienced disruptive personal problems was one of his most estimable qualities.

Former Special Agent Jack Grady of Rockville, Maryland, was one of the many who remembered Hoover for his compassion and understanding. In October 1943 while assigned to the FBI Field Office in New York City, Jack received word that his father had been killed, the victim of a furnace explosion in the family home in Springfield, Illinois. His widowed mother was left with eight of her sixteen children still living at home. About two weeks after he attended his father's funeral, a sister was rushed to a hospital and was not expected to live. When his mother, distraught and despondent, called to report this latest tragic news, Jack, who was the oldest of her children, told her immediately that he was being transferred to the Springfield, Illinois, office where he could be near the family and could assist her.

This was an off-the-cuff comment to his mother, for Jack had not even by then requested a transfer. But, having worked at FBI headquarters as a clerk before becoming a special agent, he was aware of the Director's position on hardship transfers and knew that he would be given every consideration. In view of the situation at his family home, however, he decided to go to Springfield to assist his mother even if it meant resigning from the FBI.

The morning following his telephone conversation with his mother, Jack submitted a request for a transfer through his New York supervisor. A personal letter from Hoover arrived within 24 hours granting the transfer, and he was on his way to Springfield.

Some years later it was brought to Jack's attention that on the top page of his personnel file was this note in Hoover's distinctive blue ink: "This Agent shall not be transferred from the Springfield Office for so long as he believes he is needed to help his family." [1]

In June 1982, ABC News telecast a vicious program attacking the deceased FBI Director. Members of the Society of Former Special Agents of the Federal Bureau of Investigation flooded the office of Leonard H. Goldenson, chairman of the board of the American Broadcasting Company, with letters containing information refuting the false allegations against Hoover which made up so great a portion of the program.

For instance, former FBI Inspector Lee O. Teague had related a personal experience to an investigative reporter for the ABC program. When it was telecast, that interview and many others favorable to the Director were ignored, while Hoover was severely criticized for a lack of personal interest in his employees. Here is the ignored story Lee Teague had told the investigative reporter:

> During the Vietnam War, the eldest Teague son served in the U.S. Marine Corps for over a year in the Demilitarized Zone (DMZ) near Khe Sanh. He was wounded when a contingent of 5,000 Marines was surrounded and overrun by 48,000 North Vietnam Army troops. Lee and his wife, Jean, received a tele-

gram and very sketchy information to the effect that their son had been shot, was in serious condition, and was not expected to live. Not being able to get any further details concerning his injury, or even any word on where he was hospitalized, the Teagues, as could be expected, were most concerned and distraught.

Lee had not advised FBI headquarters about any of this, although agents with whom he worked in the field office to which he was assigned knew about it. He was, therefore, understandably surprised when he received a long-distance telephone call from J. Edgar Hoover, who extended sympathy and sought such details as were available. The Director said he had a meeting scheduled that day with the commandant of the Marine Corps and would be back in touch with Lee.

Within hours Hoover called Teague again, told him the nature of his son's injuries, said the boy would recover, and reported the welcome news that he had made arrangements for Lee and his wife to speak by telephone with their son, who was being treated at the U.S. Naval Hospital in Guam.

Another agent who could have attested to Hoover's compassion was William C. Sullivan, who years later betrayed the Director, was forced into retirement, and became one of Hoover's bitterest enemies. In the 1950s Bill suffered a near collapse. It was both physical and mental. The Director personally arranged for him to spend several months recuperating in Arizona, and made certain that Sullivan received the best medical attention. He also arranged to have Sullivan's family join him for the last phase of his recovery period. After he recovered, Hoover restored Bill to his position at FBI headquarters, and before leaving the Bureau in 1971, Sullivan had been promoted to the position of Number 3 Man in the FBI hierarchy, only Hoover, himself, and Clyde Tolson, the associate director, outranking him.[2]

Emory Gregg was one of 34 of us transferred to FBIHQ in the summer of 1947 because of a marked increase in counterintelligence work occasioned by revelations of the two former Soviet intelligence service couriers, Elizabeth Terrill Bentley and Whittaker Chambers. They named dozens of American traitors who had penetrated various Executive Branch offices, including the White House, to spy for the Soviets. Emory was an expert on USSR intelligence operations, particularly those of the military intelligence organization known as the GRU.

Not long after reporting to headquarters, he developed a retina infection in both eyes which became increasingly worse, to the point that he feared becoming legally blind. I shared an office with Emory and became aware of the agony which built up in him as he faced the realization that he might have to resign from so challenging a job, one which had become a major part of his life. A morning arrived when Emory told me that he had an appointment with the Director. He said it was his intention to tell Hoover that he felt that he would be able to carry his share of the load as an FBI agent, but that if the

Director felt otherwise, he would on the spot tender his resignation. He left for the appointment about mid-morning. When he returned some two hours later, his jubilation was obvious from his broad, happy smile.

"Ray," he said, "the man is fabulous. He declined my resignation and spent the rest of the time telling me the importance he and the FBI placed in my knowledge, experience, and accomplishments. He plans to draw on these, and can't afford to lose my services. In fact, when he finished, I felt like saying, 'Mr. Hoover, you move your desk over near the window and I'll bring mine up and we'll run this outfit.' "

Emory was provided with a clerical assistant who served as his official eyes, reading letters, reports, studies, and other material for him. He had a particularly retentive memory and was able to absorb material and recall it readily. He became the principal lecturer on espionage and counterintelligence subjects at the FBI Academy at Quantico, Virginia, which trained future agents and those brought in for up-dating in these special disciplines — and his lectures usually received applause from his students. The Director received my silent applause. His compassion and concern for his agents were impressed indelibly on my mind.

Valeria (Val) B. Stewart, the chief nurse in the Bureau's health service office at FBI headquarters, saw Hoover on a regular basis. She began her career in the Bureau as a staff nurse on October 11, 1954, and was promoted to chief nurse in the mid-1960s, a position she occupied until her retirement July 3, 1980.

As chief nurse, one of her duties, and a most important one since like many Washingtonians Hoover was subject to allergy attacks, was to give him a shot each morning to keep the condition under

FBI building, Marine Barracks, Quantico, Virginia, 1942.

Chief Nurse, Valeria Stewart.

control. Usually he was quite busy when she arrived at his office just before 9 A.M. On such days he would give her a pleasant and crisp, "Good morning," and a "Thank you." as she departed. On other occasions, he would greet her then launch into an account of some matter that was occupying his mind.

One thing which was much on his mind for an extended period of time was the health of James E. Crawford, an agent who, as Hoover's chauffeur and bodyguard, accompanied him constantly. Val Stewart came to know James very well.

"Mr. Crawford was black, and very handsome, friendly, and nice," she said. "I saw him often in the office of Miss Gandy, the Director's administrative assistant, but I really got to know him after he had been admitted to George Washington Hospital because of a health problem."

Hoover asked Val to visit Crawford daily and help him and his family. Each morning the Director would ask her what tests the patient had been given, and request that each one be explained in detail. When James' condition was diagnosed as acoustic neuroma (a benign brain tumor) in the occipital area of the head, Hoover showed deep concern and asked Val to continue her daily visits until Crawford recovered. She had explained to him that, while James' condition was very serious, it was operable. The operation was a success.

During Crawford's hospitalization, Hoover visited him several times. The hospital nurses he met remarked to Val about how kind he was and expressed appreciation for how nice he was to them, although they acknowledged having been somewhat awed by him.

While visiting the patient, who recovered quite well, Val had many conversations with him and heard about incidents which occurred when he traveled with Hoover. He talked about how gracious the Director had been when his car, with Crawford driving, ran into a car in front of them when it came to a sudden stop. While neither car was moving fast and the damage was slight, there were two ladies in the other vehicle and Hoover jumped out immediately to inquire about their condition. Neither was hurt at all, but they were so impressed with his concern and graciousness that they practically thanked him for running into their car.

One day James Crawford said to Val, "I'm so tired of people saying that Mr. Hoover discriminates against the Blacks. During Mr. Hoover's younger days, he took many road trips, often accompanied by someone else When we would stop for dinner at a restaurant, Mr. Hoover was frequently told they would not serve me. He would say, 'We won't eat here either,' and he and whoever was with him would leave and eat at a place that would serve all of us." [3]

My wife and I became acquainted with another black special agent who was close to Hoover — Sam Noisette. He was an artist, and my wife, also an artist, accompanied me to exhibits of his pictures which were displayed annually in Washington.

Sam was a painter of considerable worth. The Director had sent him to New York to study, and his landscapes were particularly noteworthy. Hoover and Noisette were friends for years. Sam was in the Director's confidence more than almost anyone else among the agents, and demonstrated a deep and lasting loyalty to Hoover. [4]

Since Hoover's death, a *Washington Post* columnist, Richard Cohen, has carried out what might best be described as a personal vendetta against the Director's reputation. He repeats much of the besmirching allegations that have been made in the past, concentrating particularly on charges that the victim of his vilification, who in death is unable to defend himself, was a racist. His seeming objective was to have the name of the J. Edgar Hoover FBI Building changed to drop Hoover's name. In view of the frequency with which he writes a column on this, he obviously has adopted it as a personal cause celebre. Former FBI Inspector Ben Fulton took exception to Cohen's rantings on the subject when he included them in a December 10, 1997, column. *The Washington Post* carried Ben's reply to the columnist's charges on the 24th of the following month. In part, he stated:

> *Cohen calls Hoover a racist. But the records show that during Hoover's tenure, the FBI's hiring of black agents and employees compared favorably with other federal agencies and most private industries. Let us not forget this was an era before affirmative action. Moreover, the FBI was not responsible for societal conditions that often prevented applicants of all colors from meeting the high standards required even to be considered for one of the few FBI openings.*

> *Cohen mentions Martin Luther King Jr.'s claim that aside from the five members of Hoover's personal staff, the FBI had no black agents. But here, King was loose with the truth. The May 1962 issue of the FBI's monthly employees' magazine has a photograph of a black special agent of the Los Angeles office receiving congratulations and his 20-year service key from Hoover and Associate Director Clyde Tolson.*

The same issue of the employees' magazine mentioned by Ben Fulton also pictured the 1962 basketball team of the FBI Philadelphia office in action, with two black players among the five men on the floor.

Deke DeLoach has attested to the fact that during all the years he worked for Hoover when he had the opportunity to talk with the Director almost every day, Deke never heard him utter a single racial epithet or say anything that suggested he regarded any minority with contempt. DeLoach said, "For a man of his time, he was remarkably free of such prejudices." [5]

This was recognized in 1963 when he was the recipient of the "Pro

Deo et Juventute Award" from the National Catholic Youth Organization Hebrew Congregation "for his unswerving devotion to the betterment of brotherhood among all races, creeds and colors." [6]

During the 30 years I worked under Hoover, in six different offices of the Bureau and at FBI headquarters, I saw no signs of bigotry on his part, and heard of no other agent who did. How can a man who led the fight which destroyed the Ku Klux Klan and the equally racist neo-Nazi, anti-Semitic groups that sprang up both before and after World War II be validly labeled a racist?

Val's husband, W. Donald Stewart, was an agent with whom I worked in the same headquarters division for nine years during the late 50s and until 1965. He told me about a situation where Hoover's understanding and compassion made it possible for a young polio victim to receive treatment which resulted in his rehabilitation from the crippling disease, to the extent that he was able to lead a more normal life.

Don arrived in the FBI field office in Los Angeles on assignment in October 1951. He became a temporary roommate of Special Agent Reginald Vincent, also a new arrival in the office. Reg had been in the Bureau 12 years, was married and had a 7-year old son. His wife and son had not yet arrived in Los Angeles from Newark, New Jersey, where Reg had been assigned to the field office located there.

Reg explained to Don that in 1950 his son, Roger, the polio victim, had been a polio poster boy. To get necessary treatment, his parents decided to move to Los Angeles, which meant that Reg would have to leave the Bureau. He felt that he needed to explain his sudden resignation, so he traveled to Washington, got an appointment to see the Director, and explained the situation to him. Hoover, expressing concern for Roger, told Reg that he surely understood why his parents wanted him to get the best possible care. He remarked that Reg had a very fine record in the FBI and Hoover would like to retain him as an agent. He told Reg that it would not be necessary for him to resign and that he, Hoover, would see that he was transferred to Los Angeles, which he did. Reg had hit the Director's soft spot which often surfaced.

Soon after Roger arrived in Los Angeles with his mother, he was receiving the special treatment available for him, and shortly was in the tow of Don Stewart, a long-distance swimmer. Reg agreed to Don's taking Roger to the local YMCA pool a few times each week to teach him how to swim, knowing that this exercise would strengthen his weak limb. At first these efforts were fruitless, but finally Roger made one lap across the pool, and in time was swimming ten lengths non-stop. Roger eventually, with what he called his "broken wing stroke," was able to swim a quarter of a mile, an accomplishment he would not have attained in the absence of the concern of a fellow agent for the crippled son of another, and the kindness of Director Hoover in making the Los Angeles YMCA pool handy when a marathon swimmer was available to give a helping hand. And Roger, himself, got a big hand from parents and friends of the swim team when he received an accomplishment award during a well-attended ceremony.[7]

It was acts such as these examples that helped Hoover earn the loyalty and respect of thousands of agents who worked under him during his long and distinguished career as head of the Federal Bureau of Investigation. The Society of Former Special Agents includes most of the living ex-agents who knew and worked for him.

Hoover's compassion for those who served him was not limited to his agents but extended as well to his clerical support staff. Inspector Ben Fulton came across a prime example of this when, as part of his regular assignment, he was reviewing a young lady's personnel file. In explanation, Ben wrote:

Director Hoover was often, and sometimes still is, described as a cruel, heartless autocrat without any feelings or compassion for others, especially FBI employees who broke rules and regulations. Hoover was indeed a strict disciplinarian, and rightly so. The work, conduct, and reliability of Federal employees entrusted with responsibilities dealing with the rights and privileges of all citizens must be above reproach. Under him, this principle was a vital part of the training and supervision of FBI personnel. Many of us remember, and the records show, that quite often Hoover's decisions were based on logical, sympathetic reasoning, a fact ignored by those prone to criticize the man.

Ben's review of the young lady's personnel file revealed that she was a single employee at FBI headquarters with an excellent work record who had suddenly resigned. The reason she gave for leaving was that she was needed back at her home. One year later, she reapplied for employment, was hired, and assigned again to FBIHQ. Soon thereafter she confided to a close friend and co-worker that she had left before under false pretenses. She said that her real reason for resigning was that she had been pregnant.

Within a few days, by word-of-mouth, the young lady's secret reached her supervisor and higher-ranking officials. She was questioned and admitted her deception. She said that her pregnancy ended with a miscarriage. She begged to be forgiven, stating that her hopes and aspirations were to have a career in the FBI. She pledged that she would try to be an exemplary employee and would never again do anything to embarrass the Bureau.

A memorandum was prepared setting forth the facts. Because of her falsehoods and deception, a recommendation was made that she be dismissed.

When the memorandum reached Director Hoover, he rejected the recommendation outright. In his traditional, blue-inked script, he set forth his ruling: "No. This young employee has gone through a traumatic experience. She needs help. Give her another chance and provide guidance and assistance where possible. J.E.H." [8]

This was but one more bit of evidence illustrating his concern for the welfare of the men and women who made up what became known as the "FBI family." They benefited measurably from a recreation association which he established known as the FBIRA. It had elected officers, sponsored social and athletic events, and organized trips abroad. It fostered the esprit de corps which bound employees to one another and to the Bureau. A typical illustration of this took

Philadelphia Office Basketball Squad in 1962, sponsored by FBIRA, established by J.E. Hoover.

Director Hoover and Associate Director Clyde Tolson have been enthusiastic supportors of the FBIRA since its inception. They are shown at a baseball game between the FBI and the Baltimore Police Department in 1935. (FBI)

place during a trip the FBIRA arranged for a group of agents, staff members, and their families who desired to make a tour of several European countries.

Art Cammarota was legal attache in Rome at the time and was notified simply that the group would be spending several days in that city. He was advised that members of the touring group had been instructed not to impose upon him, and that he was not expected to spend time with them. This resulted in Art's avoiding contact with the group during business hours; however, nothing would suffice but for him to arrange for the travelers to have a private audience with Pope Pius XII. The Holy Father gave a talk and presented to each a copy of his photograph and a card containing the following:

> *Comments of The Pope During Audience*
> *at Castel Gandolfo*
> *October 19, 1957*
>
> *If We are not mistaken, this is the first time We have received such a Large group of the Federal Bureau of Investigation. On that score you are doubly welcome.*
>
> *Who has not heard of the F. B. I. and its long-experienced and trusted Director? It is a name that puts fear into evil-doers, increases a sense of security in those who would serve their country and their God in justice and charity. Upon you, gentlemen, rests a heavy responsibility. It is a responsibility that demands a more than ordinary measure of self-discipline, self-sacrifice and unselfish dedication to the common good of Society. Hence, the nobility of your profession and its great merit before all law-abiding citizens. It gives Us great satisfaction to add Our word of encouragement; and with a prayer that God's best blessings may be on you always and on those near and dear to you We impart the Apostolic Benediction.*

Art just could not stand to see close and well-liked friends, fellow employees and their families, get away without entertaining them. He and his wife Gloria invited the whole tour group to their house for cocktails and snacks after the papal audience.[9]

This was but an example of the way FBI people felt about one another. There were many indications that, having no close family of his own after his mother died in 1938, Hoover considered the whole FBI his family. That feeling certainly permeated the agent ranks and has persisted to this day among the members of the Society of Former Special Agents, men and women most of whom are not only staunch but outspoken defenders of Hoover. I consider this the sound measure of the man. He earned the lasting respect of most special agents who worked for him, who carried out his policies, who were subject to his discipline and control, and who today comprehend and appreciate, in full measure, the benefits derived from serving under a man of his stature and understanding. And throughout his stewardship of the FBI, he supported them unequivocally.

This once occurred when former Governor Grant Sawyer of Nevada criticized an FBI action. When Hoover reacted sharply to set the record straight, Sawyer said that he had not intended to attack the

FBI or Hoover personally, that his remarks had been directed only at the local FBI office. Hoover quickly responded, "Let me reiterate my oft-stated position that as long as I am Director of this Bureau, any attack upon an FBI employee who is conscientiously carrying out his official duties will be considered an attack on me personally." [10]

He is also remembered for his concern for others. Following the convictions of Julius and Ethel Rosenberg for spying on behalf of the Soviet Union, Hoover was asked for his recommendation on sentences which should be imposed. While there was no doubt in his mind about their guilt, and he concurred in a sentence of death for Julius, he said he was concerned about giving a death sentence "to a woman and mother." The Rosenbergs had two young sons to be orphaned if both were sentenced to death. He recommended against Ethel's execution, but his recommendation was not accepted. [11]

Over the years, Hoover was praised by Roger Baldwin, founder of the American Civil Liberties Union, and Morris Ernst, an ACLU guru, for his care in safeguarding the rights of citizens. [12]

During World War II, Hoover's advocacy of civil rights, laced with a strong compassion for the plight of others, was highly profiled. The "Japanese internment" issue arose soon after the Japanese sneak attack on Pearl Harbor. More than 100,000 Japanese-Americans were rounded up and herded into concentration camps. This was demanded by numerous well-known individuals, including Treasury Secretary Henry Morganthau, renowned columnist Walter Lippmann, California Governor Earl Warren who later became chief justice of the United States, even President Franklin Roosevelt.

Hoover described the demands as "a capitulation to public hysteria" and told Morganthau that arrests should not be made "unless there were sufficient facts (probable cause) upon which to justify the arrests." He contended that the rights of American citizens should be protected, and protested the dragnet procedures. He was overridden. [13]

Although information regarding Hoover's view on the "Japanese internment" issue has been and is available, journalistic prostitutes over the years since the Director's death have written media articles and stated in books that interning Japanese-Americans had been Hoover's idea.

There were signs, such as in this matter and in the Rosenberg case, that Hoover's compassion spilled over to the world outside the FBI. But without question, his concern was centered on the organization which he loved and made into one of the most respected law enforcement agencies in the world.

THE IDEA MAN

The oath of office required of all FBI agents was administered to me July 27, 1942, followed by twelve 73-hour weeks of a grueling regimen of training and indoctrination. On July 20, 1947, nearly five years to the day later, I reported as ordered to the Intelligence Division in FBIHQ where I served continuously until I retired in 1976. My assignment for the first two months was to a so-called correspondence desk with two other newly-arrived supervisors. All types of letters from other agencies and from the general public were routed to that desk to be answered within 48 hours, a deadline strictly insisted upon by Hoover. It was good but demanding training. Bureau files had to be reviewed and policy absorbed to prepare replies which went up the line of command for review and approval — frequently, it must be noted, for disapproval and return for revision. The final review before reaching the Director's office (all correspondence went out over Hoover's signature) was made in the Reading Room. There a bevy of young ladies possessing degrees in education or with similar outstanding qualifications reviewed each piece of outgoing mail for spelling, punctuation, correct form of address, etc. They saved many a supervisor's face, and at times, his career. The Director was a stickler for accuracy. Rumor had it that he established the Reading Room when, in signing a volume of mail late one evening, he put his name to one letter which described a process he had gone through as "sole-searching" rather than "soul-searching." This shoe just did not fit.

After the two months on the correspondence desk, I received my wings and was assigned to a substantive desk to handle espionage, intelligence, counterintelligence, and other national security-type violations. In the office next to mine there was a research desk manned by one supervisor, Bill Sullivan.

There was a steno pool in our division, then known as the Internal Security Division, next called the Domestic Intelligence Division, and, ultimately, the Intelligence Division. This pool was headed by one of the finest and most respected ladies at FBIHQ, Mrs. Thelma Dorset, known to all as Mrs. D. When a desk supervisor required stenographic services, he called Mrs. D, who dispatched the first available stenographer.

It was not long before I noticed that Bill Sullivan, next door, had a typewriter on a stand beside his desk, frequently turned to type a few lines or paragraphs, and seemed to have little communication with Mrs. D. In a way, I admired his typing ability — I had none and still lack any. But he was the only agent supervisor in our division who seemed to do his own typing. When I remarked about this and expressed curiosity, I was told that Bill maintained a running memorandum and sent a copy of the latest additions directly to Hoover.

The thought of having a neighbor in direct correspondence with the man whose finger was on one's career button was somewhat disturbing, to say the least. However, those in the know vouched for Bill, explaining that he was a good research man and idea generator and the Director thought highly of his ability. He was the only agent (known to them) that Hoover addressed by the first name. This was

Author at Training Session in 1942.

no doubt true. When, some years later, the boss sent me a letter of approval it was by means of a "Dear Wannall" letter, omitting the "Mr.," considered to be an indication one's career was on track and a badge of honor.

In a short time I came to like Bill and to respect him and his ability. He seemed to reciprocate this. After he became assistant director in the spring of 1961 and took over as head of our division, he approved my immediate super-visor's recommendation that I be promoted by being appointed to the very first opening that occurred in a section chief position. A few years later when I was hospitalized for surgery, he visited me and gave me two books which I still possess and prize. One was a guide to good health through nutrition and the other a select collection of U.S. Civil War photographs duly inscribed "To Ray, with all good wishes for a speedy and complete recovery. Bill Sullivan."

Bill posed as defender of the common man — and the common desk supervisor. There was a time in the early 1950s when FBI work backlogged to the extent that we were put on a six-day week. Agents throughout the organization had been volunteering about two hours-a-day overtime, for which they were not paid. The average weekly overtime of 10 hours per man was then divided by six rather than five workdays — few put in the extra two hours on Saturdays. Average per man dropped to the neighborhood of 1 hour 40 minutes a day. The bean counters up the line began putting pressure on division heads and special agents in charge of field offices to get the average back to the two-hour figure. One SAC who was known for his memorable malapropisms, called his men into conference and said he expected every one of them to be above the office average.

When, during a supervisors' conference, Assistant Director Al Belmont discussed the need to maintain a high overtime average, Bill Sullivan stood up and took exception on behalf of his fellow supervisors. He said he was a slow worker and had no objections to volunteering extra work to carry a fair share of the load, but there were some agents who produced much more rapidly than others and he thought it unfair to hold everyone to the same overtime requirements. There had been so much dissension over the demands to maintain a two-hour average for six days that almost without exception the agents were pleased to have Sullivan speak up on their behalf, although very few would own up to belonging to Bill's "slow worker" category.

Hoover was well aware of the evils of communism, his education in this regard being traceable to the post-World War I Palmer Red Raids. To handle prosecutions of aliens judged by the Department of Labor to be deportable by reason of their advocacy of, and adherence to, communism, he had studied and become an expert in its tenets. Whether from an academic interest or to curry favor, Sullivan developed an expertise in this same ideological aberration. He had developed an ability to conduct the full-day-10-hour lecture on communism which had been given to all new agents in the early 1940s. At the outset, the lecturer would get the class to agree that war was

Firearms training.

abhorrent. Building on this premise, in five hours he proceeded to convince his audience that communism was the solution to the world's problems. As he began the sixth hour, addressing his listeners as "Comrades," he proceeded in the remaining five hours to reconvert them to rationality by proving the fallacy of his previous presentation. Bill was an accomplished public speaker and excelled in making such presentations.

History has shown that Sullivan traded on the anti-communism bond with Hoover to lead the Director down two paths which have subjected Hoover to some of the most severe criticism he has suffered since his demise. One was the domestic counterintelligence program known as COINTELPRO, and the other was the Martin Luther King, Jr., investigation. The gates to both of these were set ajar by Sullivan's emphasis on the communist aspects of each. His fingerprints can be detected on other Bureau operations which in turn drew adverse reactions.

COINTELPRO

COINTELPRO was a series of covert action programs conducted by the FBI between 1956 and 1971 and directed at organizations which were the subjects of national security investigations. The objective of these counterintelligence investigations (COINTELPROs) was to use FBI resources to disrupt certain selected groups in order to counter perceived threats to national security.

To understand how Sullivan managed to get Hoover and the FBI into such a sticky morass of criticism over COINTELPRO, it is necessary to consider some pertinent background material.

When I was first assigned to counterintelligence (CI) work in Philadelphia in January 1944, the Bureau was already conducting CI programs in the foreign intelligence area of its responsibilities. These were directed against foreign intelligence services operating in the United States and had three principal goals:

1. Identify the intelligence agents;
2. Determine their activities, in advance, if possible; and
3. Take measures necessary to assure that they would not attain their objectives.

Successful CI operations involve an expertise requiring specialized training and extensive experience. Abroad, the CIA and the military services have applied counterintelligence to dampen threats against U.S. security and defense interests. Domestically, the FBI has relied on it to neutralize threats, usually those issuing from abroad, and to solve some of its more renowned espionage cases of the Hoover era. These included cases on such spies for the Soviet Union as Col. Rudolph Abel, Julius and Ethel Rosenberg, and Alger Hiss. Counterintelligence techniques were utilized by the patriots who established the United States and have been applied to protect the nation throughout its history.

The Church Committee defined counterintelligence as "those actions by an intelligence agency intended to protect its own security and to undermine hostile intelligence operations." It continued:

> Under COINTELPRO certain techniques the Bureau had used against hostile foreign agents were adopted for use against perceived domestic threats to the established political and social order. The formal programs which incorporated these techniques were, therefore, also called "counterintelligence".[1]

William Sullivan was quoted by the Committee as having testified about the use of such counterintelligence techniques in a series of five domestic programs under the COINTELPRO label as follows:

> This is a rough, tough, dirty business, and dangerous. It was dangerous at times. No holds were barred.... . We have used [these techniques] against Soviet agents. They have used [them] against us... [The same methods were] brought home against organizations against which we were targeted. We did not differentiate. This is a rough, tough business.[2]

The domestic threats referred to by the Committee involved activities of organizations and their supporters who were for the most part U.S. citizens. The domestic counterintelligence program might more aptly have been named the counter-subversion program, or the counter-terrorism program, because it had as its targets domestic subversive and terrorist groups, their members, and their advocates.

At the time I reported to the Intelligence Division for assignment in the summer of 1947 there was a unit, to which three agent supervisors were assigned, handling matters related to overthrow or destruction of the U.S. Government. It concentrated on cases involving organizations having foreign ties whose members were involved in activities deemed detrimental to the national security. Some of the operations mounted included use of techniques which would conform to the Church Committee's definition of counterintelligence and which were applied to the Communist Party, USA. The Party's devotion to and control by the Soviet Union throughout its existence has been well documented.

This was the situation when, on March 8, 1956, Director Hoover briefed the National Security Council (NSC) during a special session held in the Cabinet Room at the White House and presided over by the President. His topic was "The Present Menace of Communist Espionage and Subversion." I had the responsibility for coordinating background information submitted by supervisors throughout the Division and writing the briefing paper. The presentation was in two main sections: (I) The Domestic Menace of Communism; (II) The Soviet Espionage Pattern.[3]

Immediately upon returning from the briefing session, Hoover prepared a memorandum in which he named 18 attendees and commented that several others were there. Those he specifically named were:

President Dwight D. Eisenhower
Vice President Richard M. Nixon
Undersecretary of State Herbert Hoover, Jr.
Director of the Office of Defense Mobilization Arthur S. Flemming
Special Assistant to the President William H. Jackson
Secretary of Defense Charles E. Wilson
Vice Chairman of the Joint Chiefs of Staff General Thomas White
Attorney General Herbert Brownell, Jr.
Director of CIA Allen Dulles
Chairman of the Atomic Energy Commission Admiral Lewis L. Strauss
Director of the Bureau of the Budget Rowland R. Hughes
Special Assistant to the President Harold E. Stassen
Secretary of the Treasury George M. Humphrey
Special Assistant to the President Dillon Anderson
Governor Sherman Adams
Deputy Assistant to the President General Wilton B. Persons
National Security Council staff member J. Patrick Coyne
Assistant Attorney General J. Walter Yeagley [4]

At the briefing the highest-level officials in the Executive Branch of the government were made aware of some of the most confidential and sensitive countermeasures utilized by the FBI in its operations in the national security field. No objection to their use was voiced by the President or any other attendee and no one questioned the desirability of applying such techniques. These countermeasures were ones utilized in the pre-COINTELPRO days, but obviously served as a blueprint for the programs later conducted under this designation. Hoover described them in the following terms:

- To determine the program and activities of the CPUSA so that the national security could be protected in time of a real emergency, the FBI sought to infiltrate, penetrate and disrupt the Party.
- All means available to secure information and evidence were utilized. These included (1) interviews with cooperative former communists; (2) penetration of the party by Bureau informants; (3) use of confidential sources, including telephone surveillances, microphones, trash covers, mail covers, surreptitious entry to photograph secret records, opening a safe to secure some 400 photographs of documents revealing secret plans of the Party's operations.
- Members of the Party who might be called upon to commit sabotage and espionage should an extreme emergency develop were carefully catalogued. [The cold war was in full swing at the time.]
- As a result of prosecutable action based on admissible evidence developed by the FBI, 136 communist leaders had been indicted and 95 convicted, with many awaiting trial for violation of the Smith Act.

With regard to the special techniques utilized to secure information, Hoover explained:

> I make specific mention of these techniques because in many instances derogatory information will be attributed to a confidential source in our investigative reports. The identity of these sources cannot be disclosed outside the Bureau and in many instances, these are the sources which are publicly condemned as gossipers and "faceless informers." Communist lawyers will use any possible means to force their disclosure.

After speaking extensively on "The Soviet Espionage Pattern," Hoover concluded his briefing:

> World-wide communism has made its greatest advances through the penetration and softening of its victims with fifth columns from within. The American communist is dedicated to the infiltration of all of our cultural and industrial institutions for the single purpose of creating and maintaining the most devastating fifth column the world has ever known
>
> The ability of the Soviets in 37 years aided by their far-flung fifth column to bring under their tyrannical control one-third of the world's population and one-fourth of the earth's surface proves the effectiveness of their tactics which are to convert all the world to communism — by trickery if possible but by force if necessary.[5]

Director Hoover's briefing was well received. No one expressed any reservations about the type of techniques the Bureau was utilizing and the President "commended the report," commenting upon the fact that he did not believe the National Security Council had ever had such a complete and thorough briefing upon this subject.[6]

Four months later, on July 17, 1956, William Sullivan, the idea generator, proposed that the counterintelligence operations which were being directed against the Communist Party be considered by a committee "to discuss and formulate and recommend a *systematic program* [emphasis added]for the disruption of the Communist Party, USA." To accomplish this he proposed using as a vehicle the Socialist Workers Party (SWP), whose members were followers of the teachings of Leon Trotsky:

> *The Bureau receives reports daily showing the confusion, uncertainty, and dissatisfaction in the Communist Party, USA. There are even signs of factionalism developing. The time has never been better to take steps to systematically disrupt the Communist Party. Dissatisfaction in the Party stems in the main from developments at the 30th Congress of the Soviet Union held February 14 to 25, 1956, during the course of which Stalin was wholly denounced... .*
>
> *The Trotskyites, aware of the dissatisfaction within the Communist Party, USA, are now engaged in an organized campaign to recruit members from among the dissatisfied communists... . Also the Socialist Workers Party has acknowledged that the socialist movement in the United States includes the Communist Party, USA.*[7]

A committee was set up with Sullivan as its chairman and the COINTELPRO-CPUSA was instituted on or about August 28, 1956. A memorandum of that date showed how the Bureau hoped to seize some degree of control and direction over the Socialist Workers Party's campaign against the Communist Party:

> *The Socialist Workers Party (SWP) is making an all-out effort to win over CP members who have become disillusioned with Stalinist communism. SWP members are distributing copies of The Militant (SWP publication) at CP rallies and meetings, and are contacting individual CP members in an attempt to sell them the SWP philosophy. This SWP program could very definitely benefit the Bureau provided we can achieve through our informant coverage in the SWP some degree of control and direction over it. The ultimate goal would be to continue and intensify pressure on the CP from the left. Since the Party is already under pressure from the right, the combined pressure would contribute materially to distracting the CP from its primary goals.*

A letter was then sent to several FBI field offices to have them check into "the possibility of initiating several specific steps aimed at the Bureau's furthering, assisting and possibly adding to the current SWP disruptive program." Upon receiving positive replies, FBI Headquarters activated the program.[8]

When interviewed by the Church Committee, the FBI supervisor handling COINTELPRO-CPUSA explained the purpose of the program as being: (1) to develop intelligence to determine what the Party was doing; (2) to stop the spread of communism; and (3) to stop the effectiveness of the Party as a vehicle of Soviet intelligence, propaganda, and agitation.

The Church Committee in its report commented, "Had the Bureau stopped there, perhaps the term 'counterintelligence' would have been an accurate label for the program. The expansion of the CPUSA program to non-Communists, however, and the addition of subsequent programs, make it clear that other purposes were also at work." [9]

Of some significance is the fact that only 2370 actions were authorized under all five domestic COINTELPROs during a 15 year period, and 58% of them, 1388, were directed against the CPUSA, a target with which the Church Committee indicated it could concur. [10]

On November 6, 1958, J. Edgar Hoover again briefed the President, together with his Cabinet, and said:

> To counteract a resurgence of Communist Party influence in the United States we have a... program designed to intensify any confusion and dissatisfaction among its members.

> During the past two years this program has been most effective. Selected informants were briefed and trained to raise controversial issues within the Party. In the process many were able to advance themselves to higher positions.

> The Internal Revenue Service was furnished the names and addresses of Party functionaries who had been active in the underground apparatus. Based on this information, investigations were instituted of 263 possible income tax evasion cases. Anti-communist literature and simulated Party documents were mailed anonymously to carefully chosen members. Two of our anti-communist pamphlets were sent to the Soviet Union by the Communist Party as evidence of the problems it faces in this country.

> These programs are part of our overall counterintelligence operations. They are specific answers to specific problems which have arisen within our investigative jurisdiction.

The FBI Director made it clear to the President and Cabinet members that this investigative jurisdiction in the internal security field extended to more than CPUSA coverage. He told the assembled officials:

> The Public usually associates the FBI's internal security investigations with Communist Party activities only. Nothing could be further from the truth. Our investigations encompass any and all organizations based on a creed of force and violence to determine whether they are a threat to our internal security or whether they violated any Federal laws.

> We investigate the activities of such diverse and international organizations as the Marxist Socialist Workers Party and the Nationalist Party of Puerto Rico. [11]

It should be noted that Director Hoover referred to these two groups as international organizations as contrasted to domestic ones. The foreign aspects of the former were touched upon by David Martin, an internal security expert, a Senate staffer for about 20 years, and, during the 1970s, senior analyst for the Senate Subcommittee on Internal Security. In the fall of 1981, he explained that the Socialist Workers Party was committed to the ultimate revolutionary overthrow of the United States Government, to its defeat in war, and to the establishment of a proletarian dictatorship.[12]

If the SWP members' patron saint Leon Trotsky, rather than Joseph Stalin, had won the power struggle in Russia upon the death of Vladimir Lenin in January 1924, the SWP would have become the leading Soviet communist party. Since he did not, the SWP became the bitter enemy of the Stalin-oriented party and a natural vehicle to be selected by Bill Sullivan to support what he termed a systematic program against the Communist Party, USA.

The second organization which Hoover saw fit to mention specifically, the Nationalist Party of Puerto Rico (NPPR), had in 1949 been cited by Attorney General Howard McGrath as an organization which sought "to alter the form of government of the United States by unconstitutional means." [13]

The NPPR was charged by Governor Luis Munoz Marin of Puerto Rico with having international communist connections. On October 30, 1950, the organization instigated a revolt in Puerto Rico and attempted to assassinate him. The revolt resulted in the death of 31 persons and was described by the governor as a conspiracy helped by the communists. [14]

In an attempt to assassinate President Truman on November 1, 1950, just two days later, members of the NPPR tried to shoot their way into the Blair House in Washington, which the President and his family were then occupying while the White House was being renovated. Guards killed one of them and wounded another. In the skirmish, one guard was fatally shot and two others were seriously injured. The wounded Puerto Rican was convicted of murder and sentenced to death. President Truman commuted his sentence to life imprisonment.

Five members of Congress were wounded in the House of Representatives on March 1, 1954, by four Puerto Ricans, one a woman, who fired pistols at random from a spectators' gallery, shouting for Puerto Rican independence. The five congressmen recovered, and the attackers were sentenced to prison. [15]

So, Hoover took advantage of the November 6, 1958, briefing to put on notice, once again, the President and his advisors of the types of organizations being targeted and the kinds of counterintelligence measures being used against groups engaged in domestic violence or seeking to alter the U.S. government by unconstitutional means.

Bill Sullivan became assistant director and head of the division in June 1961. Until then, there was no expansion of COINTELPRO as such. The four remaining programs were instituted between 1961 and 1968 and were in effect under the following designations:

> Socialist Workers Party: Like the NPPR, the SWP was cited by the attorney general as an organization which sought "to alter the government of the United States by unconstitutional means." [16]

It was the major Trotskyite organization in the United States, formed during a four-day conference ending January 3, 1938, after it was expelled from the U.S. Socialist Party. It adopted a "Declaration of Principles" stating:

The main specific task of the S.W.P is the mobilization of the American masses for struggle against American capitalism and for its overthrow... .

It is, consequently, the elementary and imperative duty of all workers, and especially the revolutionary party, to defend the Soviet Union unconditionally against any and every imperialist nation. [17]

In 1941 the leaders of the SWP were indicted under the Smith Act (Internal Security Act of 1940) for advocating the overthrow of the government by force and violence. They were convicted and served jail sentences.[18]

The organization was found by a congressional committee to be the American section of the Fourth International, which was formed by followers of Leon Trotsky, a leader in Russia's October 1917 revolution and later Stalin's chief rival for power. The committee designated it the "Trotskyite Terrorist International." The SWP claimed not to be a part of this but welcomed two members from the Fourth International to participate in its closed convention in August 1973. Further, it had 24 delegates of its own attend a February 1974 congress of the International who served as the leadership of one of the factions there. [19]

During the early 1970s, the Party controlled the National Peace Action Coalition (NPAC), a group which was prominent in the protests against the war in Vietnam. Its youth group, the Young Socialist Alliance (YSL), targeted police, calling for their expulsion from the Black community and their replacement by a self-defense militia drawn from, selected by, and controlled by the Black community itself. The YSL also discussed means whereby it could handle Arab students in the United States and support their activities in defense of the Palestinian terrorist movement. [20]

Members of the SWP engaged in a considerable amount of travel to Cuba, and the Party was very friendly to the Cuban communist regime. It helped organize the Fair Play for Cuba Committee, Fidel Castro's first propaganda and information-collection network in the United States, established shortly after he seized power.[21]

During the course of the SWP COINTELPRO, it was determined that Lee Harvey Oswald, assassin of President Kennedy, claimed a connection to the Party. A famous photograph showed him holding a rifle in one hand and a copy of the official SWP publication, The Militant, in the other.[22]

In view of background information on the SWP available to the FBI, in October 1961 a survey was ordered in five field offices and it was determined that a "Socialist Workers Party — Disruption Program" was warranted. When begun the following month, it was emphasized to the five offices that the operation was "not intended to be a 'crash' program. Only carefully thought-out operations with the widest possible effect and benefit to the nation" should be considered. The program was discontinued in October 1969 after 46 counterintelligence-type operations had been implemented.[23]

White Hate Groups: In September 1964, a directive was sent to 17 field offices instituting a counterintelligence operation against the Ku Klux Klan and other white hate organizations, including the American Nazi Party and the National States Rights Party. In June, three civil rights workers had disappeared in Mississippi. President Johnson on July 2 had talked to the Director about this and was told by Hoover that his agents were convinced the White Knights of the Ku Klux Klan were behind the disappearances.

"Edgar," the President said, "I want you to put people after the Klan and study it from one county to the next. I want the FBI to have the best intelligence system possible to check on the activities of these people." [24]

This followed Attorney General Robert Kennedy's advice to the President that techniques such as the FBI had used in infiltrating communist groups should be applied to the Klan.[25]

The program ordered by the President involved a total of 289 counterintelligence actions, signaled the end of the KKK's power in Mississippi by July 1968, and was discontinued with respect to all white hate groups on April 28, 1971.[26]

Black Nationalists: In August 1967, rioting across the country had attracted the support of Black nationalist groups, and demands of officials and the public alike prompted the FBI to undertake this counterintelligence program. The primary target was the Black Panther Party (BPP). Its publications encouraged the killing of law enforcement officers. Its paper, The Black Panther, contained an article on April 25, 1970, suggesting:

The only way to make this racist U.S. government administer justice to the people it is oppressing is ... by taking up arms against this government, killing the officials, until the reactionary forces are dead, and those that are left turn their weapons on their superiors, thereby passing revolutionary judgment against the number one enemy of all mankind, the racist U.S. government.

Other targeted organizations included the Revolutionary Action Movement, Deacons for Defense of Justice, and the Nation of Islam.[27]

Attorney General Ramsey Clark added his support to the Black Nationalist COINTELPRO in a letter to Director Hoover on September 14, 1967:

In view of the seriousness of the riot activity across the country, it is most important that you use the maximum available resources, investigative and intelligence, to collect and report all facts bearing upon the question as to whether there has been or is a scheme or conspiracy by any group of whatever size, effectiveness or affiliation, to plan, promote or aggravate riot activity... .

I appreciate that the Bureau has constantly been alert to this problem and is currently submitting intelligence reports to us ... .

We must recognize, I believe, that this is a relatively new area of investigation and intelligence reporting for the FBI and the Department of Justice... .

In these circumstances, we must be certain that every attempt is being made to get all information bearing upon these problems ... .

(S)ources or informants in black nationalist organizations, SNCC [Student Nonviolent Coordinating Committee] and other less publicized groups, should be developed and expanded.[28]

Discontinued on April 28, 1971, this program had involved a total of 362 counterintelligence operations.[29]

New Left: In May 1968, this program was started when the nation was undergoing an era of disruption and violence caused to a large extent by various individuals generally associated with the New Left. Some of these activists urged revolution in the country, and called for the defeat of the United States in Vietnam. They often falsely alleged police brutality and utilized unlawful acts to further their causes.[30]

The Weather Underground Organization (WUO), made up primarily of such activists, declared itself to be:

a revolutionary organization of communist men and women. We grow from the civil rights, anti-war and youth movements of the 1960s ... .

We are part of a wave of revolution sparked by the Black liberation struggle, by the death of Che [Guevara] in Bolivia in 1967, and by the people's war in Vietnam ... .

Our goal is to attack imperialism's ability to exploit and wage war against all oppressed peoples. Our final goal is the complete destruction of imperialism, the seizure of the means of production and the building of socialism. [31]

The WUO claimed "credit" for 27 bombings committed between the 7th of October, 1969, and the 5th of September 1975. Seven of these were against state offices which were part of the criminal justice system; six against private business offices; an additional six against police targets; two, military targets; two, university targets; and one each against the San Francisco office of the U.S. Department of Health, Education and Welfare, the Washington DC headquarters of the U.S. Department of State, the Pentagon, and the U.S. Capitol Building.[32]

The COINTELPRO operation was discontinued April 28, 1971, after 285 actions were approved.[33]

Information concerning the COINTELPRO operations was surfaced after an FBI office in Media, Pennsylvania, was burglarized in March 1971. Following a law suit by NBC newsman Carl Stern, the FBI released a number of memoranda relating to the operations. As a result of the compromise of the programs, those still in existence were terminated as of April 28, 1971.[34]

The Socialist Workers Party brought a civil action against the United States, naming the FBI as a defendant, claiming damages for the counterintelligence operation which had been mounted against the organization, and, after an extended trial in 1981, was awarded a favorable decision. During the trial, a deposition of Bill Sullivan, taken March 3, 1976, was introduced as Exhibit 156. In response to a question as to his personal knowledge of the SWP, Sullivan was quoted as having responded:

"This is no criticism of the Socialist Workers Party. I never considered it to be of sufficient importance from the standpoint of its size and standpoint of its activities to warrant my giving it personal attention, you see, or picking up the phone and calling the man around who ran the operation and saying, now look, give me a rundown on this every week."

He claimed to have no recollection of a program known as the Socialist Workers Party Disruption Program. He went on to say that what he did recall was "a counterintelligence program and as to whether or not what you referred to is part of it, I have no recollection of that; in any event, if it did exist, it existed under the orders of J. Edgar Hoover, just as all counterintelligence programs existed under the order of Hoover." [35]

All FBI programs, as well as all other official FBI activities, had Hoover's approval while he was Director. But Sullivan's comment was couched in terms to conceal his own initiation of the program.

Professor John T. Elliff, who later headed the FBI task force of the Church Committee, told the Senate Judiciary Committee on March 18, 1974, that Sullivan was responsible for the counterintelligence plan against radical groups in the 1960s and also directed a program which called for "bugging, break-in, and mail cover operations against radicals," [36]

While this presentation concerning COINTELPRO was not undertaken to justify it in all its parts, in the interest of fairness to Sullivan, cognizance must be taken of the climate of the times in which the program operated. Twice in just four days President Johnson in national TV broadcasts decried the violence, the riots, the lawlessness, and warned public officials against only a "business-as-usual" response. Some elements of the media were vicious in their criticism of Hoover over COINTELPRO, but there was public support for it in various sectors.

Columnist Victor Riesel wrote on June 15, 1973, "no apologies are due from those in the highest authority for secretly developing a domestic counterrevolutionary intelligence stratagem in early 1970." Detailing the record of "dead students," "university libraries in flames," and "insensate murdering of cops," he concluded, "it would have been wrong not to have attempted to counter the sheer off-the-wall terrorism of the 1969-70 bomb seasons. And it would be wrong today. No one need apologize for counterrevolutionary action."

"Our reaction is that we are exceedingly glad he [Hoover] ordered it," reported the St. Louis Globe-Democrat in a December 11, 1973, editorial on COINTELPRO. This newspaper noted:

(T)he Federal Bureau of Investigation under the late J. Edgar

Hoover conducted a three-year campaign of counterintelligence *"to expose, disrupt, and neutralize" the New Left movement... (M)any of these New Left groups were doing everything they could to undermine the Government and some of them resorted to bombings, street riots, and other gangster tactics. Others waged war on police across the Nation and on our system of justice. Still others disrupted the Nation's campuses. The Nation can be thankful it has a courageous and strong leader of the FBI to deal with the serious threats posed by New Left groups during this period.*

On June 18, 1974, Eugene H. Methvin, senior editor, the Reader's Digest, testified before the House Committee on Foreign Affairs regarding terrorism, and said:

(T)he FBI's counterintelligence program against the extremist core of the New Left was a model of sophisticated, effective counter-terrorist law enforcement action first developed and applied with devastating effect against the Ku Klux Klan in the mid-1960s. In that context the strategy won great publicity and praise; yet now we have the Attorney General condemning it. In the current climate of justifiable revulsion over Watergate, we are in danger of crippling law enforcement intelligence in a hysteria of reverse McCarthyism in which we close our eyes to evidence and some compelling necessities of domestic and international security. [37]

Following release of COINTELPRO material to Carl Stern, a committee was set up by the attorney general to make a study of the operations, and from time to time there were leaks of information indicating that he had "condemned" parts of the program; this is what was referred to by Methvin. It was five months after Methvin's testimony before Attorney General William B. Saxbe released the results of the study committee's deliberations during a press conference, and termed "disruption of political groups" as "not something we in a free society should condone." A report he released November 18, 1974, however, said that the overwhelming bulk of the activities were:

clearly legitimate and proper undertakings within the scope of the FBI's ongoing activities and are listed as "COINTELPRO activities" only because they were reported as such... . A fair, accurate, and comprehensive understanding of the various "COINTELPRO" activities undertaken by the FBI is possible only in the light of the context and climate in which the programs were established. [38]

FBI Director Clarence M. Kelley took exception to Saxbe's criticism of some of the operations, pointing out that the measures "helped bring about a favorable change," and that failure to disrupt violence-prone groups would have been an abdication of the FBI's responsibilities to the American people.

When testifying before the Church Committee on December 10, 1975, Director Kelley called to the Committee's attention that its members and staff had "unprecedented access to FBI information." Interviews had been conducted with Bureau personnel who were involved directly in every facet of the Bureau's day-to-day intelligence operations. "It is perhaps the nature of [congressional] hearings," he said, "to focus on abuses to the exclusion of positive accomplishments of the organization," and continued:

The counterintelligence programs which have received the lion's share of public attention and critical comment, constituted an infinitesimal portion of our overall work.

A Justice Department Committee which was formed last year to conduct a thorough study of the FBI's counterintelligence programs has reported that in the five basic ones it found 3,247 counterintelligence [proposals] were submitted to FBI headquarters from 1956 to 1971. Of this total, 2,370, less than three-fourths were approved.

I repeat, the vast majority of those 3,247 proposals were being devised, considered, and many were rejected, in an era when the FBI was handling an average of 700,000 investigative matters per year.

Nevertheless, the criticism which has been expressed regarding the counterintelligence programs is most legitimate and understandable.

The question might well be asked what I had in mind when I stated last year that for the FBI to have done less than it did under the circumstances then existing would have been an abdication of its responsibilities to the American people.

What I said then, in 1974, and what I believe today, is that the FBI employees involved in these programs did what they felt was expected of them by the President, the Attorney General, the Congress, and the people of the United States. [39]

COINTELPROs were conducted during a 15 year period when the 2,370 actions were approved by FBI headquarters. It was not announced how many of these approved actions were completed, only that some were not. According to Clarence Kelley's figures, in 15 years while averaging 700,000 investigative matters each year, the Bureau would have handled a total of 10,500,000. Even if all approved counterintelligence operations had been completed, the fraction of the Bureau's work they represented would have been, as Kelley stated, infinitesimal indeed: 2,370 divided by 10,500,000.

David Martin, with a long record of expertise in internal security matters, made an in-depth study of these five basic domestic programs and concluded the results were impressive:

The Communist Party was devastated, its membership reduced in less than a decade from 70,000 to 5,000 members. The KKK, which, in the early 1960s had been involved in an orgy of attacks on civil rights workers (three civil rights activists were murdered by Klansmen in Philadelphia, Mississippi, in June, 1964) and the bombing and burning of churches and synagogues, was exposed and devastated. The Black Panther movement, which had been involved in scores of deadly attacks on law enforcement officers, was for all practical purposes put out of business.

In studying the New Left counterintelligence program, Martin commented that the Church Committee took particular note of twelve ideas generated by the FBI for disrupting activists in the group:

The suggested techniques included instituting "personal conflicts or animosities" between New Left leaders, creating the impression that leaders are "informants for the Bureau or other law enforcement agencies"; having members arrested on marijuana charges; sending anonymous letters about a student's activities to parents, neighbors, and the parent's employers ("This could have the effect of forcing the parents to take action"); using "friendly news media" and law enforcement officials to disrupt New Left coffeehouses near military bases which were attempting to "influence members of the Armed Forces"; and using "misinformation" to "confuse and disrupt" New Left activities, for example, by notifying members that events have been cancelled.

Martin concluded that a few of the proposals were open to challenge on the grounds they constituted personal harassment, but that, by far, the majority of them were "standard counterintelligence techniques for weakening and disrupting organizations which pose a danger to domestic tranquillity or national security." Acknowledging that the basic ethical problem was not a new one, Martin quoted from a letter Thomas Jefferson sent to one J. B. Colvin in 1810:

A strict observance of the written laws is doubtless one of the high duties of a good citizen, but it is not the highest. The laws of necessity, of self-preservation, of saving our country when in danger, are of a higher obligation... To lose our country by a strict adherence to the written law, would be to lose the law itself, with life, liberty, property, and all those who are enjoying them with us; thus absurdly sacrificing the end to the means. [40]

During the 1981 trial in New York of the civil action brought by the Socialist Workers Party against the U.S. government, including the FBI, testimony was introduced concerning the SWP counterintelligence program. After his June 2 testimony explaining the two separate functions of the FBI, one investigative and the other intelligence, former Attorney General Herbert Brownell was asked by the court what his understanding was about the source of the authority for the FBI to conduct countermeasures against the Communist Party and other subversive groups. Brownell replied that it was presidential directives. The following exchange then ensued:

The Court: "Just so we don't leave with any misunderstanding in this case, Mr. Brownell, there has been evidence about measures taken by the FBI against various Party groups to disorganize and disrupt specifically meaning what are called poison pen letters to attempt to cause dissension;

"Various forms of anonymous communications to cause a landlord, say, not to rent space: cause defections by leaders of the group, and even more physical types of things to break up demonstrations and so forth.

"Is that the kind of thing that you understood as being talked about when they referred to disorganization and disruption or was it something else?

"I just don't want to have any misunderstanding because of any generalities."

The Witness: "Well, I don't know of any specific instances of the type that you mention that came to my attention while I was in office.

"I think the legal situation was that the President did not give any restriction on the methods that were to be used to accomplish the ends that he sought other than in the case of wiretapping as to which I have already testified.

"Further, that the FBI was subject to correctional surveillance from time to time and questioned about its intelligence activities as well as its prosecution or investigation program and that was the legal framework under which they were operating."[41]

In Re: Martin Luther King, Jr.

Martin Luther King, Jr., the well-known civil rights advocate, was president of the Southern Christian Leadership Conference (SCLC). Born in Atlanta, January 15, 1929, he became nationally prominent during 1955 and 1956 when he organized a protest that ended bus segregation in Montgomery, Alabama. As a result of his activities in racial matters, he was arrested on numerous occasions by local officials and charged with misdemeanors. Throughout his efforts in the racial field, he stressed nonviolent action.

Since his death he has been properly recognized and honored for his forceful and successful campaign for the advancement of civil rights for all. This presentation on Dr. King has been prepared to protray information about the man which was available to the FBI and formed the basis for its investigation, as well as Director Hoover's appraisal of him. As noted in the ensuing account, the information has been corroborated publicly.

Renowned author John Barron in 1996 revealed that Jack Childs was a reliable double agent operated by the FBI for more than 25 years against the Communist Party, USA, and the Soviet Union. In 1958, James Jackson, the Party's secretary in charge of "Negro and Southern Affairs," informed Childs that the "most secret and guarded people, - - - party guys far removed from the top level," were in touch with, consulted with, and were guiding Martin Luther King.

On May 6, 1960, Jack Childs reported:

Hunter Pitts [Jack] O'Dell is working full time in connection with the King mass meeting to be held in Harlem on May 17, 1960. Working closely with O'Dell are Stanley and Roy Levison [Bennett]. The CP considers [the] King meeting of the most importance and feels that it is definitely to the Party's advantage to assign outstanding Party members to work with the [Martin] Luther King group. CP policy at the moment is to concentrate upon Martin Luther King.[1]

Baron's book disclosed that Levison met King in the 1950s and subsequently attached himself to King as a personal confidant adviser. At his behest, Dr. King employed Jack O'Dell, a secret member of the Communist Party's governing body, in the SCLC. Levison was regularly dealing with a sophisticated officer of the Soviet intelligence service known as the KGB -- his name, Victor Lessiovsky.

Syndicated columnist Joseph Alsop disclosed to the public that King had connections with two reported communists:

The subject of real headshaking is the Rev. Martin Luther King. His influence is very great. His original dedication to nonviolence can hardly be doubted. Yet he has accepted and is almost certainly accepting communist collaboration and even communist advice.

In 1962-63 the issue of the communist role in the King organization was raised because of Hunter Pitts O'Dell, commonly called Jack O'Dell. This man, a known communist, held posts in the Southern Christian Leadership Council(sic), first in the South and then in the New York office, until the late Spring of

1963. King finally dropped him when he was warned by United States Government officials that O'Dell was the genuine communist article.

Official warnings have been given to King about another, even more important associate who is known to be a key figure in the Covert apparatus of the Communist Party. After the warning, King broke off his open connections with this man, but a secondhand connection nonetheless continues. [2]

This second communist concerning whom King was warned was Stanley David Levison, whose secret membership in the Communist Party, USA, as of July 1963 was established by the FBI. King was told of his connection with the Party at the direction of both Attorney General Robert F. Kennedy and President John F. Kennedy. In mid-1963, they also separately and strongly urged that there be no further connection between Hunter Pitts O'Dell and the SCLC. O'Dell was known to be under communist influence and control. [3]

King could have known this from information published in his hometown newspaper, the *Atlanta Constitution*. It identified O'Dell as director of the New York office of the SCLC, and stated that he was in the Communist Party as late as 1958. It reported he had been identified as a member of the National Committee of the Party. [4]

Attorney General Kennedy by June 1963 evidenced growing concern about King's connections with Levison and O'Dell. A memorandum Hoover prepared reported about his being contacted by Kennedy on June 17, 1963:

The Attorney General called and advised he would like to have Assistant Attorney General Burke Marshall talk to Martin Luther King and tell Dr. King he has to get rid of Stanley Levison and Jack O'Dell, that he should not have any contact with them directly or indirectly.

I pointed out that if Dr. King continues this association, he is going to hurt his own cause as there are more and more Communists trying to take advantage of [the] movement and bigots down South who are against integration are beginning to charge Dr. King is tied in with Communists. I stated I thought Marshall could very definitely say this association is rather widely known and, with things crystallizing for them now, nothing could be worse than for Dr. King to be associated with it. *

Marshall subsequently spoke to King about both Levison and O'Dell. King, by letter dated July 3, 1963, removed O'Dell from his position with the SCLC. However, Levison continued to associate with King. It was he on whom the Communist Party pinned its hopes to progress from a supporting role in the racial unrest situation to a position of active leadership. [5]

---

*Throughout its consideration of the King case, the Church Committee referred to Levison as Adviser A and O'Dell as Adviser B. As they have been publicly identified as such, their names have been inserted where so referred to in this quoted material, taken from Page 97, Book III, Final Report, of the Church Committee; their actual names will be utilized in subsequent Committee references to them by these letters.

The attorney general was deeply concerned about King's connections with the two communist officials. Both he and his brother, President Kennedy, were closely tied in the public mind with Martin Luther King and the civil rights movement. It was no secret that Bobby realized what political damage could result for the administration if it became known that King was working with communists. It was imperative that the attorney general have the facts and then, if necessary, bring pressure on King to sever such damaging ties. Therefore, directly and through his aides, he not only authorized but pressed for an in-depth investigation. Both he and the White House, moreover, were anxious to know what Dr. King was up to, and the FBI reports which gave information about his meetings with his advisors, details of his strategy, and the attitudes of civil rights leaders were welcomed by the administration.[6]

Bobby's concern over such things was vividly brought to the Director's attention when on July 16 Kennedy initiated the idea of placing a wiretap on Martin Luther King. At the time, he was advised by an assistant director of the FBI that since King traveled practically all the time, it was doubtful technical surveillances on his office and home would be very productive. It was further pointed out that there could be repercussions if it should ever become known that such a surveillance had been put on King. Kennedy expressed a lack of concern about this because he thought that possible communist influence in the racial situation made it advisable to have as complete coverage as possible.[7]

In light of this, on July 23, 1963, a memorandum was sent to Attorney General Kennedy stating that pursuant to *his* request, authority was sought to place technical surveillances on King's residence and on his office at the Southern Christian Leadership Conference. But Kennedy now declined to approve them, telling the assistant director that he was of the opinion the surveillances would be ill advised. He referred to comments the FBI official had made earlier about King's travel status and the "serious repercussions" should it become known the government had instituted this coverage.[8]

Developments in the next few weeks indicated that Bill Sullivan seemed to be dissatisfied with Kennedy's refusal to authorize the King technical surveillances after having suggested them in the first instance. Here is how the Church Committee recorded the matter:

> On September 6, 1963, Assistant Director William Sullivan first (sic) recommended to Director Hoover that the FBI install wiretaps on Dr. King's home and the offices of the Southern Christian Leadership Conference. Sullivan's recommendation was apparently part of an attempt to improve the Domestic Intelligence Division's standing with the Director by convincing him that Sullivan's Division was concerned about alleged communist influence on the civil rights movement and that the Division intended, as Sullivan subsequently informed the Director, to "do everything that is humanly possible" in conducting its investigation.

After making this statement which ignored the fact that it was Robert Kennedy who first proposed wiretaps on King, the Committee offered a brief chart which disclosed that the first tap was activated on October 24, 1963. It had been approved on October 10 by Robert Kennedy. In approving it, the Attorney General said that he recognized the importance of this coverage if substantial information was to be developed concerning the relationship between King and the Communist Party. He ordered that he be kept advised of any pertinent information developed regarding King's communist connections. As a matter of fact, he was so interested in this that he also approved electronic surveillance coverage of Levison. This, together with similar coverage of two other individuals, was extremely productive in showing the influence of Levison on King, and Levison's behind-the-scene influence in the racial movement. This took place more than two years after Sullivan became head of the Intelligence Division.[9]

Nevertheless, in a book attributed to "William C. Sullivan, with Bill Brown," published two years after Sullivan's death in a hunting accident November 9, 1977, Sullivan was quoted as saying,

> When I took over the Intelligence Division in 1961, the FBI counterintelligence operation was already in existence and the King investigation was one that I inherited along with thousands of others. Martin Luther King, Jr., had been the subject of FBI scrutiny as far back as 1957... . Hoover singled out the King case emphasizing the need to extend great care and discretion in the wiretaps and other techniques that were being used against King. [10]

This statement was couched in terms which certainly conveyed the impression that when Bill became head of the Intelligence Division in June 1961, more than two years before any technical coverage of King was instituted, the techniques mentioned were already in effect. He concealed his paternity in the COINTELPRO operation and attempted to divorce himself from responsibility in the King case.

When he mentioned that King had been subject to FBI scrutiny as far back as 1957, he could have, with the slightest degree of honesty and integrity, cited the following instruction concerning the Southern Christian Leadership Conference, which Hoover sent to the SACs of all field offices in September of that year:

> In the absence of any indication that the Communist Party has attempted, or is attempting, to infiltrate this organization, you should conduct no investigation in this matter. However,... you should remain alert for public source information concerning it in connection with the racial situation. [11]

In conducting its mid-1970s hearings on U.S. intelligence activities, the Church Committee devoted substantial attention to the Martin Luther King, Jr., case. Its Final Report, Book II, was devoted almost entirely to the FBI, and supposedly constituted a balanced summary of its inquiries into the Bureau's intelligence activities. The slanted reporting of the Committee was evident in its discussion of the Supreme Court case Irvine v. California. With respect to the King case, the Committee bias also showed. It followed the practice of emphasizing negative data whenever an opportunity to do so was presented, scattering its comments throughout the report; examples:

- Page 49: Under the heading "Exaggeration of Communist Influence," the subject of King was first introduced by reporting that a "distorted picture" of communist infiltration served to justify the FBI's investigations of groups involved in Vietnam War protests and the civil rights movement, "including Dr. Martin Luther King. Jr., and the Southern Christian Leadership Conference." No mention was made here of the fact that Hunter Pitts O'Dell, who had been a member of the National Committee of the Communist Party, USA, served as the Executive Director of the SCLC, and Stanley David Levison was an advisor upon whom King relied.

- Page 71: Some programs concerning "general racial matters" were said to be "so overboard in their application as to include Dr. Martin Luther King, Jr., and his non-violent Southern Christian Leadership Conference in the 'radical and violence-prone' 'hate group' category," because he might abandon non-violence.

- Page 81: In the late 1960s, investigations conducted of groups which communists had targeted for infiltration were known as COMINFIL investigations. Without referring to the association of King with Levison and O'Dell, the statement was made, "As it had from the beginning, the COMINFIL concept produced investigations of individuals and groups who were not Communists. Dr. Martin Luther King, Jr., is the best known example."

- Page 211: A discussion of the use of covert actions to disrupt and discredit groups included the comment, "The sustained use of such tactics by the FBI in an attempt to destroy Dr. Martin Luther King, Jr., violated the law and fundamental human decency."

By the time an uninformed reader of the Committee's Book II arrives at a discussion of the King case, he is well primed to expect the worst, and that is what he is spoon fed. Comments such as the above, lead to a four-page dissertation on the case, which at Page 220 reports:

The FBI's campaign against Dr. Martin Luther King, Jr. began in December 1963, four months after the famous civil rights March on Washington, when a nine-hour meeting was convened at FBI Headquarters to discuss various "avenues of approach aimed at neutralizing King as an effective Negro leader." Following the meeting, agents in the field were instructed to "continue to gather information concerning King's activities... in order that we may consider using this information at an opportune time in a counterintelligence move to discredit him."

The Committee footnoted these statements showing the information came from a memorandum from William C. Sullivan to Alan Belmont dated December 24, 1963. It commented that although FBI officials were making derogatory references to Dr. King and passing personal information about him to their superiors, "Prior to December 1963, the Committee had discovered no document reflecting a strategy to deliberately discredit him prior to the memorandum relating to the December 1963 meeting."

Thereafter, in the four pages, the Committee recounted actions of a disruptive nature instituted against King, but there was no mention whatsoever of the names of Levison and O'Dell. Among the actions were the following:

- An anonymous letter was mailed to King in November 1964 which the Committee concluded was an effort to induce him to commit suicide.
- Efforts were made to undermine "ambassadorial receptions" when King was in Europe, and to diminish support for a special "day" planned in his honor.
- Attempts were made to rescind plans of two schools to confer special degrees upon him, and to block a Ford Foundation grant to him.
- In attempts to "undermine" him, information was provided to religious leaders, journalists, and a congressional committee in "off the record" testimony.
- Attempts were made after his death to prevent his birthday from becoming a national holiday.

After ruminating about these actions, the Church Committee concluded, "The actions taken against Dr. King are indefensible. They represent a sad episode in the dark history of covert actions directed against law abiding citizens by a law enforcement agency."

The only reference to communists or communism in this supposedly unbiased summary of the Committee's inquiries into FBI intelligence activities was found in an introductory sentence at the bottom of Page 219: "The FBI's claimed justification for targeting Dr. King — alleged Communist influence on him and the civil rights movement — is examined elsewhere in this report."

If one takes the trouble to review the "elsewhere," he might agree that the evidence was fairly substantial and the Committee's final summary of the FBI's handling of the King case could have presented a more objective picture despite some easily questionable operations. The "elsewhere" is in a completely separate volume, the 989-page Book III, Final Report, captioned "Supplementary Detailed Staff Reports on Intelligence Activities and the Rights of Americans." In a half-dozen pages beginning at Page 95, staff members reported the information showing efforts by the Kennedy administration (Democratic, as was the Church Committee Congress) to get King to divorce himself from reliance on Levison and O'Dell. Burke Marshall told the Committee that rumor of communist infiltration of the civil rights movement had caused the administration considerable concern. The staff reports, nonetheless, highlighted exculpatory statements by both the President and the attorney general. On July 17, 1963, two weeks after Jack O'Dell was removed from his position with King's SCLC at the urging of the two Kennedy brothers, President Kennedy was able to say at a news conference, "We have no evidence that any of the leaders of the civil rights movement in the United States are Communists." Attorney General Kennedy on the 23rd of the same month, 20 days after the removal of O'Dell from his job, was able to convey the same message to a congressional committee: "(W)e have no evidence that any of the top leaders of the major civil rights groups are Communist or Communist controlled. This is true as to Dr. Martin Luther King, Jr., about whom particular accusations were made, as well as other leaders."

The Church Committee's clearly fathomable efforts to protect the Democratic administration, and its neglect in failing to report in its final summary on the FBI the Kennedy administration's view of, and concern over, the communist connections of King, might be said to "represent a sad episode in the dark history" of politicized congressional hearings.

The staff reports published as Book III helped explain the basis for the campaign which began against Dr. King following the civil rights march on Washington, which took place August 28, 1963. Five days before the march began, Bill Sullivan submitted to Hoover a 67-page brief which assessed efforts by the Communist Party to inject itself into and exploit the struggle for equal rights for Negroes. The brief presented the conclusion that there was no evidence that the march "was actually initiated or is controlled by the CP."

When testifying before the Church Committee November 1, 1975, Sullivan said that this brief precipitated a dispute between his division and Hoover over the extent of communist influence in the civil rights movement, and the resulting "intensification" was part of an attempt to regain Hoover's approval. Hoover was reportedly concerned that the movement was strongly influenced by communists.

The Director began penning what were described as "sarcastic notes" on memoranda originating in Sullivan's division and, according to Bill, a few months went by before the Director would speak to him.

Sullivan reversed his tactics. On September 16 he recommended "increased coverage of communist influence on the Negro," this time stating that all indications pointed toward the increasing attempts by the Communist Party to exploit racial unrest. Hoover rejected the proposal, noting that he could not understand how Sullivan could "so agilely switch your thinking and evaluation." Despite the Church Committee's documentation of this 180 degree turnabout on his part, Sullivan, during an interview years later, similarly misrepresented Hoover's policies while heading the FBI. He acknowledged that the Director wouldn't speak to him for three or four months and said, "but I stuck to the facts." This was as false as many accusations he made against the Director after splitting with him in 1971.[12]

The incident over the 67-page brief may well have been the beginning of Hoover's reevaluation of Sullivan's reliability. The latter certainly demonstrated a chameleon-like approach to what should have been objective investigations.

As an aftermath of the incident, on September 25, 1963, Sullivan wrote a mea culpa memo, stating, "We are in complete agreement with the Director that communist influence is being exerted on Martin Luther King, Jr., and that King is the strongest of the Negro leaders... [w]e regard Martin Luther King to be the most dangerous and effective Negro leader in the country." He resubmitted his proposal for intensification of coverage. [13]

Thus, Sullivan cajoled the Director into concurring in this recommendation, and this led ultimately to the utilization of approximately 25 questionable tactics against Martin Luther King. This was the number mentioned by Deputy Associate Director James B. Adams when appearing before the Church Committee on November 19, 1975.

The first question posed by Senator Frank Church that day was directed to me: "Was Dr. King, in his advocacy of equal rights for black citizens, advocating a course of action that in the opinion of the FBI constituted a crime?" Since I had little knowledge of the King case at the time, Jim Adams (who was there beside me) answered in the negative, and took over the testimony. He made the point that King's nonviolent advocacy of civil rights was not the basis of the Bureau's investigation of him.

The Senator ignored that and asked on what legal basis the FBI had the right to interfere in the conferring of an honorary degree on Dr. King. Adams said he knew of no basis for this, and mentioned the true basis for the investigation, which was to determine communist influence on King. He explained that, because of a very sensitive aspect of the investigation, details of it had previously been made known to Senator Church. Adams was referring to Jack Childs' 1958 and 1960 revelations about communist connections on King's part. Church had been briefed concerning these on a highly confidential basis and knew that their disclosure could have compromised the most sensitive FBI foreign counterintelligence operations ever targeted against the Soviet Union, and put in jeopardy the lives of Bureau-controlled double agents involved. However, with the extensive TV coverage being afforded the hearing, Church seemed bent on draining as much political advantage from the situation as possible. He next posed the question, "Is it true that the FBI on another occasion intervened in an attempt to prevent Dr. Martin Luther King from seeing the Pope?"

Mr. Adams replied, "I believe that is correct, sir. There were approximately 25 incidents, I believe, of actions taken in this regard. I think Mr. Schwartz [chief counsel of the Committee] has those available, that I would lump basically all of them into the same situation of I see no statutory basis or no basis of justification for the activity."

This reply obviously took the wind out of the Senator's sails. He seemed to be prepared to recite all 25 of the incidents and ask for explanations for each. He limited the remainder of his time to concentrating on the anonymous letter sent to King in November 1964.[14]

With respect to Sullivan's 1975 testimony about his dispute with Hoover over FBI coverage of King, the following precautionary statement was included in Book III:

> Sullivan's comments, however, should be considered in light of the intense personal feud that subsequently developed between Sullivan and Director Hoover, and which ultimately led to Sullivan's dismissal from the Bureau.[15]

Book III issued by the Church Committee to record the findings in its inquiries about U.S. intelligence operations contained the results of investigations conducted by the Committee staff. The investigations were extensive and in depth. The staff must surely have learned of other aspects of Martin Luther King's support of communist causes, which information would have been available to Senator Church. However, information of this type was neither included in Book III nor brought up during the public hearings relating to King.

There was no indication that King attempted to conceal or disavow such support. It was a matter of public record, easily available to investigators. At the time Congress was considering declaring a national holiday to honor King, it was the subject of news commentaries. On October 13, 1983, columnist James J. Kilpatrick wrote in *The Miami Herald:*

> *The record is replete with evidence linking King to the notorious Highlander Folk School, a Communist training center... . The shadowy figure of the late Stanley Levison floated in and out of King's life... .*
>
> *King lent his name and his prestige freely to events sponsored by Communist fronts, for example, the National Conference for New Politics in Chicago in 1967, where he served as keynote speaker. Among the sponsors: The W.E.B. DuBois Clubs, the Communist Party U.S.A., the Socialist Workers Party, the Revolutionary Action Movement, and the Draft Resistance Union.*
>
> *King dabbled in foreign affairs. His American Committee for Africa supported the Communist terrorist Holden Roberto. In a major address at Riverside Church in New York City, a year before his assassination, King denounced the United States in a speech that might have been drafted in Hanoi. Even The Washington Post was appalled by King's excesses... .*
>
> *Congress ought to wait 50 years before formally memorializing anyone...*

Acting under general authority granted by the attorney general, after December 1963 microphone surveillance coverage was effected on Martin Luther King, Jr., when he traveled to cities away from home, especially when the possibility existed that he might make contact with communists. This was to comply with Attorney General Kennedy's orders that he be kept advised of any pertinent information developed regarding King's communist connections. Such coverage was established, often for just a one-day visit, in Washington, New York City, Milwaukee, Honolulu, Detroit, Los Angeles, San Francisco, Sacramento, Savannah, and Atlantic City. [16]

Notations on a January 21, 1966, memorandum addressed from Bill Sullivan to Assistant to the Director Cartha D. DeLoach suggested that some of the microphone surveillances approved by or for Sullivan in his division may have been conducted without the personal approval of Hoover or Associate Director Clyde Tolson, a normal requirement. The memorandum reported that the FBI office in New York City had been authorized to activate such a technical surveillance in a hotel room to be occupied by King. Tolson wrote on it, "Remove this surveillance at once," and the Director wrote, "Yes. H." In addition, Tolson wrote, "No one here approved this. I have told Sullivan again not to institute a mike surveillance without the Director's approval." Beside this notation, Hoover blue-inked, "Right. H." [17]

The microphone surveillances and the telephone taps on King and the SCLC demonstrated conclusively that the civil rights leader continued his contacts with communists. There was another revelation, according to Deputy Director Mark Felt:

> When the puritanical Director read transcripts of the tapes disclosing what went on behind Dr. King's closed hotel doors, he was outraged by the drunken sexual orgies, including acts of perversion often involving several persons. Hoover referred to these episodes with repugnance as "those sexual things."

> Hoover was an extremely straitlaced man who did not tolerate even the appearance of alcoholic or sexual irregularities involving Bureau personnel. He was incensed that a man preaching morality to the Nation should comport himself as Dr. King did. [18]

With regard to King's moral character, in preparing for a televised program on ABC (aired June 3, 1982) a reporter named Ms. Patricia Lynch requested from a member of the Society of Former Special Agents of the FBI "documentation of Dr. King's sexual activities." She was advised that no such information could or would be provided. Approximately a week later, she called back and stated that she had talked with the attorney at the Department of Justice, name not revealed, who had handled the King reports and heard tapes from the microphone coverage. According to Ms. Lynch, he had advised her that she could be assured that King's reputation for "moral degenerate acts" was true. Ms. Lynch said this had satisfied her superiors at ABC in New York, as far as using such data on the program. [19]

The Washington Post reported on February 26, 1984, that during an interview by Stephen Baker, publisher of Tapes for Readers, television commentator Bill Moyers was asked whether, with respect to his service under President Lyndon B. Johnson, he had ever distributed scurrilous information about Martin Luther King. Moyers replied in the negative, and said he had distributed only one document to members of the National Security Council under a top secret classification. This, from J. Edgar Hoover, was a long list of efforts by the Communist Party to infiltrate King's campaign. Saying that he had done the right thing, Moyers explained, "Johnson said to me, 'There's nothing old man Stennis and old man Eastman wouldn't [sic] like better than to prove that I've got my arms around a communist agent.' King was flawed, there's no question. So are we all."

Moyers said that this scared Johnson because he had determined to put "our administration" solidly behind King. The most important speech the President had made on the civil rights movement was to Southern Baptists, saying, "It's your moral responsibility to be on the side of justice." Moyers then continued, "Well, you know Southern

Baptists. The sexual life of Martin Luther King and his ties to the communist movement could have — unintentionally and unwittingly on King's part — lost a huge constituency Johnson was determined to win."

Long-time secret Communist Party member Stanley Levison continued as King's principal adviser until King's death. On March 28, 1968, just one week before he died, King led a march composed of 5,000 to 6,000 people through the streets of Memphis, Tennessee, which resulted in a riot. As the march developed, acts of vandalism broke out, including the breaking of windows in stores and some looting. A few months earlier he had announced that he would create massive civil disobediences in the nation's Capital and in 10 to 15 major cities throughout the United States in the spring of 1968 if certain commitments were not forthcoming from Congress in the civil rights field. An aide of King's had commented, "Jail will be the safest place in Washington, D.C. this Spring."

This comment, followed by the actual Memphis riot on March 28, obviously concerned King, for he had a wide reputation for non-violence. On March 29 he was in conference with Levison about the events of the previous day, and stated that he was considering calling off the Washington march. Levison advised him to continue his plans for the march.[20]

Rev. Ralph David Abernathy eleven years after Rev. King's assassination wrote *And the Walls Came Tumbling Down* (1989, Harper & Row), a book chronicling Abernathy's life as a preacher and civil rights activist, including his many years as King's closest friend and confidant in the movement. He wrote about the last 24 hours of King's life following the Memphis riot, saying that he felt compelled to write of "my friend's weakness for women." He devoted part of a chapter to King's extramarital affairs and explained that King:

> believed in the biblical prohibition against sex outside of marriage. It was just that he had a particularly difficult time with the temptation... . He was a man who attracted women, even when he didn't intend to, and attracted them in droves... He was a hero... the greatest hero of his age... and women are always attracted to a hero."

He commented that he saw no evidence that King was disturbed by the knowledge that "FBI agents were spreading tales about his exploits."

Detailing the night before King's April 4, 1968, assassination, Rev. Abernathy wrote that after King's famous "I have been to the mountain" address in Memphis, King, Abernathy and a colleague went to the home of "a friend of Martin's." Abernathy saw Martin and his "friend'" come out of the bedroom after 1:00 AM. Later that night at the Lorraine Motel, Martin was with "a black woman... a member of the Kentucky Legislature" with whom he shared a "close" relationship. Abernathy added that King did not return to the room he shared with the writer until after 7:00 AM.

That morning, King asked Rev. Abernathy to mediate a dispute involving "another young woman Martin knew well" who apparently had come looking for the civil rights leader in the middle of the night and could not find him. In an ensuing argument, King shouted at the woman and "knocked her across the bed." [21]

At 6:00 PM that evening, April 4, 1968, Rev. King was shot and killed while standing on a balcony of the Lorraine Motel.

Years later, on January 25, 1995, the first black woman to serve in Kentucky's Senate confirmed that she was with Rev. King the night before his assassination. She was Georgia Powers, who wrote of her year-long relationship with King in her autobiography *I Shared the Dream.*[22]

The revelations of Abernathy, coming from King's closest friend and confidant, did much to confirm the tales of King's sexual exploits, at least to many who had attributed them to vicious rumors. Nationally syndicated columnists followed the revelations with their own observations:

- *Clarence Page: Perhaps the Rev. Ralph D. Abernathy should consider changing the title of his autobiography from And the Walls Came Tumbling Down to something like The Last Temptation of Martin Luther King.*

- *Patrick Buchanan: While Mr. Abernathy has not well served the cult built up around his old friend, he has certainly served the cause of truth.... Is rampant promiscuity consistent with a reputation for high integrity? Is relentless adultery consistent with moral character? To both questions, most Americans would answer "no".... How ask people to worship at the shrine of a preacher, the files on whose private life are so sulfurous and radioactive that a federal judge had to order them sealed for 50 years?*

- *Cal Thomas: What bothers me most about Mr. Abernathy's account is the immediate absolution Dr. King gets from some black leaders for his alleged adultery. They say the revelation has hurt Dr. King's widow, Coretta. But, according to Mr. Abernathy, she was well-aware of the infidelities, and he writes of third-party interventions directed at repairing damage to Mrs. King by her husband's alleged philanderings.... Abernathy has not betrayed Dr. King or the civil rights movement or those who followed in Dr. King's footsteps. If Mr. Abernathy's reports are true, it was Dr. King who betrayed his wife and children, and who committed a grave disservice to the family, especially the Black family.*[23]

Walter Scott's "Personality Parade" in the January 29, 1989, issue of *Parade Magazine* carried a revealing item: "King, who was no angel,... in fact had confessed to a friend: 'I'm away from home 25 to 27 days a month. [Extramarital sex is] a form of anxiety reduction.'"

In the Fall of 1990, long after Rev. King's death, another controversy raged regarding his character, this relating to his questionable truth and honesty. It had to do with his extensive plagiarism in his graduate school term papers and doctoral dissertation in the early 1950s.

Pulitzer Prize winning author David J Garrow, after making extensive inquiries into the charges, concluded:

There is no getting around the fact that the scale of King's unattributed borrowings — almost word-for-word copying of sentences and whole paragraphs without benefit of quotation marks on scores of occasions, often without minimal footnoting — is extensive and substantial. In particular, King's heavy reliance on an unpublished dissertation completed three years earlier by Boston University doctoral candidate Jack Boozer is especially egregious... .

There is no gainsaying the depth of one's emotional disappointment over King's plagiarism... .

Only speculation is available to answer the question of whether King was conscious of his offense and whether in later years he regretted what he had done.   My own tentative guess is that it did gnaw at him, even though in later years King's daily life was so hectic as to leave him few opportunities to reflect upon the past.

Still, after 1965, King spoke movingly of his own shortcomings and imperfections, of how he, like everyone else, is inescapably a sinner.[24]

This observation takes on some significance when considered in the light of two events which took place in late 1964 and which have aroused considerable interest and speculation. The first involved a meeting between J. Edgar Hoover and Rev. King; the second concerned an anonymous letter sent to the Reverend.

The meeting followed a false charge against the FBI mouthed by King during an interview conducted by *The New York Times.* King claimed:

One of the great problems we face with the FBI in the South is that the Agents are white Southerners who have been influenced by the mores of the community. To maintain their status, they have to be friendly with the local police and people who are promoting segregation. [25]

This was patently untrue. Some 70% of the agents then assigned in the South had been born in the northern part of the United States.[26]

Always sensitive to criticism of the Bureau, Hoover reacted strongly to King's charges. At his instruction, two calls were made to King so that he would have the facts — one by Deke DeLoach and the other by the SAC of the Atlanta field office. In both instances, an SCLC secretary took the message and promised that the Reverend would return the call. He never did.[27]

On November 18, 1964, during a press briefing session, Hoover called Dr. King "the most notorious liar in the country." Reacting to this, King told the press, "The time has come to bring this controversy to an end." He traveled to Washington and met with Hoover on December 1st. Emerging from the Director's office after the conference, King had no criticism for Hoover, and the Church Committee described the meeting as "amicable." [28]

This description lends credence to Rev. Abernathy's comment that King appeared undisturbed about FBI agents allegedly "spreading tales about his exploits."

In December 1964, Robert Kennedy, after resigning as attorney general, spoke about the Hoover-King controversy, defending Hoover and the FBI against charges that the Bureau was anti-civil rights.

With regard to Hoover's characterization of King as a "notorious liar," Kennedy said that King was in a very vulnerable position because of his association with members of the Communist Party and because of information the Bureau possessed about his private life. He explained that "to protect ourselves" when he heard that King was tied up "perhaps with some communists," he asked for an intensive investigation and gave permission for the wiretap on King's telephone. He spoke of his and Burke Marshall's efforts to persuade King to break his ties with Levison. Kennedy described the President's own warnings to King, the latter's promise to sever the connection with Levison, and how King nevertheless remained in touch with him through a third party. This greatly bothered Robert Kennedy.[29]

With regard to the anonymous letter, the Church Committee, in the final report covering the FBI, stated that in late 1964 a "sterilized" tape was prepared in a manner that would prevent attribution to the FBI and was anonymously mailed to King just before he received the Nobel Peace Prize. Enclosed in the package with the tape was an unsigned letter which warned Dr. King, "your end is approaching... you are finished." [30]

According to the Committee, a technician in the FBI Laboratory had been ordered to prepare a "composite" tape from tapes made while microphone surveillances were being conducted covering rooms in hotels occupied by King in Washington, San Francisco, and Los Angeles. A copy of the composite tape was left with Sullivan.[31]

When Bill was forced to retire in October 1971, he was unable to remove from his outer office the contents of a file cabinet in which he had maintained not only official Bureau records but also a folder marked "Personal." In it was found the original of a typed letter addressed "KING" which read in part as follows:

> KING,
>
> In view of your low grade... I will not dignify your name with either a Mr. or a Reverend or a Dr. And, your last name calls to mind only the type of King such as King Henry the VIII... .
>
> King, look into your heart. You know you are a complete fraud and a great liability to all of us Negroes. White people in this country have enough frauds of their own but I am sure they don't have one at this time that is anywhere near your equal. You are no clergyman and you know it. I repeat you are a colossal fraud and an evil, vicious one at that. You could not believe in God... . Clearly you don't believe in any personal moral principles.
>
> King, like all frauds your end is approaching. You could have been our greatest leader. You, even at an early age have turned out to be not a leader but a dissolute, abnormal moral imbecile. We will now have to depend on our older leaders like Wilkins a man of character and thank God we have others like him. But you are done. Your 'honorary' degrees, your Nobel Prize (what a grim farce) and other awards will not save you. King, I repeat you are done.
>
> No person can overcome facts, not even a fraud like your-

self.... . I repeat - no person can argue successfully against facts. You are finished.... . And some of them to pretend to be ministers of the Gospel. Satan could not do more. What incredible evilness... . King you are done.

The American public, the church organizations that have been helping - Protestant, Catholic and Jews will know you for what you are - an evil, abnormal beast. So will others who have backed you. You are done.

King, there is only one thing left for you to do. You know what it is. You have just 34 days in which to do [sic] (this exact number has been selected for a specific reason, it has definite practical significant [sic].) You are done. There is but one way out for you. You better take it before your filthy, abnormal fraudulent self is bared to the nation.

This letter was surfaced for the first time in early 1975 when the Intelligence Division, which I then headed, was called upon to provide the services of an agent supervisor to assist in inventorying the contents of the file cabinet in which the original was located. By then the Church Committee had been established by the Senate and was making such heavy demands for information from the Bureau that I had to set up a task force to meet the demands.

I received a telephone call about this same time from Lish Whitson, a retired special agent whom I had known as a co-worker in the division for several years. He asked to drop by my office, and when he did, he told me that he had been interviewed by the Church Committee. He was questioned by staff members about the King case and told them about a telephone call he had received at his home one Saturday from Bill Sullivan. This occurred before Whitson retired. Sullivan told him that he had a very important mission for him. He instructed Whitson to go to National Airport, just outside Washington, receive a package from somebody who would be there to deliver it to him, take the package by plane to Miami, then call Sullivan for further instructions. Whitson went to the airport where an agent whom he knew by sight and who worked in the FBI Laboratory delivered a small package to him. Lish then flew to the Miami airport. When he telephoned Sullivan, as instructed, he was furnished the address of Rev. King in Atlanta, told to place it on the package, then mail it. He complied, stayed overnight in Miami, and flew back to Washington the next day.

Shortly after Lish told me about this, a request was received from the Church Committee for any material in Bureau files which would verify his trip to Miami. Our task force was able to locate verifying information in the form of an expense voucher submitted by Lish to reclaim the cost of his overnight accommodations in Miami on November 21-22, 1964. Also located was a copy of a Government Transportation Request (GTR) issued by Whitson to purchase the round-trip plane ticket covering those dates. This information was sent to the Committee.

The task force made a concentrated effort to develop whatever information was available regarding the anonymous letter addressed "KING" and sent it, together with a copy of the letter, to the Committee. What the task force established follows.

There was no record in Bureau indices or files regarding the letter. The only evidence that it even existed was the original copy found in Bill Sullivan's folder marked "Personal." It was concluded that a copy of the original had been made and mailed, possibly to prevent identification of the typewriter on which it had been prepared.

The portion of the letter excised before its public release indicated there was an enclosure.

A review of logs covering the Martin Luther King wiretap disclosed that following November 21, 1964, a conversation was overheard between King and an assistant during which King said a tape had been received recording some activity of a very personal nature, and it was very disturbing. But nothing was said about a "suicide letter."

It was established that three or four special agent supervisors were working in the office across from Sullivan's on Saturday, November 21, 1964. One of them (at Sullivan's request) located some unwatermarked paper in a secretary's desk and gave it to Bill, who was then heard typing in his own office. He later asked for and received King's address in Atlanta. Following that, he had one of the agents deliver a package to the office of either Alan Belmont or Deke DeLoach, whose offices at that time were located in a building about a mile away. It was not known whether this package contained the anonymous letter and tape sent to King. Its subsequent delivery that same day to Whitson would suggest that if it did contain the letter and tape, it was sent by Sullivan to one of the two offices in the other building for the FBI Laboratory agent who gave it to Whitson at National Airport.

A person of credibility who requested confidentiality advised the author that about two months after Sullivan testified before the Church Committee on November 1, 1975 about the anonymous letter, he acknowledged that an FBI Laboratory man delivered to him a box containing a tape sanitized so it could not be traced to the FBI. He said that the tape was "done up with great security and wrapped in brown paper."

Since DeLoach did not occupy a position in 1964 which placed operational responsibilities under his control, it seems unlikely he would have been involved in this operation concerning King. In his book *Hoover's FBI,* he wrote, "The person who sent King the tape and the note had the sensibilities of a bushwhacker." [32]

Considering Hoover's penchant for written records — his insistence that all employees record complete details of investigative results, actions taken, and information received — the fact that there was absolutely no information in official records relating to the anonymous letter and the tape indicated that the operation was not an FBI-sanctioned one. It is inconceivable to one subjected to Hoover's discipline to believe that DeLoach, Belmont, or someone else involved in the incident, other than Sullivan, would have risked his career by not complying with Hoover's strict requirements. The fact that Bill did conceal things from Hoover is attested by the manner in which he maintained and, without authority, removed from the FBI material relating to wiretaps, which resulted in the dismissal of an espionage case against the man who stole the Pentagon Papers.

On April 24, 1976, long after his retirement, Al Belmont was interviewed as to his possible role in the King anonymous letter incident. The interview was conducted by Clarence M. Kelley, who was then FBI Director. Al said he had no recollection of his discussing, knowing about, or participating in any plan to mail to King a tape and/or an anonymous letter. He made the point that if a plan such as this had actually been undertaken, it not only would have required Hoover's approval, but would also have had to go through him, Belmont, in the chain of command, and, he added, Hoover would have expected to have something in writing. The lack of any record and the lack of any recollection on Belmont's part indicated to him that any such mailing was an individual's enterprise. Such conclusion, Belmont emphasized, was based on "known facts or lack of facts, and not on conjecture or surmise."

Belmont indicated that Sullivan in correspondence to him had attempted to "trigger" his recollection to support Sullivan's claim that the anonymous letter incident was approved by Hoover. Belmont commented that claims alleging Hoover had a vendetta against King were absolutely false. As he put it, Hoover "couldn't care less" about how King directed his personal and business life; he had "far more important things to think about and concern himself with."

Loch K. Johnson, as a staff member of the Church Committee, was an investigator and personal aide to its chairman, Senator Frank Church. He reported the Committee's findings concerning, and interpretation of, the anonymous letter incident as follows:

> In what was interpreted as an attempt to force King to commit suicide, the FBI had sent him... a tape recording and a note from an anonymous source. The tape, obtained from electronic listening devices placed by the bureau in various hotel rooms across the country where King had stayed, apparently contained sounds of King in moments of amour outside the confines of matrimony. The package was mailed in November 1964, thirty-four days before King was to receive the Nobel Peace Prize. The note inside read: "King there is only one thing left for you to do. You know what it is. You have just 34 days in which to do it."

After quoting the remainder of the final paragraph of the anonymous letter, he concluded, "A month later, the bureau sent a copy of the tape to Mrs. King, who joined her husband in rejecting the FBI blackmail attempt." [33]

This Committee version, as reported by Johnson, resulted in a wide acceptance of the theory that the anonymous letter was a "suicide note," and this is usually how it is referred to today. However, there are four things about the Committee version *as presented by Loch Johnson* which don't ring true.

First, it did not give the day of the month, the 21st, when stating, "the package was mailed in November 1964." It was known to the Committee since it was evident from the expense and travel vouchers of Lish Whitson supplied by the FBI in response to its specific request. The complete date was used by the Committee in its official report. It disclosed and discussed the anonymous letter incident under the caption "Tapes Are Mailed to King: November 21, 1964." [34]

Secondly, thirty-four days from November 21 was actually Christmas Day. The media, including *The New York Times*, reported that King received his Nobel Peace Prize in Oslo, Norway, December 10, 1964. This was just 19 days after the letter was prepared and mailed. [35]

Thirdly, the reference to the letter's having been an "FBI blackmail attempt" was gratuitous on Johnson's part and unsupported. The concluding phrase of the letter referred to action King should take before he was "bared to the nation." The writer did not say that "I" or "the FBI" will bare you to the nation, which, by dictionary definition, could constitute blackmail. It is arguable whether the letter writer threatened to do this himself or was warning King that his character faults were so obvious that, by reason of his promiscuity, knowledge of them could become ubiquitous.

Finally, there is no information in the Committee's discussion of the tape incident even suggesting that a month after the tape was sent to King the FBI sent a copy of it to his wife. The charge is completely unsupported and, as far as can be determined, is made up of whole cloth. Nothing was located at the Bureau indicating or suggesting that Mrs. King was separately sent a copy of the tape a month later or at any other time by Sullivan or anyone else.

The manner in which Loch Johnson presented the anonymous tape incident left the writer with the impression that Johnson was personally prejudiced against J. Edgar Hoover. This impression was sustained by the follow-up comment, "Bureau officials were forced by J. Edgar Hoover, at the risk of losing their jobs, to rewrite reports on the civil rights leader, falsely charging him as a national security risk." The accusation was undocumented and unsupported by any examples or facts. [36]

Bill Sullivan, when called upon by the Church Committee to testify November 1, 1975, about the anonymous letter, laid the blame for it off on Hoover, Tolson and Belmont. He said the Director wanted a "sterilized" tape mailed to King's wife, Coretta, to "precipitate their separation, thereby diminishing Dr. King's stature." Sullivan owned up to being responsible for the "project," but said he had opposed it. He acknowledged the parts Lish Whitson and the FBI Laboratory employee (not identified) had played. Incidentally, both of them had been interviewed by the Committee and it would have been somewhat less than brilliant of Sullivan not to do so.

With regard to the letter itself, Sullivan testified under oath that he did not recall ever having seen it, although it was "possible" that he had something to do with it and simply could not remember. In light of the fact that the original of the letter was found among Sullivan's personal papers left behind when he retired, this disclaimer reflected on his lack of credibility. As a saving grace, he suggested to the Committee that the original may have been "planted" in his personal material.

He also testified that he could not recall any conversations at the FBI concerning the possibility of King's committing suicide. After reading the last paragraph of a copy of the letter as provided by the Committee, he conceded it could be interpreted as an invitation to suicide, although he said that so far as he knew, the FBI's goal was simply to convince King to resign from the Southern Christian Leadership Conference, not kill himself. This conflicted with what he previously described as the Director's reason — to precipitate King's separation from his wife to diminish his stature.[37]

Having known Bill Sullivan by reason of our rather close business association from July 1947 until October 1971, I offer some observations which may be appropriate. He had a knack for symbolism. He was a devout Catholic and as such must have considered King's inordinate sexual desire one of the seven deadly sins — lust. He felt that faithfulness to one's wife and family, as well as to his religion, was paramount, especially for a "man of the cloth" as King was. Bill's own religious convictions were evident on an occasion when he learned of the marriage of a young female colleague. She was Catholic and her husband was the son of a Protestant minister. Bill was highly critical of her and even became verbally abusive of her mother with whom he was acquainted. I was told this by the young woman.

When Sullivan learned in August 1964 that Dr. King might have plans to visit the Pope while on a European tour, he mentioned this during a conference with the section chiefs in his division. He sounded quite upset and voiced the opinion that it would be shocking for such an unscrupulous character to be granted an audience with the head of the Catholic Church. Subsequently, an agent was dispatched to impress upon Cardinal Spellman the likely embarrassment such an audience might engender.[38]

Based on my assessment of Sullivan and the facts about the anonymous letter developed by the Intelligence Division task force established to handle requests of the Church Committee, I felt that Bill was urging King to repent and confess his sins before Christmas Day. It is a high holy day for Christians, one on which ministers from their pulpits commemorate the birth of Christ. Sullivan considered King, a Christian minister, unworthy to do this because of his sins unless he would confess them, repent, and be forgiven. There were still 34 days for King to do this before facing his congregation, otherwise he might be "bared to the nation" as a result of his notorious sinful activities.

Sullivan was urging King to do what he seemed to have done before. David Garrow, in his article about King's plagiarism, stated that King viewed himself as highly imperfect, once telling his Atlanta congregation, "I make mistakes tactically. I make mistakes morally, and get down on my knees and confess it and ask God to forgive me." Perhaps some significance should be attached to Garrow's comment that after 1965 King spoke movingly of his shortcomings and imperfections, and how he considered himself "inescapably a sinner." Was it possible that Rev. King interpreted Sullivan's 1964 letter as suggested and took it to heart? [39]

I don't condone what Bill Sullivan did and doubt that Hoover, who took the blame for it, would have. We developed no information indicating that the Director even knew about it.

When J. Edgar Hoover headed the Bureau it was known as Hoover's

FBI. Press releases extolling its successes and accomplishments were issued in his name. By the same token, when a mistake was made or something went wrong, Hoover was charged with it even though it was one of his men who was personally responsible. When disciplining his agent personnel in such matters, the Director was not averse to reminding them of this.

For William C. Sullivan's misdeeds, Hoover has borne a heavy burden.

THE HUSTON PLAN

Surreptitious entry, in intelligence parlance "black bag job," was used most sparingly in the FBI and only in cases deemed to have the potential of impacting on the nation's security. The Director insisted that if a surreptitious entry was felt to be warranted in such a case, full justification must be submitted to him and that either he or Associate Director Clyde Tolson must personally approve its use. Hoover acknowledged during the 1956 briefing of the President and other high-level government officials that the Bureau utilized this covert investigative technique.

In July 1966, a request for approval of a black bag job was submitted by Bill Sullivan and the Director asked to be advised concerning the authority which existed for the use of this technique. Bill explained in a memorandum that authorization for its use was not obtained from outside the Bureau, that it was used sparingly, but that it was an invaluable tool in combating subversive activities of a clandestine nature aimed directly at undermining and destroying the nation. The Director's decision came back in the form of an order penned in blue ink at the end of Bill's memo: "No more such techniques must be used."

When he continued to receive requests for approval of bag jobs, he sent down his own memorandum on January 6, 1967, in which he reminded that he had previously indicated he would not approve them and ordered that no recommendations be submitted for approval of such matters.[1]

The loss of this technique disturbed Sullivan, as it did other Bureau officials sharing the responsibility for countering efforts inimical to the welfare of the country. It was some three years later before Bill recognized an opportunity to recover its use, and undertook to develop it to what he was obviously convinced was the FBI's advantage.

In the fall of 1969, he became acquainted with Tom Charles Huston, a staff assistant to President Nixon who (in effect) was a presidential advisor on internal security affairs. From this association a plan developed which ultimately took on the name of Sullivan's friend, "Huston Plan."

Huston saw himself as a kind of White House Gauleiter over the intelligence community, riding herd on the FBI, the CIA, the Defense Intelligence Agency (DIA), and the National Security Agency (NSA), imposing his ideas on how they should move against subversives and dissidents. Sullivan believed that with Huston's backing he could undermine Hoover's position with the President and succeed to the job of FBI Director.

Tom Huston knew that the White House had become transfixed by the wave of domestic protest that had swept the country. His plan had as a major objective the eventual creation by President Nixon, at Huston's urging, of an interagency committee on intelligence to review and suggest improvements in intelligence-collection procedures against the New Left.[2]

On June 5, 1970, President Nixon, at Huston's suggestion, called a meeting to make sure that the intelligence community was aware of the seriousness with which he viewed the escalating of revolutionary violence. He ordered that an ad hoc committee be formed to assess the threat, with Hoover as Chairman and including as the other members the directors of CIA, DIA, and NSA. Its orders were to prepare a report assessing the threat, specifying restraints under which the agencies thought they were operating, and presenting a series of options of how to deal with them. A working group headed by Bill Sullivan was established to carry out the President's orders.[3]

It did not take a clairvoyant to discern that, through Tom Charles Huston, Bill Sullivan's hand was behind this enterprise.

The Church Committee conducted three days of hearings on the Huston Plan in September 1975 and issued a 403-page volume on the results. Testifying at the hearings, Tom Huston admitted that prior to June 1970 he had numerous conversations with Sullivan during which there were discussions about inhibitions upon intelligence collection. He said that it was Sullivan's opinion that the FBI was operating under restraints, that it did not have available for use the tools that it was felt necessary to do the job. He had become close to Sullivan when, in October and November 1969, Huston was responsible for the coordination of intelligence relating to antiwar demonstrations in Washington. They enjoyed each other's confidence and, according to Huston, "I do not think there was anyone in the Government who (sic) I respected more than Mr. Sullivan."

James J. Angleton in 1970 was head of CIA counterintelligence operations and a member of the Huston Plan working group headed by Sullivan. He told the Committee that it was his understanding that Bill had known Tom Huston more than a year before the plan was developed, and that Huston reflected Bill's views. He said that while Sullivan chaired the group and was the primary drafter of the Huston Plan, he did not represent the views of his boss, J. Edgar Hoover. When asked about Hoover's views regarding things of "questionable legality," Angleton replied:

> I believe that Mr. Hoover's real concern was that during the Johnson administration, where the Congress was delving into matters pertaining to FBI's activities, Mr. Hoover looked to the President to give him support in terms of conducting those operations. And when that support was lacking, Mr. Hoover had no recourse but to gradually eliminate activities which were unfavorable to the Bureau and which in turn risked public confidence in the number one law enforcement agency. [4]

After a series of meetings throughout June 1970, a special report was prepared for the President by the working group and delivered to him June 25. In the words of Senator Church, "It set forth several options which ranged from the innocuous to the extreme, from doing nothing to violating the civil rights of American Citizens." According to Frank Church, in a memorandum Tom Charles Huston recommended to Nixon that he approve the extreme options, those the Senator termed violations of Americans' civil rights. These were the options Nixon approved.[5]

The ad hoc committee's report had previously been footnoted by

Hoover to register his opposition to a half-dozen options falling into the extreme category. He opposed:

- Expanding FBI electronic surveillance coverage, beyond major internal security threats, to produce intelligence. However, the FBI would not oppose other agencies' seeking Attorney General authority for coverage required by them and thereafter instituting such coverage themselves.
- Implementing covert mail coverage (opening mail surreptitiously), because it was clearly illegal.
- Surreptitious entry of the premises of subjects under investigation.
- Removing controls and restrictions on the development of sources on college campuses, which could result in charges of interfering with academic freedom.
- Use of military undercover agents to develop domestic intelligence information, which would violate a pre-existing agreement with the military services.
- Creation of a permanent interagency group to provide evaluations of domestic intelligence; however, the FBI would approve of preparing periodic domestic intelligence estimates. [6]

Senator Church noted that five days after the President approved the Huston Plan, he revoked it "at the insistence of the FBI Director and the Attorney General — to the dismay of those CIA, NSA, and FBI representatives who had helped Huston develop it."[7]

Attorney General John N. Mitchell's opposition to the Plan resulted from Hoover's informing him in writing of his own opposition, but assuring him, "The FBI is prepared to implement the instructions of the White House at your direction. Of course, we would continue to seek your specific authorization, where appropriate, to utilize the various sensitive investigative techniques involved in individual cases."

Since John Mitchell was Hoover's boss, this was not an out-of-line procedure for Hoover to insist upon. The illegal or unconstitutional aspects of at least some of the techniques were such that he desired separate, outside authorization for each of them, something which was lacking when Bill Sullivan sought unsuccessfully to get approval for black bag jobs in 1966. During the sizzling sixties, Lyndon Johnson admonished public officials they could not meet the threats of violence, riots, and campus disturbances with merely a business-as-usual attitude. He announced to the public that the FBI would exercise its full authority to investigate "in accordance with my standing instructions." Following this, Hoover moved into the breach, knowing he had Johnson's backing even to the extent of utilizing disruptive COINTELPRO-type tactics, some of which, as Attorney General Saxbe acknowledged, were outside the framework of "business-as-usual." However, as explained by Jim Angleton in his testimony, when Congress began to delve into FBI activities, many undertaken to combat the threat which so concerned Lyndon Johnson, the latter hit the silk, and Hoover was left dangling in the wind. Surely the old adage "once burned twice shy" must have crossed Hoover's mind.

John Mitchell declined the dubious honor of personally

authorizing the use of each and every act of questionable legality which might be forced upon the FBI if the Huston Plan were implemented. He saw to it that it was not, and it met an early demise.

Sullivan's explanation of Nixon's turnaround and cancellation of the Huston Plan was quite interesting. "Of course," he said, implying blackmail, "Hoover had his files." Bill had done his best to push through the plan, but while doing so, he had protected his position with Hoover. In a series of memoranda to Deke DeLoach, while the plan was under discussion, Sullivan placed the blame (for what was for the most part his brainchild) on the heads of the three other agencies on the ad hoc committee and "warned" that there could be "problems involved for the Bureau" if it was implemented. He also urged the FBI to oppose "the relaxation of investigative restraints which affect the Bureau." At the same time he was privately belaboring other Bureau officials for not going down to the mat with the Director to lift the ban on surreptitious entries and increased wiretaps.[8]

After Bill Sullivan's retirement from the Bureau, his performance during the development of the plan seemed to have been looked upon favorably by Dick Nixon. During a meeting he had in the Oval Office on March 13, 1973, with Counsel to the President John Wesley Dean, III, the two men referred to allegations of use of the FBI for political purposes. Dean commented that everything was cast "that we are the political people and they are not — that Hoover was above reproach, which is just not accurate, total (expletive omitted)."

Dean then continued, "The person who would destroy Hoover's image is going to be this man Bill Sullivan. Also, it is going to tarnish quite severely... some of the FBI. And a former President. He is going to lay it out, and just all hell is going to break loose once he does it... ."

After a brief discussion of the political aspects of the situation which brought on this comment, the conversation continued.

Nixon: "Why is Sullivan willing to do this?"

Dean: "I think the quid pro quo with Sullivan is that he wants someday back in the Bureau very badly."

Nixon: "That's easy."

Dean: "That's right."

Nixon: "Do you think after he did this, the Bureau would want him back? Would they want him back?"

Dean: "I think probably not. What Bill Sullivan's desire in life is, is to set up a domestic national security intelligence system, a White House program. He says we are deficient. He says we have never been efficient because Hoover lost his guts several years ago. If you recall he and Tom Huston worked on it. Tom Huston had your instructions to go out and do it and the whole thing just crumbled."

Nixon: (inaudible)

Dean: "That's all Sullivan really wants. Even if we could put him out studying it for a couple of years, if you could put him out in the CIA or someplace where he felt — put him there... ."

Nixon: "We will do it."

Dean: "I think that is a simple answer. Let me just simply raise it with him."

Clarence Kelly. (FBI)

Nixon: *"There is no problem with Sullivan. He is a valuable man."* [9]

The Nixon administration did look out for its own. During the summer of 1972, after he had retired from the FBI, Sullivan received a telephone call from Nixon's attorney general, Richard G. Kleindienst, who offered him the position of director of a newly established Office of National Narcotics within the Justice Department. Sullivan accepted and by August 1972, less than a year after his departure from Washington, he was back in a prestigious position. Assistant Attorney General Robert Mardian confided to an FBI official that Sullivan had been given the high-paying job to keep him from writing a book about what he knew.

Despite his new and well-paying position, Sullivan did not forsake his pursuit of the directorship of the FBI. When the candidacy of L. Patrick Gray, III, for the permanent appointment to that position seemed in danger of foundering, he inundated Bob Mardian, then attached to the Committee for the Re-election of the President, with letters extolling his own qualifications for the top Bureau job. Mardian encouraged the letters, hoping to keep Sullivan quiet until after the November elections. When John Dean called Sullivan to the White House and asked him point blank to prepare a memorandum listing examples of political use of the FBI by previous presidents, Sullivan gave him two memoranda. He saw this as a chance to ingratiate himself further with Nixon. Both of the memos were later turned over to the Senate Watergate Committee by Dean.

Nixon paid what seemed to amount to at least lip service to Sullivan's craving to become Director of the FBI. After Pat Gray was publicly disgraced over destroying documents relating to the Watergate case and on April 27, 1973, resigned as Acting Director, Sullivan was one of three candidates considered for nomination to the permanent position. Fortunately for the Bureau, Clarence M. Kelley was nominated and confirmed for the job. [10]

It was John Dean who, within two months of the decision to abandon the Huston Plan, somewhat replaced Tom Huston. He set up a new committee, the Interagency Domestic Intelligence Unit, for both operational and evaluation purposes. Senator Richard S. Schweiker commented on this and the fact that the notorious White House "plumbers" unit thereafter performed some of the same illegalities, such as breaking and entering, that the Huston Plan proposed. [11]

DR. KISSINGER'S ROLE IN WIRETAPPING

Director Hoover and Attorney General John N. Mitchell were guests of President Nixon at the presidential retreat at Camp David April 25-26, 1969. Nixon told them that he was most disturbed about White House (National Security Council — NSC) leaks of information and something had to be done about it. Mitchell had a record in his files confirming his being at Camp David on those dates. While he could not recall Hoover's being there, he did remember having participated in one or more meetings in late April or early May 1969 involving Nixon and Dr. Henry A. Kissinger, assistant to the President for national security affairs and executive secretary of the NSC. They had discussions concerning the use of wiretapping in an effort to check for leaks of information relative to foreign policy matters. A decision was made by Nixon to proceed with a program of wiretaps to trace the source of the leaks, and he directed that this program be carried out. It was concluded that parties to be subject to them would be the individuals who had direct access to the information leaked; individuals who might obtain such information from others and who, because of their backgrounds, might have motives to leak such information; and individuals becoming suspect as the investigation developed.

There was a series of leaks from the NSC concerning foreign policy matters. One, the substance of a council meeting on a delicate situation in the Middle East, occurred in February 1969. Another, revealing deliberations concerning the shooting down of an EC-121 reconnaissance plane off the shores of North Korea, hit the newsstands in April. The deliberations were about the courses of action that might be pursued, including consideration of military actions that had been planned then rejected. Again in April, *The New York Times* carried an article regarding consideration of the unilateral withdrawal by the United States of its military forces engaged in the war in Vietnam. The same paper in a May 1 article summarized a study of the posture of U.S. strategic forces; it had been prepared in connection with the Strategic Arms Limitation Talks (SALT). Some of the leaks had political aspects to them in that they afforded ammunition to those who disagreed with the policies of the Nixon administration, permitting them to lobby against them.[1]

The wiretap program decided upon by President Nixon went into effect on Friday, May 9, 1969. William Beecher, Pentagon correspondent for *The New York Times*, had a front- page story in the paper that morning concerning American bombing raids in Cambodia while the United States was engaged in the Vietnam war. It was based on highly classified government information. The U.S. military forces were, of course, aware of the identity of their bombing targets in that country, and the Cambodians knew they were being bombed. But the United States had not acknowledged publicly that it was carrying out the bombing raids, and the U.S. electorate had not been apprised of this. By 1969 the participation of American forces in the war in Vietnam had become a controversial political issue and the bombing of Cambodia exacerbated this issue.

Early the same day the Beecher article was published, Director Hoover received a telephone call about it from Dr. Kissinger, who requested that the FBI "make a major effort to find out where [the story] came from." He called the Director twice more that day, once to request that additional articles by Beecher be included in the inquiry and once to request that the inquiry be handled discreetly "so no stories will get out."

At 5:05 P.M. Hoover telephoned Kissinger to advise him that contacts of the FBI believed that the Beecher leak came from a staff member of the NSC, and the speculation was that Morton Halperin* may have been responsible. Hoover noted that Halperin knew Beecher and was of "the Kennedy era."

Kissinger expressed appreciation for the information and the hope that Hoover would follow it up as far as he could take it, saying "they" would "destroy whoever did this if we can find him, no matter where he is." [2]

A wiretap covering Halperin's residence was instituted during the late afternoon of May 9, 1969.[3]

At this point, an explanation is appropriate regarding Halperin's long-known ideological orientation, not as disclosed in FBI records but from public sources. In June 1993 President Clinton nominated Halperin as his choice to become "assistant secretary for democratization and peacekeeping" in the Department of Defense, a position created just for him. On the 28th of that month *The Washington Times* dug up his background in an editorial captioned "Who is Morton Halperin?" in which it was stated:

> Going forward with the nomination of Morton Halperin, an avowed enemy of military intervention, intelligence operations and nuclear weapons — the very things that have safeguarded democracy and kept the peace for the past 50 years — would surely send another message of contempt for the military and its mission.

Backing up this conclusion, the editorial contained selected items from Halperin's past record, including the following:

> He is a former American Civil Liberties Union lawyer who defended the right of the ultraradical Progressive magazine in 1979 to publish a recipe for the hydrogen bomb; who aided and abetted ex-CIA agent Philip Agee in his campaign during the 70s to expose the identities of CIA agents overseas, which is believed to have resulted in the murder of the CIA's Athens station chief; who unabashedly avowed, in print and in congressional testimony, his opposition to any and all covert intelligence operations; who, just before the Persian Gulf war, urged federal employees to come forward with any information indicating the Bush administration was withholding the full truth about its actions in the Gulf. He is a former member of the Carnegie Endowment for International Peace who believes the United States should never intervene

---

*Source providing this information did not name Morton Halperin but his identity and the identities of other individuals subsequently wiretapped under this program have been disclosed publicly.

militarily anywhere without an invitation from the United Nations.

In the latter connection, Halperin evidenced strong support for United Nations interventions with the United States carrying the brunt of military support. Senator Strom Thurman, ranking Republican member of the Committee on Armed Services, before which Halperin's nomination to the Department of Defense position was pending, issued a public statement, in part as follows:

Mr. Halperin's record shows a man whose judgment about the nature of conflict and international relations is deeply flawed. He is a leading advocate of subordinating U.S. military power to multinational interests in the apparent belief that the United States can't be trusted to act unilaterally for the good of mankind ... .

Republican members [of the committee] have good reason to believe that Mr. Halperin's advice will lead to more United Nations "peacekeeping" operations like Somalia. Possibly more Americans will be killed or wounded for no clear national purpose. Consequently, we have no choice but to oppose him. I believe senators of both parties have a moral obligation to make sure that his kind of misguided and discredited policy does not gain a beachhead of influence in the Pentagon. [4]

Halperin's background with regard to such matters, known at the time he was wiretapped in May 1969 and highlighted in 1993 by Senator Thurmond and *The Washington Times,* resulted in his being dropped from consideration for the Department of Defense position. Instead, he was placed by President Clinton in a position on the National Security Council which did not require Senate confirmation.

At the outset of the 1969 wiretapping program, Dr. Kissinger requested his aide, Colonel (later General) Alexander M. Haig to talk to Assistant to the Director William C. Sullivan, who had been designated by Hoover to be the point of contact in the Bureau for matters regarding this program. Haig's mission was "to lay out parameters under which the system would be established and reports rendered to Dr. Kissinger and the President." Kissinger had given Haig the names of the four individuals who, Haig assumed, would be subjected to a "surveillance" that might or might not include wiretaps, but would not be limited to that. [5]

The meeting between Haig and Sullivan took place in the latter's office on Saturday, May 10, 1969. According to Sullivan, Haig asked that wiretaps on the four individuals be instituted "on the highest authority," taken to mean on the authority of the President of the United States. Haig made it clear that he was there on orders, was following instructions, and had a message to relay. The message was that extremely serious — this was emphasized — leaks of very sensitive information were occurring and this was gravely damaging United States foreign policy. In fact, he explained, "they would ruin this policy completely if the leakers were not identified and stopped." It was desired that the FBI take immediate action to stop them, and this would include the placing of wiretaps on people suspected of being directly or indirectly involved. Haig was reported to have said the taps would be necessary for only a few days to resolve the issue and that he would come to Sullivan's office to review any information developed.[6]

Director Hoover at the outset of this investigation, because of its sensitivity, ordered that all records be retained in his office. They would have become a part of his so-called Official and Confidential files. As the case dragged on, however, and obviously to facilitate its handling by Sullivan, who had been designated to do so, the records were moved to his office; but they were not made a part of the general records of the FBI, nor were they indexed in the regular indexing system. Hoover told Sullivan that all mail in the case destined for the White House should be sent to him for his approval and, since it was strictly a White House matter, similar communications should not be sent to the attorney general regularly, only "general periodic summaries." [7]

Since the President had made a decision to proceed with the program of FBI wiretaps to trace the source of leaks of highly classified foreign policy information, Hoover was in no position to oppose FBI participation in it despite the political ramifications involved. A former agent who had been assigned by Sullivan to assist on the program said that Hoover did not like it and consistently referred to the wiretaps utilized as "White House taps." [8]

Sullivan confirmed this when writing to the Senate Foreign Relations Committee about his participation in the program:

In late 1969 or early 1970, I sent through a memorandum to Mr. Hoover requesting that these wiretaps be discontinued. I pointed out that I needed the manpower, not necessarily for more important work, but for more urgent work and I wanted to put these taps on these urgent cases, criminal as I recall. I asked him to take this matter up with the Attorney General and get the taps taken off. Later, on talking one day with Mr. Hoover on the telephone, we discussed these taps. He told me that these wiretaps were not FBI taps; not an FBI operation; that they were White House taps; a White House operation and because the White House had made the request to put on these taps they would stay on until the White House asked that they come off. I agreed with Mr. Hoover that it was a White House operation and not an FBI one... . [9]

Sullivan's communication had been written while the committee was looking into Kissinger's role in the wiretapping program. Kissinger had been nominated by President Nixon on August 22, 1973, to succeed William P. Rogers as secretary of state. He had been confirmed by the Senate Foreign Relations Committee one month later after rigorous hearings which focused on his role in the controversial program. However, the committee had not, at that time, had access to basic FBI documents involved in the wiretaps. The documents were subsequently the basis for a number of news stories raising questions concerning Kissinger's testimony during the confirmation hearings and his qualification to continue as secretary of state. On June 10, 1974, Kissinger wrote to the chairman of the committee stating that the news reports involved fundamental issues concerning the truthfulness and completeness of his prior testimony;

thus, they raised issues of public confidence and directly affected the conduct of U.S. foreign policy. He requested that the committee review his former testimony in order that the matter might be resolved. Complying with this request, the committee, after holding hearings during July 1974, released a report to the public containing its conclusion that his role in the wiretapping did not constitute grounds which would have barred his previous confirmation as secretary of state. The report contained an exchange of letters between the chairman of the committee and Nixon in which the President confirmed that he had assumed full responsibility for the entire program in a public statement which he had issued May 22, 1973, reading in part:

> I authorized this entire program. Each individual tap was undertaken in accordance with procedures legal at the time and in accord with long-standing precedent.
>
> The persons who were subject to these wiretaps were determined through coordination among the Director of the FBI, my Assistant for National Security Affairs, and the Attorney General. Those wiretapped were selected on the basis of access to the information leaked, material in security files, and evidence that developed as the inquiry proceeded.

In his letter to the chairman, which was dated July 12, 1974, Nixon reaffirmed his 1973 public statement, stating categorically, "Secretary Kissinger and others involved in various aspects of this investigation were operating under my specific authority and were carrying out my express orders." His statements went far toward resolving the issue regarding Kissinger's continuing in office as secretary of state.[10]

Dr. Kissinger had taken an active role in the program. For example, on May 20, 1969, accompanied by Haig, he called at Sullivan's office and read logs in which was recorded information picked up on two of the four wiretaps that by then had been placed on the individuals the FBI had been requested to cover.

After reading them, he remarked, "It is clear that I don't have anybody in my office that I can trust except Colonel Haig here."

He said that he wanted the coverage to continue on the first four individuals for a while longer. One of them was an adviser to the secretary of defense while Morton Halperin and the remaining two were NSC staff members. All were associated with internal governmental opposition to the Vietnam war.

On the same day, May 20, wiretap coverage was instituted on two additional NSC staff members whose names had by then been furnished to the Bureau. When no information was developed from them relevant to the leaks, Haig agreed to their discontinuance one month later at Sullivan's suggestion.

By July 8, from the standpoint of the leak in question, nothing had come to light of significance from any of the wiretap coverage. Sullivan informed Hoover that he was suggesting that some of the coverage be removed. While some were discontinued, there were continuing requests for coverage of other individuals during 1969, one as late as September 10. This was on a news reporter on whom Hoover had sent information to Attorney General Mitchell the previous day. President Nixon reviewed the information, thought that the man "might be receiving information," and ordered an immediate wiretap on him.

Colonel Haig indicated on September 15 that Dr. Kissinger wanted all surveillances discontinued except two.[11]

A leak of information in May 1970 resulted in the institution of five more wiretaps involving two NSC staff members not previously covered, a newspaperman, and two State Department officials. On May 2 the White House learned that an article by William Beecher concerning stepped-up bombing of North Vietnam was scheduled to appear in *The New York Times* the next day. Haig sent word to the Bureau that the President had called him about this and the leak had been "nailed down to a couple of people." He requested coverage of two individuals "on behalf of the President." As a matter of fact, wiretap coverage was instituted on three individuals May 4, and on two additional ones on May 13, as requested by Kissinger through Haig.[12]

Director Hoover had a meeting at the White House with President Nixon on May 13, 1970, immediately following which he sent word to Bill Sullivan that any requests from "General Haig, Dr. Kissinger, et al." for wiretaps or other "super secret technical surveillance" must first be cleared by Assistant to the President H. R. Haldeman. He also ordered that neither Kissinger nor anyone else at the White House was to receive wiretap information directly from the FBI. Apparently the President had indicated to Hoover concern over leaks of the wiretap information within the White House. Haldeman separately informed the Bureau that reports on wiretaps were to be sent to him, "at the President's specific instructions." [13]

With two exceptions, this procedure was thereafter followed until the last of the wiretaps were discontinued on February 10, 1971. Prior to this time, letters had been sent regularly summarizing information produced by the wiretaps only to the President and Dr. Kissinger, as specified by Haig when he first called on Sullivan at FBI headquarters on May 10, 1969.

Regarding the two exceptions, one occurred on November 3, 1970, when a letter was sent to Kissinger reporting information developed on two wiretaps. The letter was approved for transmittal by Hoover, but there was no indication why it went to Kissinger rather than Haldeman.

The other was somewhat revealing of possible favor currying, or perhaps even duplicity, on the part of Bill Sullivan who, later developments revealed, was by this time opposed to Hoover's continuing as FBI Director and hopeful of taking over this position himself. When writing to the Senate Foreign Relations Committee to explain his participation in the wiretapping program, Sullivan acknowledged having met Kissinger when the latter was a professor at Harvard, and also once socially after Kissinger came to Washington. On that occasion, the two talked for two or three minutes. He advised the Committee, "If my memory is correct, except for this very brief social meeting, I have not seen or talked to Dr. Kissinger or received any requests or communications from him since he entered government."

This statement is in conflict with the information on record in the wiretapping program to the effect that Kissinger called at Sullivan's office May 20, 1969, and commented that the only person in his own office he could trust was Haig. Sullivan, himself, recorded this in a communication to Hoover on the same day. He also recorded numerous contacts with Haig during which the Colonel told him he was conveying communications from Kissinger. It is also in conflict with the second exception to Hoover's orders to send all communications regarding the wiretapping after May 13, 1970, to Haldeman.

Without the approval or knowledge of the Director, Sullivan sent a "Dear Henry" letter to Kissinger reporting a conversation that one of the individuals wiretapped engaged in a discussion Kissinger had with the President about some "book project." [14]

All wiretapping under the program came to a sudden and complete demise in February 1971. On the 7th of the month, the first article of a two-part series highly critical of FBI wiretapping practices appeared in *The Washington Post*. Three days later, responding to a request of Associate Director Clyde Tolson, Sullivan sent him a memorandum listing the names of the individuals then being wiretapped under the White House program, together with the date each wiretap started. Bill reported that Haig had indicated that "they" intended to remove some of them, but no definite word relative to this had been received. In a handwritten note on the memorandum Hoover instructed that Haig be asked if any of them could be removed. When contacted, Haig requested that all of this special coverage be discontinued, and it was as of February 10, the date of Sullivan's memorandum.

Afterwards, Colonel Haig indicated that the wiretaps had been invaluable and of considerable assistance in helping to control leaks to the press. He also described them as invaluable to both him and Dr. Kissinger in making a determination as to whether, in terms of leaks, NSC personnel could be trusted with highly classified information. Those at the White House who reviewed the tap results felt that they were justified by what they had received from them. The identities of these individuals and the bases on which they drew their conclusions were not disclosed. No information was developed as a result of the electronic surveillance coverage indicating a violation of federal law had occurred, nor was there any specific instance developed of information leaked in a surreptitious manner to an unauthorized person. [15]

In the words of President Nixon, the wiretaps never helped — they produced "just gobs and gobs of material: gossip and bull... ." He told John Dean during a conference with him in the Oval Office, "The tapping was a very, very unproductive thing. I've always known that. At least, I've never (sic), it's never been useful in any operation I've ever conducted." [16]

While Nixon denied that the Kissinger wiretapping operation had been productive insofar as establishing the identities of White House personnel who were leaking information, it was looked upon at the White House as part of "a discreet information-gathering machine of considerable effectiveness." Other parts of the machine included a physical surveillance conducted by Secret Service agents and the intelligence-gathering arm of the Internal Revenue Service.[17]

The February 26, 1973, issue of *Time* magazine carried an article in which it was stated that four different sources in the government had reported that newsmen had been wiretapped, starting three years before. The White House was reported to have claimed that no one on President Nixon's staff had ever requested or been aware of any telephone taps on newsmen's telephones.

Nixon's press secretary, Ronald L. Ziegler, said that the use of such taps "would be counter to our philosophy, of course."

Despite this disavowal, the White House became alarmed. Efforts were made to determine how the leak to *Time* magazine had occurred when Nixon had a conference in the Oval Office on February 28 with John Dean. Bill Sullivan was one of the first persons contacted for help:

> Dean: *"I haven't probed Sullivan to the depths on this thing because I want to treat him at arm's length until he is safe, because he has a world of information that may be available."*
>
> Nixon: *"But he says that what [sic] happened on the bugging thing. Who told what to whom again?"*
>
> Dean: *"On the '68 [sic] thing — I was trying to track down the leaks. He said that the only place he could figure it coming from would be one of a couple of sources he was aware of that had been somewhat discovered publicly. He said that Hoover had told Pat Coyne [NSC staff member] about the fact that this was done. Coyne had told [Nelson] Rockefeller — now Rockefeller had told Kissinger. I have never run it any step beyond what Sullivan said there. The other thing is that when the records were unavailable for Mr. Hoover, all these logs, etc., Hoover tried to reconstruct them by going to the Washington Field Office and he made a pretty good stir about what he was doing when he was trying to get the record and reconstruct it. He said that at that time we probably hit the grapevine in the Bureau that this had occurred. But there is no evidence of it. The records show at the Department of Justice and the FBI that no such surveillance was ever conducted."*
>
> Nixon: *"Shocking to me!"*
>
> Dean: *"[That's] what the White House had from reporters in Life [magazine]. The other person who knows and is aware of it is Mark Felt, and we have talked about Mark Felt before."*
>
> Nixon: *"Let's face it. Suppose Felt comes out now and unwraps. What does it do to him?"*
>
> Dean: *"He can't do it."*
>
> Nixon: *"... . Hoover to Coyne to Nelson Rockefeller to Kissinger. Right?"*
>
> Dean: *"That's right."*
>
> Nixon: *"Why did Coyne tell it to Nelson Rockefeller? I have known Coyne for years. I haven't known him well, but he was a great friend of one of my Administrative Assistants, Bob King, who used to be a Bureau head."*

> *Dean: "Now this is Sullivan's story. I have no reason to know whether it is true, but I don't have any reason to doubt that it is true."*
>
> *Nixon: "Hoover told me, and he also told Mitchell personally, that this had happened."*
>
> *[Discussion regarding "surveillance of Anna Chennault, the South Vietnamese Embassy, and the Agnew plane."]*
>
> *Nixon: "...So Hoover told Coyne, who told Rockefeller, that newsmen were being bugged."*
>
> *Dean: "That tickles you. That is right."*
>
> *Nixon: "Why do you suppose they did that?"*
>
> *Dean: "I haven't the foggiest idea. It is a Sullivan story as to where the leak might have come from about the current Time magazine story, which we are stonewalling totally here."*
>
> *Nixon: "Oh, absolutely.... You still think Sullivan is basically reliable?"*
>
> *Dean: "I have nothing to judge that on except that I have watched him for a number of years. I watched him when he was working with Tom Huston on domestic intelligence, and his desire to do the right thing. I tried to stay in touch with Bill, and find out what his moods are. Bill was forced on the outside for a long time. He didn't become bitter. He sat back and waited until he could come back in. He didn't try to force or blackmail his way around with knowledge he had. So I have no signs of anything but a reliable man who thinks a great deal of this Administration and you.... I have got to say one thing. There has never been a leak out of my office. There never will be a leak out of my office. I wouldn't begin to know how to leak and I don't want to learn how you leak."*
>
> *Nixon: "Well, it was a shocking thing."* [18]

In seemingly accepting Sullivan's story involving Hoover in the leak, Nixon overlooked two salient factors: (1) Sullivan's enmity toward Hoover since being forced to retire from the FBI in October 1971, which laid open to question any charges he made against the Director; and (2) at the time the information leaked regarding the tapping of the newsmen it was in records which were under the exclusive control of the White House, the source of numerous leaks during the Nixon administration.

Among the allegations, Sullivan later leveled against Hoover, were that he was "a master blackmailer," had lost control of himself, and was on the verge of senility before his death. He charged that the FBI posed a threat to the civil liberties of the country.

"The weaknesses of the FBI," he said, "have always been the leadership in Washington."

It was Bill Sullivan who was responsible for the location in the White House of the entire set of records created as the result of the wiretapping program. They made up the files which contained the information which had leaked to *Time* magazine. Sullivan was responsible for their theft from the FBI. Just before his retirement, he had one of his supporters, remove and deliver them to Assistant Attorney General Robert C. Mardian, who turned them over to the White House.

Sullivan had previously contacted Mardian and told him that he, Sullivan, was in trouble with the FBI Director and expected that he might be fired, but didn't explain why. He said he had information which was "out of channels" that he wanted to turn over to the President. It was wiretap information and, in his opinion, Hoover could not be trusted with it. He claimed to be afraid that Hoover would use it to "blackmail" President Nixon into keeping Hoover in his job indefinitely. This was at a time when Sullivan was trying to get Hoover removed from his position so he, Sullivan, could succeed to it.

Mardian was requested by him to contact the President personally and pass to him Sullivan's information. After Mardian told Attorney General Mitchell about the request, he received a call from Assistant to the President John D. Ehrlichman, who directed him to fly immediately to the Summer White House in San Clemente, California, where the President was staying. Mardian did so, met with Nixon, and told him about Sullivan's request. The President directed him to obtain the material from Sullivan and deliver it to Ehrlichman, which he did.[19]

Prior to his departure from the Bureau, Sullivan declined to offer any explanation for his action in causing the removal from the FBI of some of its official records. It was simply discovered that they were missing when Mark Felt, having learned that Sullivan had complete control of the records, talked to Hoover about it several days before Sullivan retired. Hoover instructed Felt to obtain them and keep them in his own office.

At Felt's request, Inspector Thomas J. Smith searched through the file cabinets in Sullivan's office and all logical places where the files might be lodged, but they could not be located. When Sullivan was questioned about their whereabouts, he acknowledged having had them delivered to Mardian but refused to discuss the matter further, telling Felt, "If you want to know more, you'll have to talk to the Attorney General." [20]

As a result, Hoover became aware that Sullivan had taken the files, but no effort was made by the FBI to recover them after Attorney General Mitchell reportedly informed Hoover that they had been destroyed. [21]

There were other files in the cabinets in Sullivan's office from which the wiretap records had apparently been removed. As a safety precaution, Mark Felt ordered the combinations on their locks changed. This led to newspaper accounts that Sullivan found himself locked out of his office when he returned from annual leave he had taken.[22]

William D. Ruckelshaus became acting director of the FBI April 27, 1973, when papers and TV reports were filled with the February 26 *Time* magazine story of the wiretapping of media types. He was informed by Bureau officials that such wiretapping had, in fact, been conducted but that the records relating to them were missing from FBI files. At the same time, District Court Judge W. Matthew Byrne was preparing to conduct a trial in Los Angeles of Daniel Ellsberg who was accused of leaking highly classified documents relating to the war in Vietnam. Ellsberg's telephone conversations with Morton Halperin or with others while he was a guest at Halperin's home had been overheard on 15 occasions during the period when electronic surveillance coverage of Halperin's home was in effect. The judge had called for the production of the records of the overhearings to determine whether information from them had been used by the prosecution in any way and thus tainted the evidence. Ruckelshaus, upon taking over as acting director, had the mission of determining what had happened to the records.. He ordered an investigation into the facts surrounding the taps and the missing records.

The investigation began under the coordination of Inspector Tom Smith, and 42 separate interviews were conducted, including ones with John Ehrlichman, General Alexander Haig, and Robert Mardian. Mardian told about his receiving the wiretap records from Sullivan and their subsequent delivery to the White House. Ehrlichman advised that they were in his possession there prior to April 30, and Haig said they were still there as of May 11.

Accompanied by Inspector Smith, Ruckelshaus went to the White House the very next day and the two FBI officials retrieved the records from Leonard Garment and J. Fred Buzhardt, both special consultants to President Nixon. They were located in a vault where they had been placed when Ehrlichman left his position at the White House.

Tom Smith gave a receipt to Garment and Buzhardt for the records and emerged from the White House with two large boxes containing hundreds of pages of secret wiretap transcripts and memoranda. A Secret Service agent drove him back to the Federal Triangle Building about a mile away, where they were returned to the FBI Intelligence Division, completing an unscheduled journey which had begun some 22 months before.

Unfortunately, the records were not located in time to respond to Judge Byrne's inquiries about the potential taint of evidence in the Ellsberg trial, and this played a role in the government's eventual decision to drop the indictment of Ellsberg. [23]

Halperin was scheduled to be a witness for Elsberg. He and his family filed a tort action against Dr. Kissinger in 1973, alleging invasion of privacy and that the wiretap of his home telephone was illegal. The family phone was covered from May 9, 1969, to February 10, 1971. It was instituted while Halperin occupied a position at the National Security Council, which he left in September 1969. The tort action was doggedly pursued, and Halperin later explained that a key purpose for it was to establish the principle that government officials could be held responsible for their actions.

The FBI files on the wiretapping program were being held under court seal in connection with the Halperin suit. In June 1974 when the Senate Foreign Relations Committee was conducting its hearings regarding Kissinger's appointment as secretary of state, it desired the files to complete its task. The Department of Justice agreed to release to the Committee, under rigid controls, one copy of all material related to Kissinger's role in the program. This done, Halperin on the 14th of June asked a district judge to make public all the documents except logs of conversations tapped on his phone and materials relating to other persons.

In 1976, the district judge ruled that the Nixon administration had illegally wiretapped Halperin's phone. Two years later an appellate court ruled that the case could go to trial, but that Halperin would have to prove that the defendant, Kissinger, had no national security reason for permitting the wiretap to continue after Halperin left the National Security Council.

Kissinger sent a letter to Halperin on December 19, 1991, accepting "moral responsibility" for the fact that he "acquiesced in the tap" and later had simply left the matter of termination to others. He explained that if the same circumstances were repeated, he would not do it again. In exchange for an apology from Kissinger, Halperin settled the suit November 12, 1992, saying that he was glad that it was over and that Kissinger had accepted moral responsibility.[24]

Thus the controversial Kissinger wiretapping program with its many ramifications finally came to an end. But the administration was still plagued with leaks. Just three months after the last of the Kissinger taps were removed, Nixon was still preoccupied with the leak of highly classified information. During a relaxing cruise on the Potomac River in the presidential yacht *Sequoia* with Kissinger as a guest, Nixon made a passing reference to a secret trip he was about to make to China. There being other guests present, Kissinger, who had arranged the trip through delicate negotiations with the Chinese, blanched, fearful that the President might reveal details about it.

Turning to Kissinger, Nixon said, "Relax, relax. If those liberals on your staff, Henry, don't stop giving everything to *The New York Times,* I won't be going anywhere. The leaks, the leaks, that's what we've got to stop at any cost. Do you hear me, Henry?"[25]

The leak of the Pentagon Papers less than a month later to *The Times* by Henry's close friend Daniel Ellsberg seemed to have made a far greater believer of him than had the President of the United States.

THE PENTAGON PAPERS CASE

A 1968 "History of U. S. Decision-Making Process on Viet Nam Policy" was commonly known as the Pentagon Papers. It consisted of some 7,000 pages of a study, with supporting documents, ordered by Secretary of Defense Robert S. McNamara in June 1967 to chronicle U.S. involvement in Vietnam. It covered nearly two decades during which the country had been engaged in the war in Indochina either directly or through support of forces combating communism on the Indochina Peninsula. It was eighteen months before the study was completed and it covered U.S. policy up to and including the summer of 1968. The study was also frequently referred to as the McNamara Papers and included documents classified as high as top secret.[1]

Following the takeover of China in April 1949 by the communist leader Mao Tse-tung and the realization five months later that the Soviets had a nuclear capability, the Truman containment policy went into effect to take steps to prevent the further spread of communism. The so-called domino theory also fueled U.S. policy in Southeast Asia — if one nation in the area fell to the communists, neighboring nations would follow suit.

Efforts to prevent the spread of the red tide launched the United States into the Korean war in 1950 as a principal participant when the United Nations joined the conflict on the side of the South Koreans. The fighting ended inconclusively in 1953. American support then followed for the French who were fighting a guerrilla war in Indochina, locking horns with the communist leader of North Vietnam, Ho Chi Minh. Between 1954, when the French were defeated, and the second war, which erupted in 1959, the United States began paramilitary operations in Indochina and ultimately they blossomed into the commitment of more than a half million American troops to fighting the Vietnam war by 1968.

The mid-1960s in the United States will be remembered for the urban riots and outbreaks of racist acts which resulted in violence, death, and extensive property damage. They will also be remembered for the traces of anti-Vietnam war protests which began to surface. Opposition to the war rose sharply in the winter of 1967-68 as casualties mounted and victory for either side seemed impossible. It was during the stirrings of this opposition that McNamara ordered a study of the policy and developments that had brought the country to this position. By 1968 the war was the major issue and the administration of Lyndon Johnson was so severely criticized that LBJ in March declared he would not run for another term as President in the fall election.[2]

Nixon, winner of the election, had been in office less than four months when a hemorrhage of leaks relating to his policy regarding the war led to the wiretap program embroiling Henry Kissinger, his national security affairs advisor. The program was kicked off' when the William Beecher article on the bombing raids on Cambodia was published by *The New York Times* in May 1969.

President Nixon spoke to the nation on television April 30, 1970, defending his decision to order an "incursion" (read invasion) of Cambodia to release pressure on our armed forces in Vietnam. This was at a time when the bombing raids had been going on for more than a year and were to continue for three more, totaling, in all, more than 3500.[3]

Following Nixon's TV address, there was a backlash across the country from governors to church leaders. Four senators introduced legislation to cut off funds for support of the Vietnam military action. The outrage resulted in a student demonstration on the campus of Ohio's Kent State University. National guardsmen fired upon the students, killing four and wounding eleven. The picture of a father weeping about a daughter who was killed and shouting "the President is to blame" was flashed across television screens that evening. The incident was followed by student and faculty strikes on campuses across the country. Officials under Nixon began leaking stories to friends in the media, assuring them that they opposed the President's decision. [4]

The leak doing the greatest damage to U.S. foreign relations occurred some 14 months later. On Sunday morning, June 13, 1971, *The New York Times* ran on its front page a modest headline spanning columns five, six, and seven:

Vietnam Archive: Pentagon Study Traces
3 Decades of Growing U. S. Involvement

A small box underneath said, "Three pages of documentary material from the Pentagon study begin on page 35." [5]

The disclosed Pentagon study was relished by Vietnam war opponents, those inside the government as well as those on the outside. It provided fodder for their cause. But the major leak of information, impinging as it did on foreign policy and the course of the war, stunned U.S. officials having responsibilities for its successful termination, distressed and alarmed them. The 7,000 documents laid bare decisions made during some 20 years by one Republican and two Democratic administrations which had plotted the course of the war. In retrospect, some of the decisions were open to pointed criticism. There was also the strong possibility that information included in the leaked material could influence and adversely affect the outcome of the conflict.

The leak caused Henry Kissinger deep concern. The next day, Monday June 14th, he paced the floor in his office angry enough to bite nails.

"There can be no foreign policy in this government," he said. "We might just as well turn it all over to the Soviets and get it over with." He avowed that the leaks were slowly and systematically destroying the United States.

Charles Colson, one of Nixon's closest advisors, upon reading the material published in *The Times* felt it to be nothing more than a collection of old memos, position papers, and cables detailing how President Kennedy's New Frontiersmen had gotten involved in Vietnam. However, listening to Kissinger, he began to understand that the material disclosed could undermine the secret negotiations with the North Vietnamese in which Kissinger was then engaged.

Kissinger drew his attention to cables he had received from Australia, Great Britain, and Canada protesting the leak.

"They can't trust us," he fairly shouted. "If our allies can't trust us, how will we ever be able to negotiate with our enemies?"

A review of *The Times* article at the White House resulted in the conclusion that continued publication of material from the Pentagon Papers could compromise not only vital national security secrets but also U.S. decoding capabilities. Disclosures from as yet unpublished documents might reveal the identities of some CIA agents and the results of U-2 flights over communist China. Revelations about the U-2 flights could result in the cancellation of a secret visit to China by Nixon, final preparations for which were in a most delicate stage. The decision was made that afternoon to seek a court order to stop publication. [6]

It proved to be the first step toward providing the "fourth estate" carte blanche to publish whatever government secrets it can get its hands on by whatever means. Unanswered was the question whether a criminal action against the media for doing this might be sustained if material were published potentially damaging to the security of the country and the national defense.

The injunctive relief sought by the government against both the *Times* and *The Washington Post*, which by now had started a series on the Pentagon Papers, moved rapidly through the district and appellate courts and was heard and disposed of by the U.S. Supreme Court all within 15 days, surely a record for such an important landmark case: "New York Times Co. v. United States, 403 U. S. 713."

The government argued that the authority of the Executive Branch to protect the nation against publication of information whose disclosure would endanger the national security arose from the power of the President to conduct foreign affairs and his authority as commander-in-chief.

The two newspapers argued that the Pentagon Papers belonged in the public domain.[7] The *Times*, itself, had a substantial investment in the papers. Following the receipt of them from Ellsberg the paper had set up a staff in a suite in the New York Hilton Hotel which, working secretly, prepared for publication a series of articles based on this prized scoop which had fallen into its hands.[8] The *Times* pressed for an immediate decision, as much to take full benefit of this scoop as to serve the public's "right to know."

By a decision of 6 to 3, the Supreme Court held that injunctive relief to prevent publication as granted by lower courts could not prevail. The majority of the justices held to the conclusion that enjoining publication would "make a shambles of the First Amendment." Arguments supporting this were that a ban on prior judicial restraint may be overridden only when the nation is at war, and that "the press must be left free to publish news, whatever the source, without censorship, injunctions, or prior restraints. The press was to serve the governed, not the governors."

Leading in the arguments for the minority, Chief Justice Burger acknowledged that there was "little variation among the members of the Court in terms of resistance to prior restraints against publication." He highlighted the fact, however, that rights of the press came into conflict with the effective functioning of a complex modern government, and, "We do not know all the facts in the case. No District Judge knew all the facts. No Court of Appeals judge knew all the facts. No member of this Court knows all the facts." Haste, he argued, precluded reasonable and deliberate judicial treatment of the cases, and was not warranted. He presented as argument in support of this:

> A great issue of this kind should be tried in a judicial atmo-sphere conducive to thoughtful, reflective deliberation, especially when haste, in terms of hours, is unwarranted in light of the long period the Times by its own choice deferred publication.
> It is not disputed that the Times has had unauthorized possession of the documents for three to four months, during which it has had its expert analysts studying them... . During all this time, the Times, presumably in its capacity as trustee of the public's "right to know," has held up publication for purposes it considered proper and thus public knowledge was delayed... . After these months of deferral, the alleged right-to-know has somehow and suddenly become a right that must be vindicated instanter.

Joining in the dissenting opinion, Justice Blackmun also took exception to the Court's rush to judgment. He observed that two federal district courts, two U. S. courts of appeal, and now the Supreme Court — within a period of less than three weeks — had been "pressed into hurried decision of profound constitutional issues on inadequately developed and largely assumed facts without the careful deliberation that, hopefully, should characterize the American judicial process."

It was true that during oral argument of the case before the Supreme Court, counsel were frequently unable to respond to questions on factual points. They simply had been unable in the time available to review the 7,000 documents that gave rise to the action and, accordingly, were not familiar with them although they were the very the core of the case.

The New York Times, despite being the successful litigant, came in for some pointed criticism from the Chief Justice:

> To me it is hardly believable that a newspaper long regarded as a great institution in American life would fail to perform one of the basic and simple duties of every citizen with respect to the discovery or possession of stolen property or secret gov-ernment documents. That duty, I had thought — perhaps na-ively — was to report forthwith, to responsible public officers. This duty rests on taxi drivers, Justices and the New York Times.

Presidents and movers and shakers who developed and executed the government's policy on Vietnam must certainly have taken some comfort in the Chief Justice's recording for posterity this observation in the annals of the Supreme Court. The U. S. intelligence community surely accorded him a hearty, if silent, salute for his footnote to his discussion of the performance of the *Times*. He reflected upon whether it would have been unreasonable for the paper to have given the government the opportunity to review the documents to determine if an agreement could be reached on publication. He remarked on the fact that, since the information spanned a period ending in 1968, much of the material could no doubt have been declassified. To this observation he added the footnote:

> *Interestingly the Times explained its refusal to allow the government to examine its own purloined documents by saying in substance this might compromise their sources and informants! The Times thus asserts a right to guard the secrecy of its sources while denying that the Government of the United States has that power.*

It was soon learned that copies of the Pentagon Papers had been made available to other newspapers: the *Boston Globe* and the *Los Angeles Times.* A double agent of the FBI, who was a strategically placed Soviet intelligence agent serving at the United Nations, reported that a complete set of the top secret documents had also been delivered to the Soviet Embassy in Washington. Eventually, the Soviet ambassador, supposedly anxious to avoid an incident, returned the set of papers to Kissinger's office. Of course, they were hardly needed by his government. They were available through the U.S. free press.[9]

On Monday, June 28, a scant two weeks after publication of the first article by *The New York Times,* Ellsberg admitted having stolen and disseminated the Pentagon Papers. Kissinger began urging the President to take revenge on the thief. [10]

Ellsberg was a former Marine officer and an avowed "hawk." By his own admission he had once experimented with LSD. With his release of the Papers he became a folk hero of the anti-war movement. The press hailed him as a courageous champion of the "public's right to know." Nixon viewed his conduct as treasonous and wanted to let the country know what kind of "hero" he was. [11]

The avowed "hawk" had been one of Dr. Kissinger's collaborators during the doctor's earliest days at the White house, having been personally engaged to do special studies. Working at the Rand Corporation, the think tank, he was given the assignment to propose every possible Vietnam option. With his close friend, Morton Halperin, he drafted Nixon's first top secret option paper on Southeast Asia, "National Security Study Memorandum Number One." It outlined strategy for resolving the Vietnam war. As Kissinger's former protege and a former official of the Department of Defense, Ellsberg was in possession of retaliatory missile plans and other critical defense information.

Kissinger became deeply involved in the formulation of White House strategy to handle problems created by release of the Pentagon Papers. He strongly denounced Ellsberg and urged a thorough investigation of him. He also dropped tidbits about the thief's private life and use of drugs. Both he and the President were pressing hard to find out why Ellsberg had stolen and released the Papers and what he was liable to do next.[12]

Both also asked Charles Colson to disseminate derogatory

information about Ellsberg. It was their stated desire to get out everything available to counter public views which Ellsberg was expressing. For his activity in acceding to this request, in 1974 Colson was charged with responsibility "for devising a scheme to obtain derogatory information about Daniel Ellsberg, to defame and destroy Mr. Ellsberg's public image and credibility." He entered a plea of guilty to this charge and on June 21 was sentenced to one to three years in prison and fined $5,000. Neither Nixon nor Kissinger was charged and tried for his part in this scheme. [13]

Two days after the first *Times* article on the Pentagon Papers, Director Hoover received a White House request for an immediate investigation to determine who was responsible for the leak of the highly classified material. The request was referred to the Nationalities Intelligence Section, which I headed at the time, with instructions to give the case very special handling and to have a memorandum on the Director's desk reporting daily developments at 9:00 A.M. each work day. It was assigned as an espionage investigation to Supervisor James R. Wagoner, a dedicated and experienced agent.

While our section had handled all leak investigations from the time it was established in the mid-1950s, there had never been one involving such a huge amount of top secret information and the pressure on us was in proportion to the importance of the case. We began gearing up for the job. It was necessary to establish two 12-hour work shifts to operate around the clock. This permitted us to analyze results reported each day from FBI field offices across the country, and furnish investigative developments daily to the Director by memorandum, and by separate letters to the White House and the attorney general. The section had been required to gear up many times to respond to special situations — during crises involving the Middle East, Cuba, and the Dominican Republic, as examples — and the esprit de corps among our personnel was excellent. By 3:00 A.M. the next morning we were reviewing Bureau files on the names of the administration officials who were on a limited dissemination list to receive copies of the Pentagon Papers, and setting out leads for FBI field offices to begin the active investigation.

This case turned out to be one of the most vigorously pressed investigations the Bureau ever handled. Results received at FBI headquarters, in keeping with regular filing practices, were placed in volumes secured with acco fasteners, each one being about two inches thick. As an indication of the investigative activity, during its first five months 40 such volumes were required to file the results. Investigative results in the Watergate case which brought down the Nixon presidency did not fill 40 volumes until the case had been under investigation for 14 months. This fact was called to the attention of the Watergate special prosecutor's office by letter dated August 14, 1973.

We were not long into the case before field offices established that it was Daniel Ellsberg who was responsible for the theft of the Papers and the leak to the press of their contents. In fact, it was established that he converted the documents to his possession in the Washington, DC, area and carried them across country to the Rand Corporation. With the assistance of an associate, Anthony Joseph Russo, Jr., he made copies of them, eliminating the classification markings, Top Secret, Secret, and Confidential, and sent the copies to various newspapers. Soon after receiving the early results of our investigation, Attorney General John Mitchell drew the conclusion that Ellsberg was part of a communist spy ring, and so informed the White House.[14]

Early July 6, the Director called me on the phone. He said that President Nixon was leaving for the Summer White House in San Clemente that afternoon. Hoover ordered that we send Nixon a summary of the results of the investigation up to that date and, especially, the information developed regarding Anthony Russo. He ordered that the summary be sent to the White House by noon. It was a big order; quite a bit of evidence had been developed by then, but we were able to meet the deadline.

Charles Brennan, head of the Intelligence Division, at the suggestion of his mentor, Bill Sullivan, on August 2 had lunch with George Gordon Liddy. Liddy, an ex-FBI agent, was then working under Egil "Bud" Krogh, a member of John Ehrlichman's staff at the White House. He later gained notoriety and served time in prison for his part in the June 17, 1972, burglary of the office of the Democratic National Committee in the famous Watergate case. After the lunch engagement, Brennan summoned Jim Wagoner and me to his office to meet Liddy. After the introductions, Brennan said that Liddy desired to discuss the Pentagon Papers investigation and asked that we take him to my office for that purpose. Brennan did not volunteer any information regarding the nature of his discussion of the case with Liddy.

Complying with this request, Jim and I gave Liddy a briefing on the developments in our investigation and the intensive attention which was being afforded to it. During the twenty eight years and seven months I served in the Intelligence Division, no other case, in fact no other national emergency which affected my assignment — including the 1962 Cuban missile crisis — received closer, more concentrated attention. It was necessary to keep in continuing, direct contact with field offices involved. It was the only investigation during all those years that required the installation of a second telephone on my desk to respond to calls about the case coming in to headquarters. This was the picture painted for Liddy.

When we had finished the briefing, he startled both of us by saying, "The case should be handled as a Bureau special." It was as if he had not been listening or could not absorb what we had been telling him. We explained to him we were doing everything possible to assure that a "clean" case could be made against Ellsberg. Having worked on cases in the Bureau as a special agent, Liddy knew that we meant that we had no tainted evidence, such as might arise through our utilizing wiretaps, surreptitious entries, or other investigative techniques which might endanger a successful prosecution.

Again, before leaving, Liddy said the case should be handled as a

Bureau special. What he considered this to mean became obvious to us later when we learned of White House intrusion into the investigation of Ellsberg. This was ordered by Nixon and carried out by Liddy and others connected with the so-called White House "plumbers."

A case can be tainted by wiretap evidence. So when it is proceeding toward prosecution, special care must be taken to assure that information received directly as a result of the use of this technique, or developed by using the information to lead to other evidence (the "fruit of the poisonous tree" principle), is not utilized.

At FBI headquarters, at the instigation of the attorney general, in the mid-1960s a special electronic surveillance index, known as the ELSUR index, was established. It contained the names of all individuals overheard, even incidentally, on electronic surveillances after January 1, 1960. [15]

During the month of July, before Liddy was briefed, this index had been checked on Ellsberg and Morton Halperin, who was to be a witness on behalf of Ellsberg at his trial. There was no record of overhearings regarding them. Bill Sullivan, knowing that information generated by the wiretapping program involving Henry Kissinger had not been indexed anywhere in Bureau records, had an agent check through the Kissinger material for possible overhearings involving Ellsberg, but not Halperin. The agent came personally to my office and said there were no Ellsberg overhearings during this special wiretap program. The criminal division of the Department of Justice was advised of the negative results of the ELSUR check. [16] As a matter of fact, as developments later showed, Halperin had been the subject of one of the Kissinger wiretaps and Ellsberg had been overheard 15 times on this technical coverage.

In his 1982 book, *Witness to Power: The Nixon Years* (Pocket Books, New York, N.Y.) John Ehrlichman reported that Egil Krogh told him the FBI was not vigorously investigating Daniel Ellsberg. He proposed that Howard E. Hunt (a former CIA operative) and Gordon Liddy be permitted to investigate him. Ehrlichman asked Nixon what he thought about White House employees acting as investigators, pointing out that Krogh felt Liddy and Hunt might be able to answer some of the questions the President and Henry Kissinger had raised about Ellsberg. Nodding, Nixon reportedly said, "If Krogh thinks they can do it, let's go ahead."

Testifying before the Senate Committee on Foreign Relations on July 23, 1974, Dr. Kissinger referred to an affidavit prepared by Ehrlichman which disclosed that just seventeen days after the White House requested Hoover to investigate the case, Nixon ordered the recruitment of a person to assume full responsibility for investigating the Ellsberg case. David Young, Kissinger's assistant, was proposed for this responsibility. On July 9, 1971, the decision was made to make Young and Egil Krogh of Ehrlichman's staff jointly responsible.

The *World Almanac and Book of Facts* in 1974 (published by the Washington Star News) reported that on December 7, 1972, White House secretary Dorothy Chenow named Krogh, Young, Hunt and

Liddy as members of a White House "plumbers" unit assigned to investigate leaks to the news media. Their reports were sent to Ehrlichman and their telephone bills to her house. She forwarded the bills to Ehrlichman's office. The White house confirmed the existence of the plumbers unit but denied that Hunt and Liddy were members.[17]

The one man Nixon wanted for the job of nailing Ellsberg was Hunt. He was hastily interviewed, hired by Ehrlichman as a $100-a-day part-time consultant, and assigned by Charles Colson to office space in a tiny room in a remote corner on the third floor of the Executive Office Building. Colson, who had recommended Hunt to Bob Haldeman, described him as "debonair, smooth talking, unobtrusive," and said, "He knew foreign policy, but more important, was a conservative true believer, fanatically loyal."

When Hunt reported for duty, Colson told him:

Howard, your job will be to research the Pentagon Papers — beginning to end. Analyze the political opportunities we can salvage now that we have taken the lumps. Work with the congressional committees investigating the leaks and this madman Ellsberg.

Colson considered it a relief "to get a professional in here to deal with such matters." [18]

He also gave a candid appraisal of Gordon Liddy after observing this rugged individual's operations in the Ellsberg and Watergate burglary cases. When Colson was sentenced on June 21, 1974, for his own role in the Ellsberg case, Liddy was in the courtroom. Colson described the dramatic moment:

Seated at the table was the strangest of all the characters in the Watergate cast: Gordon Liddy, the Kamikaze mentality, ideologue, and original Plumber. Despite months of incarceration in the D.C. jail, and the twenty-year sentence (Judge) Sirica had hung on him to make him talk, he had remained stoically silent, fervently worshiping (sic) a self-conceived deity of high authority. At the sight of me Liddy bounded to his feet and saluted snappily. Adhering to his own vow of absolute courtroom silence, he said not a word, but his eyes showed the fire of defiance, sparkling against a drawn, pallid face. To him I was a high priest of the government order he revered because I had not turned on the President. How the demon of Watergate had warped men's values and lives! For only a few minutes I would have this proud man's esteem.

Never again would the man with the Kamikaze mentality salute him. Throwing himself on the mercy of the court, Colson rose and entered a guilty plea.[19]

In a court affidavit released in May 1974, Ehrlichman, much to Henry Kissinger's chagrin, suggested that Kissinger knew more about the "plumbers" than he had acknowledged, based on his objections to the President's decision to assign his aide David Young to this special investigative unit as co-director. In another affidavit, Charles Colson reported that Kissinger was present during a conversation aboard a helicopter when Nixon decided upon Young's assignment.

Under oath, Kissinger stated he recalled no discussion of the "plumbers" by that or any other name during the flight. He testified that he did not know of their existence and had nothing to do with their activities.

"After Mr. David Young left the NSC staff," he said, "I knew only that he had gone to work for Mr. Ehrlichman with duties related largely to a declassification project to be terminated in three months." [20]

This appears to have been the cover utilized at the White House to afford protection to the "plumber" operation. The "plumbers" attained not one but two 15 minute-increments of fame in history; unfortunately, they were for burglary jobs. One was targeted against the Democratic National Committee Office at the Watergate. The other, not quite as well known, was just as daring and considerably more foolhardy: the office of Ellsberg's former psychiatrist in Beverly Hills, California, Dr. Lewis Fielding.

In his book *Witness to Power*, Ehrlichman stated, "It seems clear that Hunt and Liddy first proposed the Fielding break-in." They felt that his files on Ellsberg might contain information which would help in carrying out their mandate to nail the Pentagon Papers thief. Assistant Attorney General Robert Mardian claimed that Liddy had given him the clear impression that Nixon had authorized the burglary. John Ehrlichman, on the other hand, told the Senate Select Committee on Campaign Activities (Watergate Committee) that neither he nor Nixon had authorized it. This was representative of his part in the conspiracy by the White House mafia to preserve the presidency of Richard Nixon. In a further protective move, he maintained that the break-in had been well within the constitutional duty and obligation of the President. He claimed the right came from the President's legal authority to prevent national security information from falling into the hands of foreign powers. [21]

As for Dick Nixon, he was perfectly willing to look with benevolence upon the conspiracy. He said that he first learned of the break-in on March 17, 1973! [22]

In 1982, long after all the dirty laundry in the Ellsberg and Watergate cases had been washed and hung out to dry, Ehrlichman stated that privately Nixon was by then admitting that he knew of the Fielding break-in before it occurred and encouraged it. According to Ehrlichman, it was an attempt to get information on Ellsberg's motivation, his further intentions, and the identity of any possible co-conspirators. [23]

Under the direction and control of Hunt and Liddy, the Fielding job was pulled off during Labor Day weekend 1971 by a group of Cuban refugees, the same ones utilized the next year in the attack mounted against the Watergate headquarters of the Democratic National Committee. As a burglary, the endeavor proved to be considerably less than successful. It was discovered that Fielding's files on Ellsberg were not in his office. Speculating that they might be in his residence, Hunt and Liddy proposed a break-in of his apartment. Ehrlichman, learning of the break-in for the first time, flatly refused to approve the last proposal of Hunt and Liddy. Krogh told him that the two had not personally engaged in the actual break-in.

Because Ehrlichman failed to have Krogh, Young, Hunt and Liddy arrested upon learning of the Fielding caper, he was charged with having obstructed justice and was prosecuted and found guilty in 1975. The trial was a media event. Crowds gathered outside the court room to take a look at the witnesses as they arrived and departed. There were five or six film crews with lights glaring, and on a normal day, dozens of reporters and photographers milled around. When a particular celebrity, such as Henry Kissinger, appeared for testimony, the media representatives would triple or quadruple in number. At the conclusion of this media circus, Ehrlichman was sentenced to prison for 20 months to five years. He was released after serving 18 months in the Federal Prison Camp in Safford, Arizona.[24]

Howard Hunt cooperated with the prosecution of Ehrlichman in this trial and, in return, was not indicted. For his testimony in the Watergate case, David Young was granted immunity in both that case and the Fielding break-in violation.[25]

Egil Krogh was the first Nixon man indicted. Following the advice of John Dean, he committed perjury when questioned under oath about the Fielding matter, denying having any pertinent knowledge. Dean had counseled him to do this "for national security reasons." In the spring of 1973, he recanted this testimony and admitted that he had ordered the break-in. On January 24, 1974, he was sentenced to two to six years in prison, all but six months of which was suspended. He served the six months at Allenwood Prison in Pennsylvania, working hard driving a tractor. It was an experience he would never forget. To maintain a sense of balance, he and his wife, Suzanne, would study the same Bible course during the week and then discuss it when she visited him each weekend. Asked about conditions inside a prison by Charles Colson, who was about to be sentenced for his role in the Ellsberg case, Krogh gave him a graphic description:

> It's hell, Chuck. But you're tough; you'll do okay. Be careful whom you associate with. You'll see a lot of ugly things going on around you — a guy once had his skull crushed changing a TV station in the middle of a program. Just stay out of it and keep to yourself. The blacks will test you. Stand up to them if threatened; if they find any weakness in you, your goose is cooked... .
>
> I was in the bull pen in Montgomery County for the first twelve days. There were men in there waiting trial for murder, some real tough customers, twelve of us in one cell. I slept on the floor right next to the toilet and one night a dude urinated all over me. Could have been ugly, but I knew I was outnumbered so I just talked to him, and thank God it didn't happen again. [26]

Liddy was sentenced to serve one to three years in the Fielding break-in case on August 3, 1974. This was to run concurrently with a six-year, eight-month to 20-year sentence for his part in the Watergate case.[27]

In order to get immunity from prosecution in return for implicating others, John Dean told the United States attorney about the Fielding break-in as part of his quid pro quo during plea-bargaining with the

Watergate special prosecutor. This came to the attention of Henry Peterson, the head of the Department of Justice criminal division during the Watergate investigation. While at the Aspen Lodge at Camp David April 18, 1973, President Nixon telephoned Peterson and discussed the break-in. He specifically instructed Peterson that there was to be no investigation of the burglary.

"I know about that," Nixon told him, "and it is so involved with national security that I don't want it opened up. Keep the hell out of it."

Hanging up the phone, Nixon turned to John Ehrlichman, who was with him at the time, and said, "That should keep them out of it. There is no reason for them to get into it. What those fellows did was no crime; they ought to get a medal for going after Ellsberg."

Disregarding Nixon's instructions, Peterson, one of the most honorable Justice Department officials I ever dealt with, recommended that the Fielding break-in be disclosed to Ellsberg's lawyers and to Judge W. Matthew Byrne, who was conducting the Ellsberg trial in Los Angeles. [28]

As for John Dean, on October 19, 1973, he entered a plea of guilty to one count of conspiracy to obstruct justice in plotting to cover up the Watergate break-in. He agreed to testify for the prosecution against alleged cover-up participants in exchange for immunity from prosecution for any Watergate-related case. He faced a maximum five-year prison term and a $10,000 fine.[29]

The trial of Daniel Ellsberg for his theft of the Pentagon Papers got underway in Los Angeles before Judge Byrne on January 18, 1973, just two days before Nixon's second inauguration. In early April, Richard Kleindienst, then attorney general, suggested that Nixon nominate Byrne to head the FBI — this while the case was still pending before him. Nixon was seeking a successor to Acting Director Patrick Gray because Gray's confirmation as permanent director was in serious trouble during Senate hearings since it had been disclosed that he had destroyed evidence relating to the Watergate burglary.

Disregarding any consideration of the ethical aspects of the matter, Ehrlichman, on Nixon's orders, met Byrne in San Clemente on April 5 and told him that the President was considering several people for FBI director and asked the judge if he was available for consideration. Byrne immediately said he was. The conversation took place outside the building at the Summer White House where Nixon was working. As it ended, Nixon just happened to walk out of the building, met Judge Byrne, shook hands with him, and engaged in small talk. It must have left Byrne with a very favorable impression.

The very next day Gray's nomination was withdrawn. On the 7th of April, Byrne initiated a contact with Ehrlichman. He called him on the telephone and requested a second meeting. The two men met again and Byrne said that he wanted the President to know of his very strong interest in the FBI job, now that Gray's nomination had been withdrawn. When questioned about his availability, he said he didn't know how soon the Ellsberg case would be concluded since a lot depended on what the verdict would be. He promised to keep Ehrlichman informed as the case wound up.[30]

He wound up the case quite suddenly.

As a result of the negative ELSUR checks resulting from Bill Sullivan's failure to disclose the wiretap on Morton Halperin and the 15 overhearings of Ellsberg among the Kissinger wiretap records, Judge Byrne had been given false information. The government had filed affidavits with the court certifying there had been no electronic surveillance information which might have tainted evidence.

The interviews ordered by William Ruckelshaus in May 1973 to trace the missing Kissinger wiretap records soon revealed the incorrect information which had been provided to the court. On May 9, Judge Byrne was advised of the lost records and that Ellsberg had been overheard on the Halperin wiretap.

On May 11, Byrne dismissed the case, charging government misconduct, especially in the loss of the records. This was the day before they were retrieved from the outer office of John Ehrlichman in the White House. [31]

The charge of government misconduct was bolstered. Byrne disclosed in court the approach made to him about the FBI directorship while the case was still pending before him. It seemed to many lawyers a clear breach of ethics.[32]

The Pentagon Papers case had ramifications in several directions. The most serious and lasting one was the landmark Supreme Court decision in New York Times Co. v. United States (403 U.S. 713). It was clearly established that in the United States, the news media must be left to publish news, whatever the source, without censorship, injunctions, or prior restraint, "The press was to serve the governed, not the governors."

The Executive Branch concluded that recourse for leaked government secrets, if it is to be had, must be assessed against those doing the leaking, not the press to which they are leaked.

The pursuit of the war in Vietnam suffered both an immediate and long-range set back. Even before the Supreme Court rendered its decision, the U. S. Senate on June 22, 1971, by a 57 to 42 vote adopted an end-the-war amendment calling for unilateral withdrawal from Vietnam in nine months. Four days later, the North Vietnamese, who during peace talks in Paris were negotiating terms for ending the war, rejected a peace proposal Kissinger had left on the table in May.[33]

Assistant Director Charles D. Brennan of the FBI was personally adversely affected. He was severely disciplined for the action he took in the case in authorizing an interview after Hoover had specifically forbidden it. When the Director learned of this, he was livid. He considered it a deliberate insubordination, and knowing that Brennan was Bill Sullivan's right-hand man made him doubly angry. Brennan was ordered out of FBI headquarters to a position in the field office in Cleveland. Two days later, Attorney General John Mitchell called Hoover and indicated the White House was displeased about this action and did not want Brennan transferred because, in the opinion held there, he was so important to the Ellsberg investigation. Hoover felt he had little choice but to cancel the transfer. To those of us at headquarters, it was clear that Bill Sullivan had used his White House contacts to force Hoover to capitulate.[34]

The problems Hoover was having with Sullivan had reached a head, and now Brennan was just adding to them. Hoover discussed the unpleasant situation with Mark Felt, who counseled him:

The White House ordered you not to transfer Brennan because he was so important to the Ellsberg case. Why not set up a separate unit to handle the case and put Brennan in complete charge with no change in salary? This would permit him to devote full time to the case, giving the White House exactly what it asked for.

We've got to do something. Morale under Brennan is deteriorating badly. He is not a popular leader. Many of his employees still resent his having been promoted at Sullivan's request over the heads of others who had served longer and he does not know how to assuage them. He exerts his authority unnecessarily. His removal is a necessary step to bring the... Intelligence Division back under control. [35]

Hoover followed Felt's advice. Brennan was demoted from his position as the assistant director over a division having more than three hundred employees and having responsibility for all FBI security, intelligence, and counterintelligence operations. On September 9, 1971, he was designated to head a single unit whose entire responsibility was to investigate the Ellsberg case.

The most serious ramification of the case as far as the FBI was concerned was its use as a vehicle to attempt to get rid of J. Edgar Hoover as its director.

According to John Ehrlichman, during the first week of 1971 the President "began to evidence some concern about Hoover." In another eight months, "Nixon felt compelled to end Hoover's long career. In part, his decision rested on Hoover's failure to carry out the President's wishes in the Pentagon Papers case." [36]

From subsequent developments in the White House handling of the case through the illegal "plumber" operations and dirty tricks — such as efforts to degrade Ellsberg by circulating derogatory information about him — it is possible that Nixon had requested Hoover to do things of this nature. Considering Hoover's stand on the Huston Plan recommendations and how he caused the plan to be abandoned, even after Nixon gave it his approval, it is understandable why he would have declined such a request. If the President made any specific requests of this nature, those of us responsible for the investigation were unaware of them. We would have voiced objection to doing anything to clutter up the possibility of a successful prosecution of Ellsberg. We had developed sufficient legally admissible evidence for use in a trial.

On October 22, 1971, Gordon Liddy wrote a memorandum on White House stationery on the subject of the directorship of the FBI. The course of action recommended was that the President terminate J. Edgar Hoover immediately.[37]

Ehrlichman was called into the Oval Office to help Nixon prepare to confront Hoover and ask for his resignation. The next morning the President met Hoover alone in the White House residence. It was more than a month before Nixon told Ehrlichman the result of the meeting.

"It was," Nixon said, "a total strikeout. Hoover hinted that the President would have to force him out. Mitchell was surprised."

Evidently, the attorney general who, of course, was Hoover's immediate superior, had assured Nixon that the Director was ready to leave office. Also evidently, as much as Nixon was desirous of having Hoover leave office, he would not risk the public outrage and backlash which would surely follow if the FBI Director were forced to resign.

No one at the White House shed any crocodile tears when Hoover passed away. Ehrlichman completed his recital of the confrontation between Nixon and the Director:

> About six months later Hoover died, and we all went to his elaborate funeral. Nixon cemented forever his connection with Hoover on that day with his attendance at the rites and his public statements. He even ordered that the enormous, unfinished FBI building be named for Hoover. [38]

THE SLIDE DOWN THE TOTEM POLE

J. Edgar Hoover had the following quotation of Elbert Hubbard framed and hung in each FBI field office:

LOYALTY

If you work for a man, in heaven's name work for him, speak well of him, and stand by the institution he represents.

Remember — an ounce of loyalty is worth a pound of cleverness.

If you must growl, condemn, and eternally find fault, why — resign your position and when you are on the outside, damn to your heart's content — but as long as you are a part of the institution do not condemn it, if you do, the first high wind that comes along will blow you away, and probably you will never know why.

This could well-describe the road map for the course pursued by William C. Sullivan during his 30-year FBI career: staunch, outspoken support for the Director and the institution he represented, followed by a gradual replacement of loyalty with concealed cleverness and deception, and finally buffeted by a high wind that blew him to the outside where his rancorous criticism of Hoover and the FBI continued until his dying day.

A fall from grace might be likened to a parachute jump from a high-flying plane. The skilled jumper aims for a specific target and his decision to pull the ripcord is dictated by his experience and his estimate of the most appropriate time to make his move. Nevertheless, however he may attempt to guide his path to his selected target area by manipulating the shroud lines on his 'chute, he may be buffeted by a wayward wind, and the landing, no matter how gentle the descent, can be sufficiently jarring to fracture a bone.

Bill Sullivan's slide down the FBI totem pole was such a fall from grace. He was an intellectual, a former school teacher, an idea man, a voracious reader, a collector of books and literature on espionage and subversion. He cultivated an interest in communism — a subject on which Hoover was an authority — to the point that he was able to use it as a stirrup to mount and climb the Bureau totem pole. On June 10, 1970, he attained a position just two steps removed from the lofty one to which he aspired: the directorship of the FBI. It was on that date that he was appointed assistant to the director, tantamount to his being personal counselor to Hoover. Significantly, this was but five days after President Nixon established the committee which, under Sullivan's guidance, produced the Huston Plan. Ultimately, the plan was designed to undercut Hoover's decisions which eliminated the use of certain operational techniques and, obviously, to discredit him in the eyes of the President and the U.S. intelligence community.

There were wayward winds along his path, but he was a survivor, sailing with the prevailing breeze but tacking sharply if he encountered rough waters created by his own ambitions. An early example of this was his 180 degree turn from his position that there was no evidence that the August 1963 civil rights march on Washington was initiated or controlled by the CPUSA. This surely raised a question in Hoover's mind about Bill's credibility since he expressed a lack of understanding how Sullivan could "so agilely" switch his thinking and evaluation.

When Hoover decreed in July 1966 that black bag jobs should not thereafter be used, Sullivan continued submitting requests for the Director's approval. Mr. Hoover evidenced a loss of patience with Bill by writing instructions that no further recommendations for use of this technique should be sent to him.

The Huston Plan fiasco did nothing to enhance Sullivan's standing. The Director knew that Bill had chaired the working group that developed the plan and presented it to Nixon for approval, despite Hoover's pointed exceptions to parts of it. Hoover would have to be judged devoid of his senses to not see maneuvering by Bill to regain the surreptitious entry technique which had been eliminated a mere two years before.

There was another huge stumbling block along the road leading to Sullivan's fall from grace. This, like his conclusion that there was no communist threat to the civil rights movement, was his denigration of that threat to the country as a whole by ignoring it. On October 12, 1970, he gave a major and scholarly address before the United Press International Conference which was held at Williamsburg, Virginia.

Extolling the virtues of our nation under a constitution which British statesman William Gladstone described as "the most wonderful work ever struck off by the brain and purpose of man," Sullivan declared, "We must challenge the defeatist, the ignorant critic, and the self-seeking protester, whatever his motives... . The competition between conflicting values and ideas occasionally has been marked by bitterness and even violence."

Expounding on this theme, he proceeded to catalog what he considered constituted the threat to America: "The growing commitment to violence on the part of small, willful, emotionally unstable, dangerous, and destructive minorities of alienated groups and individuals... extremists of the far right, black extremists, and youthful anarchists of the so-called New Left."

In a lengthy presentation on this topic, he named a string of such groups, detailing their disruptive and criminal activities: Ku Klux Klan, National States Rights Party, National Socialist White Peoples Party, Minutemen, Fedayeen, Fatah, Black Panther Party, Black Liberation Army, Students for a Democratic Society, Weatherman, Venceremos Brigade, New Mobilization Committee to End War in Vietnam (New Mobe), East Coast Conspiracy to Save Lives, White Panther Party.

Even the casual reader may have noted that Bill's list did not include the Communist Party, USA. It was mentioned by him only as one of several groups attending an anti-war conference in Cleveland in June 1969.

During the question and answer period, Sullivan was specifically asked about the threat of the CPUSA and possible communist connections with the New Left. He answered that the Communist Party had been greatly contained through the years and that he did not feel the threat was serious. Even though he waffled in his answer, it made headlines across the nation. A high FBI official, the press reported, had minimized the communist threat.

Hoover was furious, and understandably so. What Sullivan over the years had fed to the Director on the threat of communism when courting his favor had certainly helped reinforce Hoover's own concern over, and outspoken opposition to, that alien ideology. Hoover had publicly emphasized that the Communist Party was an integral part of an international conspiracy. It was also his very defensible contention that the Party, however circumscribed by the FBI, was still giving secret aid and comfort to the New Left and to its terrorist off-shoots.[1]

In critiquing media action with respect to the threats he outlined, Sullivan exhibited what may have been either a demonstration of courage or a display of naiveté. He told his audience of media moguls and their entourage:

> Vigorous action by law enforcement against Klan-type individuals and other white extremists has generally been applauded in the press, but some press elements seem to contend that arrests are making martyrs of the [Black] Panthers and police should bend over backward in dealing with them. The question can logically be asked: does such criticism mean Panthers should not be arrested despite their criminal acts?

> (T)here is an aim to make the campus a base for political action directed against the social structure and ultimately against the Government itself. A small nucleus of professors occupy (sic) a very important role in this strategy. To date, this role has not been adequately treated by the press.

> The mass media, of course, has (sic) a fundamental responsibility for pursuing truth. It (sic) also has (sic) the responsibility to report in a rational and balanced manner. Unfortunately, certain segments of the media — either wittingly or unwittingly — have given impetus to student extremists through slanted coverage of their activities, or through excessive concern for the sensational in their reporting.

Bill certainly should have recognized that at the time of his Fall 1970 speech his audience could have been well-peppered with students and activists from the sizzling sixties who now pursued careers in the mass media field. There was a veritable flood of letters to Hoover following Sullivan's address. There were needling inquiries about why the FBI felt that communism no longer was a threat. Hoover began sending such letters to Sullivan for reply. Frustrated, Bill made efforts to intercept the incoming letters before they reached the Director's office. To say that he was deeply exasperated by the turn of events would be a gross understatement. Coming close upon the heels of the ill-fated Huston Plan, the incident marked one of the final warning signs of Bill's slide down the totem pole.

Another such sign was his disagreement with Hoover over the latter's decision to comply with a presidential order to increase the FBI's presence abroad, a matter which Sullivan had strongly supported and pushed in the past.

In May 1971, President Nixon commented most favorably on the value of having Bureau representatives assigned to various U.S.

embassies. These FBI agents were accredited to several foreign nations and each bore the title "legal attache", with the responsibility to maintain liaison with the law enforcement and intelligence agencies of the country to which accredited. Nixon ordered Hoover to expand this program and assign agents to additional countries. These operations being within the purview of the section in the Intelligence Division I headed, we sent to the Director our recommendation regarding where this expansion should be made. Sullivan, for some unexplained reason, took exception to this action, despite its being responsive to a presidential order. The Director, in keeping with his philosophy of confining Bureau interests outside the country to law enforcement and intelligence matters, was not in favor of increasing the FBI complement abroad. He sought the opinion of top Bureau officials as to the advisability of doing this. Except for Sullivan, they were in unanimous agreement that since the President had ordered the expansion and there was no valid reason for refusing him, compliance was the only course. It was possible, nevertheless, to confine the expansion to countries where the FBI could derive benefits by having agents located there. Sullivan, however, continued bitter in his outspoken opposition and once more found himself crossing swords with Hoover.

By the time the Ellsberg case broke in mid-June 1971, Hoover showed such a lack of confidence in Sullivan that he excluded him from the line-of-command when forwarding instructions to the Nationalities Intelligence Section and approvals of recommendations relating to the handling of the investigation. Whether this resulted in Sullivan's removal of the Kissinger wiretap records from FBI control, as well as his failure to reveal during the ELSUR check that they contained information vital to the success of the prosecution in the Ellsberg case, is subject to speculation. However, the fact that his removal of the records and his failure in revealing the pertinent overhearings on the Halperin tap were major contributions to Ellsberg's getting off scot-free is not speculation.

During its 1975-6 inquiries into operations of the U.S. intelligence community, the Senate Church Committee reported:

> The dismissal of charges against Ellsberg in 1973 was largely due to the belated discovery of the fact that Ellsberg had been overheard on a wiretap indicated in these [the Kissinger wiretapping] records, which were withheld from the court, preventing its determination of the pertinency of the material to the Ellsberg case. [2]

As recognized by John Dean during his March 13, 1973, conference with President Nixon, Bill Sullivan was out to destroy Hoover's image. This was obviously recognized also by the Director when, on September 3, 1971, he acknowledged a letter Sullivan had sent to him August 28. Hoover told Sullivan it had been apparent that the Director's views concerning his administration and policies in the Bureau did not meet with Sullivan's approval. This, he said, had brought about a situation "which, though I regret, is intolerable for the best functioning of the Bureau." He suggested that Sullivan submit an application for retirement effective upon the expiration of annual leave he had accumulated. [3]

Sullivan did take some of the annual leave which he had earned but did not request retirement. He returned to his office. On September 30, Hoover sent another letter to him advising that he was being relieved of all duties, and placing him on annual leave pending receipt of his application to retire. The next day Bill found that the combinations on the file cabinets in his office had been changed by Mark Felt, and the official appointed as his successor, Alex Rosen, was occupying the office. He stewed over this, recognizing that he was fighting a losing battle, and on October 6 requested retirement.[4]

This was also the same date on which he sent a highly critical letter to Hoover at his home address, explaining, "in order that you may hold it privately for as you are aware the Bureau has become a bit of a sieve and this letter if seen would be the subject of gossip which, I am sure, we both wish to avoid." He then proceeded in 12 pages to tell the Director what he considered was wrong with his operation of the FBI and what he considered was wrong with him personally.

From an operational standpoint, here are some examples, in Sullivan's words, which he cited to Hoover:

- The FBI should not try to dominate the police.
- You want the FBI to have as little to do jointly as possible with other members of the [intelligence] community.
- We have been conducting far too many investigations called security which are actually political... investigations mainly of students, professors, intellectuals, and their organizations concerned with peace, anti-war, etc... .
- FBI and organized crime: Here is where we should concentrate more time, money, and manpower.
- FBI and foreign liaison: I have discussed this with you in my August letter and will say no more other than to stress the great waste of taxpayer's money in maintaining so many needless offices in foreign nations.

Some of Sullivan's comments of a personal nature bordered on the vicious, of a type just about everyone would find offensive:

- The damage you are doing the Bureau and its work has brought all this on.
- One of your minor faults — overstatement and overkill.
- You caused a communist scare in the nation which was entirely unwarranted.
- You abolished our main programs designed to identify and neutralize [illegal agents in the United States]... . Mr. Hoover, are you thinking? Are you really capable of thinking this thing through?
- FBI and statistics: We all know they have never been either definitive or wholly reliable. More than one scholar has pointed this out down through the years and instead of appreciating their interest we looked upon them as enemies to be attacked.

Why do we have such an attitude? Is it because long ago you projected the image of infallibility and now you are stuck with it?

• As you know, you have become a legend in your lifetime with a surrounding mythology linked to incredible power. This is not good for either you or the Bureau... . Let's face it — everyone knew of your ego.

• A few years ago I could see the beginning of the breakup of the FBI.

• Why don't you sit down quietly by yourself and think this all over, and then get some of the men together and work out a plan to reform, reorganize, and modernize the Bureau.

• Mr. Hoover, if for any reasons of your own you cannot or will not do this, may I gently suggest you retire for your own good, that of the Bureau, the intelligence community, and law enforcement.

It was hardly necessary for Sullivan, in making some final observations in his 12-page diatribe, to state, "I am no typist so please pardon the mistakes and organization," but it was the only meaningful apology he offered.

Bill was extensively investigated by the Watergate special prosecutor for his role in removing the Kissinger wiretapping records from the FBI. The question was: had Sullivan conspired to remove from FBI control the so-called Kissinger wiretaps for the purpose of concealing these taps from Judge Byrne who was presiding over the Ellsberg case? On September 16, 1975, the special prosecutor issued a statement to the effect that evidence did not warrant criminal charges against him.[5]

In May 1977, Sullivan was also subjected to questioning by attorneys of the Department of Justice about his knowledge of alleged illegal activities. He reportedly denied knowing that former departmental officials Attorney General John Mitchell and Assistant Attorney General Robert Mardian had knowledge of or ran any illegal Bureau activities. He claimed that President Nixon "and all those who preceded him with the exception of Harry Truman" had been aware that the FBI used break-ins and other questionable methods in both foreign and domestic intelligence investigations. When questioned about his own alleged role in granting requests for surreptitious entries, he reportedly told the attorneys about vague incidents. The only one about which he seemed to have a better recollection involved a case in the Boston area when he was informed of it "after the fact." He then condoned a break-in which agents had committed in a hunt for a fugitive wanted in connection with a national security matter, according to his story.

A good portion of questioning by the departmental officials was devoted to Sullivan's role in helping to draft the Huston Plan.[6]

He had to be cautious in assigning any blame to himself. By the time of his death in a hunting accident on November 9, 1977, Bill had been named in civil suits stemming from almost every infraction, real or imagined, that the Bureau had been accused of committing against citizens since World War II, and could rarely step outside his house without being served with another subpoena.[7]

Information relating to Sullivan's deceitfulness and his sullied reputation for integrity appears many times in public print. He authored many of the alleged abuses by the FBI. At the time of his death, *The Washington Post* took note of the fact that when he joined the organization in August 1941,

the FBI saw itself — and was seen by others — as a crime-fighting organization and as the country's first line of defense against Nazis and other subversives. By the time he left, the bureau was coming under increasing attack for violating the rights of American citizens.... . Mr. Sullivan played a role in these transformations, first as a loyal lieutenant of Hoover who initiated many of the abuses that have been uncovered by Congress and the press in recent years, and then as a bitter critic of his late boss. [8]

Book reviewers have found much to criticize about Sullivan and his book "My Thirty Years in Hoover's FBI."

• *New York Post*, July 2, 1979, article "How FBI boss Hoover upstaged RFK funeral." *William C. Sullivan, once Hoover's third-in-command, writes of his former boss' alleged dislike of the Kennedys and blacks.... . Sullivan, who despises his boss, also charges Hoover hated black Americans, 'particularly Martin Luther King, Jr'.... . FBI Agents told Newsweek that Sullivan was known to them as "Crazy Bill" and was guilty of "gross misstatements of tone and fact."*

• *Parade Magazine*, September 30, 1979, "Parade Special Intelligence Report." *During the Nixon Administration, Bill Sullivan tried to bring J. Edgar Hoover down.*

• *The Washington Post*, September 30, 1979, review of Sullivan's book by Anthony Marro in <u>Bookworld.</u> *This book... adds up to little more than a diatribe against Hoover and the Bureau he created, coupled with a scattering of self-serving (and not entirely believable) justifications for Sullivan's having stayed in the organization for so long and for being a part of so many things — the anti-communist hysteria, the harassment of political and civil rights groups, among them — that he later found reason to denounce Hoover for. (It should be noted in this context, that Sullivan was the sort of person who, while in government believed that the government should have great power to involve itself in people's lives, but who, after retirement to New Hampshire, questioned the right of the state to make him have his car inspected each year.).... . The purpose [of the book] seems to be getting even, pure and simple, and the result is a series of assaults on Hoover and almost all his lieutenants that should cause even veteran Hoover-haters to wince.*

• *Law Enforcement News*, <u>Book Reviews,</u> October 22, 1979. *The image of the author that emerges in this book is that of a deceitfully ambitious man. Sullivan continuously refers to himself as a "liberal democrat" but at the same time tries to justify official use of illegal wiretaps, break-ins and "dirty trick" letters. His book might be compared with John Dean's "Blind Ambition" except that Sullivan's ambition, after thirty years in the very shadow of a boss he considered to be "one of the most balefully powerful men in America," can hardly be called blind.*

This documentation of Sullivan's bias, hatred for Hoover, deceitfulness, lack of integrity, and disregard for truthfulness, taken entirely from public source material, is by no means complete, but certainly sufficient to paint a picture of his character.

After Bill left the Bureau, he spent the rest of his life circulating half-truths and non-truths about the FBI Director in an effort to get his job. He said many things which warped the true facts or disregarded them entirely. An example was his disavowal in his book of responsibility for initiating COINTELPRO operations and Martin Luther King investigative techniques, claiming they were already in effect when in 1961 he became head of the division handling the case.

In an interview with *The Los Angeles Times* in 1973, he called Hoover "a master blackmailer." He suggested that the Director had lost control of himself and was verging on senility before his death. [9]

In November 1974 when speaking before a conference of the Roscoe Pound-American Trial Lawyers Foundation, Sullivan described the Bureau as a threat to civil liberties and voiced the opinion that its internal security responsibilities should be taken away from it. He said, "The weaknesses of the FBI have always been the leadership in Washington." [10]

Even after Mr. Hoover passed away, Sullivan agitated to have all internal security responsibilities removed from the FBI and placed in a domestic national security intelligence system, as mentioned by John Dean during his March 13, 1973, meeting in the Oval Office with Dick Nixon, and with Sullivan, himself, of course, heading it.

He concocted easily refutable arguments in efforts to attain this goal. An example: He claimed that the United States was the only country in the free world naive enough to combine both criminal and security investigative responsibilities in the same agency. He was well aware that under Hoover there was no penetration of the FBI by Soviet intelligence while the Cambridge spy ring, with British turncoat and Soviet master spy Kim Philby in a leading role, accomplished high-level penetrations of the two British intelligence agencies who had no criminal jurisdiction — a strong argument in favor of the American system. [11]

With respect to some of Sullivan's FBI associates referring to him as "Crazy Bill," there surely were signs of certain irrationalities on his part beginning about a year before he retired from the FBI. However, during the time I worked under him, he impressed me as brilliant. Those of us who came to know him well felt that he may have suffered a mental collapse the last year or so he was in the Bureau, perhaps brought on by his obsession to become FBI Director. His tirades and false charges so alienated him from his fellow agents that he was refused membership in the Society of Former Special Agents of the FBI after he retired.

The strain under which he lived during the last years of his life must have had a telling effect upon him. A person of credibility who requested confidentiality provided information regarding Sullivan's reactions following his November 1, 1975, testimony before the

Church Committee. Bill stated that he was deeply embittered against the country, the presidency, the Congress, and "all their toadies." He complained that he had nothing but the utmost contempt for the Federal Government. Claiming to have been made the scapegoat in the Martin Luther King, Jr., case, he said that he was going to see that everyone involved was brought to justice, either in court <u>or outside of court at his hands</u>. [12]

Sullivan's threat seemed ominous. He had a violent streak and once offered to fist-fight a man half again his size, Deputy Associate Director Mark Felt.[13] And as a 30-year FBI agent he was well trained in the use of side arms, rifles, and shot guns.

Sullivan's betrayal obviously impacted Hoover. Months later, it was still much on his mind. In connection with my promotion to an inspector's position, I had a half-hour appointment with him April 6, 1972, 26 days before his death, just six months after Sullivan submitted his official retirement request. Hoover began to speak of Bill Sullivan. His first words were, "That son of a bitch Sullivan pulled the wool over my eyes, he completely fooled me. I treated him like a son and he betrayed me."

He berated himself for this, saying, "Sullivan kept sending me notes and making remarks critical of Deke DeLoach," and seemed to accept blame for not recognizing Sullivan's duplicity.

He commented, "DeLoach was not making any such snide remarks about Sullivan, and it didn't occur to me just what Sullivan was doing. I have never been so disappointed in anyone in my life."

When thwarted by another Bureau official, Sullivan often threw a tantrum, followed by the sort of stab-in-the-back technique that he directed against Deke DeLoach, and which the Director had come to recognize.[14] DeLoach as assistant to the director was Sullivan's superior. It was a position Sullivan had wanted when Deke was appointed to it and Sullivan obviously was trying to undercut him.

During this, my last meeting with the Director, once he got on the subject of Sullivan, he didn't even notice whether I was taking notes. At the end of the half-hour, he thanked me for coming in and dismissed me.

Hoover died of a heart attack May 2, 1972. Years later when his doctor, Robert V. Choisser, told me that the Director had no heart condition, no angina during the 20-years he had treated him, I could not help but wonder just how deeply the Director was affected by the break with one on whom he had relied and for whom he had had such a high regard that he "treated him like a son."

On Sullivan's last day at the Bureau, Hoover told Mark Felt, "The greatest mistake I ever made was to promote Sullivan." [15]

Bill, in your lifetime you certainly proved the validity of a favorite quotation of yours, one I heard you repeat so many times:

Oh what a tangled web we weave
When once we practice to deceive.

HOOVER AND THE KENNEDYS

JOSEPH P. KENNEDY

Joseph P. Kennedy was the father of John, Robert, and Edward (Ted) Kennedy and from 1937 to 1940, served as ambassador to the Court of St. James in London. In June 1939, the British were bewildered as to why Ambassador Kennedy was allowed to remain in his post considering his record as an appeaser and apologist for Prime Minister Neville Chamberlain.[1]

His ambassadorship to Britain was widely regarded in the United States as demonstrating that Kennedy was, in fact, an appeaser, and believed that Great Britain would lose World War II. His appeasement attitude was thought to be important only as far as it threw light on his views about the Soviet Union.

Arthur Krock of *The New York Times* described Kennedy as spokesman for a group of industrialists and financiers who believed the Soviet Union should not be opposed at any point and all American energies should be devoted to keeping America prosperous. Thus, when communism failed in the Soviet Union, or more properly in the rest of Europe, the people whose faith in communism had been destroyed by its failure would return to democratic beliefs. The only country to which they would be able to turn would be the United States, and the complete superiority of the democratic over the communistic system would be demonstrated.[2]

While J. Edgar Hoover could hardly be regarded as an appeaser, his strong aversion to communism in all its forms must certainly have been stroked in the proper way by this theory, and over the years a warm, first-name-basis friendship developed between him and Joe Kennedy.

The ambassador in September 1943 offered to assist the FBI in any way possible should his services be needed. He commented to a representative of the Boston office of the Bureau that if he were ever in a position to make any official recommendations, there would be only one federal investigative unit, and that would be headed by J. Edgar Hoover. [3]

He had extensive interests in real estate, the motion picture and liquor industries, and the general field of corporation finance. He maintained numerous contacts among the international diplomatic set and expressed a willingness to use his entree to those circles for any advantage the Bureau might desire in this field.[4]

From September 1943 until May 1, 1964, when he entered a rehabilitation center in Philadelphia due to an illness, he was in frequent contact with the Boston office while living at Hyannisport, Massachusetts, and the Miami office whenever he stayed at his summer home on North Ocean Boulevard in Palm Beach, Florida. He entertained Hoover at his Palm Beach estate and the two men carried on a frequent exchange of letters. When Joe's daughter Eunice married Robert Sargent Shriver, Jr., Hoover received an invitation to the wedding and reception.[5]

In an April 12, 1957, letter, the ambassador remarked that his son Bobby "is more enthusiastic than ever about J. Edgar Hoover and the FBI and he has many incidents to back up his enthusiasm." Subsequently, Bobby's enthusiasm seemed to have waned with age. [6]

A year later when referring to the FBI, "Joe" told "Edgar," "This is the greatest organization in the Government and you have performed the greatest public service of any man that I know." [7]

Hoover's regard for Joe Kennedy and his family also came through. In a letter on November 9, 1960, he told Joe how pleased he was with John Kennedy's election as President, writing, "You may be certain my associates and I will be glad to do anything we can to be of assistance to him." [8]

When Robert Kennedy was gunned down by an assassin on June 5, 1968, Hoover sent an urgent telegram to Ambassador and Mrs. Kennedy expressing heartfelt sympathy and saying, "It is my fervent hope that his strength and courage will help pull him through this crisis and that his recovery will be swift and complete." At the time, no one was aware of the fatal nature of Robert Kennedy's wounds, and the very next day Hoover by telegram conveyed his deepest regret and sympathy over Robert's death. [9]

Joseph P. Kennedy suffered a severe stroke in December 1961 and lived another eight years until November 18, 1969. On that same day, Edward M. Kennedy advised Hoover by telegram of the death of his father, and said that he and his mother wanted to thank Hoover for the warm ties of friendship Joe Kennedy shared with him throughout many years, which "he so deeply appreciated." A telegram of sympathy was sent by Hoover to Mrs. Joseph Kennedy the same day and a letter went out to Edward the following day expressing sympathy and stating that the Director was grateful for the close friendship he had shared with his father over the years. [10]

While Joe Kennedy often spoke very highly of his regard for Hoover, perhaps the most edifying information in this regard was revealed in a letter he sent to the Director on October 11, 1955. The ambassador said the only two men he knew in public life, for whose opinion he gave "one continental," both happened to be named Hoover — one John Edgar and the other, Herbert. (Joe served on the Herbert Hoover Commission in 1954 which studied U.S. intelligence operations.) Referring to a Walter Winchell broadcast during which the commentator mentioned Hoover as a candidate for President, Kennedy wrote:

> If that could come to pass, it would be the most wonderful thing for the United States, and whether you were on a Republican or Democratic ticket, I would guarantee you the largest contribution that you would ever get from anybody and the hardest work by either a Democrat or a Republican. I think the United States deserves you. I only hope it gets you.
>
> My best to you always.
> Sincerely,
> /s/ Joe

JOHN F. KENNEDY

Starting when John Kennedy was a senator, he and Director Hoover exchanged friendly correspondence concerning such matters as an operation performed on Jack in 1954 to correct crippling effects of a World War II PT-Boat crash; the 1956 awarding to Jack of the Cardinal Gibbons Medal for outstanding service to the country; and Kennedy's re-election to the Senate in 1958. The Bureau and the Director enjoyed friendly relations with the senator and his family, and Jack was one of three members of the family — the others being Joe Kennedy and Bobby Kennedy — to whom Hoover sent autographed copies of Don Whitehead's *The FBI Story* and the Director's own book, *Masters of Deceit.* [11]

On his part, Senator Kennedy was very complimentary of both the Director and the Bureau, and stated he was anxious and willing at all times to support Hoover and the FBI. He commented that he felt the Bureau to be the only real government agency worthy of its salt, and expressed admiration for the Director's accomplishments. [12]

In January 1953, he expressed a desire to see Hoover and go on a tour of the Bureau. Receiving a favorable reply, he indicated that as soon as things settled down on Capitol Hill he would take the tour and would appreciate it if he could have the opportunity to shake hands with Hoover. [13]

At Jack's wedding reception on September 12, 1953, while speaking to a Bureau agent in attendance, he was quite complimentary of Hoover and the FBI and volunteered that he was anxious and willing at all times to support both. [14]

At the home of his father a month later, the senator told the special agent in charge of the FBI Boston office how much he admired Hoover for his accomplishments, repeating his previously expressed belief that the only real governmental agency "worthy of its salt" was the FBI. The Director, in appreciation, acknowledged the compliment and invited him to visit the Bureau. [15]

When writing to Jack about his 1954 surgery, Hoover commented upon "the gallant courage and determination which you have displayed in the past," expressed the hope that these would give him the fortitude he needed, and conveyed his wishes for a speedy and complete recovery. [16]

Following Kennedy's selection by the Democratic Party to be its candidate for President in 1960, he made a campaign promise on August 3 that if he won in November he would continue Hoover as Director of the FBI. Incidentally, this was interpreted as beating candidate Richard Nixon to the draw. [17]

Upon Kennedy's election on November 9, 1960, Hoover offered his congratulations, writing, "Our nation will benefit immeasurably from your leadership. America is most fortunate to have a man of your caliber at the helm in these perilous days." [18]

This may or may not have been a subtle reminder by Hoover of Kennedy's campaign promise. Who can say? In any event, on November 10, the very next day, Kennedy pressed the right button, as far as Hoover was concerned, by announcing he would continue the Director in his job. While serving as President, he invited Hoover to the White House for a discussion of conditions generally, and accepted the award of an FBI badge following an address he gave to a graduating class at the FBI Academy. [19]

The *Melbourne Times* of Melbourne, Florida, carried an editorial in its November 14, 1960, edition, reporting that Las Vegas gamblers were laying bets of something like seven to five odds that Kennedy would not live to be inaugurated. There were, in fact, three threats against his life and one against the life of his wife Jacqueline prior to the January 20, 1961, inauguration. [20]

When a threat of this nature was received, it was immediately called to the attention of the Secret Service, which had the responsibility for the safety of the President and his family. This dissemination was made by the FBI both on a field level and at the headquarters level. In addition, whenever the President traveled, and Kennedy made numerous trips in the United States, the FBI field offices covering the areas he visited alerted FBI sources to provide any information coming to their attention, however remote, bearing upon his safety or that of his family members. All such information reported by these sources was given similar dissemination on an immediate basis.

On November 21, 1963, the day before the President was assassinated, the Dallas office of Secret Service was advised that a bundle of leaflets was discovered in the 300 block of South Poydras Street in that city. Found at 6:30 A.M., they were of various colors, had front and profile views of Kennedy, and contained the wording "Wanted for Treason." He was accused of "Turning the sovereignty of the U.S. over to the communist controlled United Nations;" being lax in "enforcing Communist Registration laws;" other actions showing support for communist and "anti-Christian" actions; and telling lies to the American people "(including personal ones like his previous marriage and divorce)." There was no stated threat against the President.

A Dallas Police Department detective said there were numerous complaints about the leaflets' being distributed all over the downtown area and the wealthier residential areas of the city, but the identities of the distributors were unknown.[21]

On the same day, the FBI office in Dallas advised the Secret Service office that a reporter for the Dallas *Morning News* had furnished information to the effect that signs were being printed to be used in picketing President Kennedy during his visit to Dallas.[22]

When John Kennedy was shot, Hoover was immediately notified by the Dallas FBI office and he promptly conveyed the information by phone to the President's brother, Attorney General Robert Kennedy. He later was the first one to break the tragic news to Bobby that his brother had died. [23]

With regard to the charge in the leaflet that John Kennedy had lied about a previous marriage and divorce, according to a book titled "The Blauvelt Family Genealogy," John F. Kennedy, son of Joseph P. Kennedy, one-time ambassador to England, was the third husband of twice-divorced Durie (Kerr) Malcolm.[24]

When this was brought to Attorney General Kennedy's attention, he said the person who prepared this item for the genealogy book was dead and the executor of his estate could find only one reference to the girl in a newspaper clipping. This was to the effect that the President had gone out with her only once.

Bobby told newspapermen he hoped they printed the story of

Jack's previous marriage, because then "we" could all retire for life on what "we" collect in a libel action. [25]

Allegations of immoral activities on the part of John Kennedy were reported to the Bureau over the years beginning with World War II. They included data indicating that he carried on an illicit relationship with another man's wife during the War; that he was "compromised" with a woman in Las Vegas, probably in January 1960; and that he had an affair with Judith Exner, nee Campbell, a free-lance artist who was reported to have associated with prominent underworld figures John Roselli and Sam "Mo Mo" Giancana, with whom she also shared her favors. Reportedly, he and Frank Sinatra had been involved in "parties" in Palm Springs, Las Vegas, and New York City, and *Confidential* magazine had affidavits from two mulatto prostitutes concerning this. Allegations were also made regarding hoodlum connections of President Kennedy. [26]

In January 1942, the FBI was advised that a woman who was under investigation for alleged espionage on behalf of the Germans had been carrying on an affair with John Kennedy, then an ensign in the U.S. Navy. It was determined the following month that she had spent several weekends with him in a hotel in Charleston, South Carolina. Investigation of the woman was closed in 1945 as no espionage or other subversive activities were determined.[27]

The Jack Kennedy-Judith Campbell relationship has been the subject of speculation and stories since it became known following Kennedy's assassination. Even for many who were his strong supporters, it left a bitter taste in their mouths. Columnist Mary McGrory, who found it easy to put a pro-Democratic Party spin on matters and things affecting Party politicians, more than 34 years after Kennedy's demise commented somewhat mournfully on how this disillusioned the Kennedy cult:

> What was Judith Campbell Exner doing at the White House? Why did the president go to such lengths to arrange for this exceptionally ordinary Chicago woman to come to the White House many times?... .
>
> To keep her around, Kennedy willingly took risks with his wife, the Secret Service and the public — as he did with so many women he kept in his life. Even so resolute an opponent of monogamy has to have a better reason... .
>
> Exner is a matter of an official Senate report. Sen. Frank Church, a gentle and good Democrat, reluctantly made the affair public in 1975. The fact that she was a friend of Chicago mobster Sam Giancana rocked the Camelot myth so delicately arranged by Jackie Kennedy after the national trauma of Nov. 22, 1963. The idea that the laid-back Irishman, a paragon of elegance and taste, would be sharing a moll with Giancana dismayed the Kennedy cult... .[28]

Le Ore, a weekly magazine in Turin, Italy, on January 31, 1961, quoted one Alicia Purdom, wife of English actor Edmund Purdom who was attempting to obtain a divorce from her, concerning a relationship she claimed to have had with President Kennedy. She said she had been engaged to him and could have been "First Lady of America," but the marriage was opposed because she was a Polish-Jewish refugee. [29]

In mid-1963, from information provided by an aide to Senator John G. Tower of Texas, as supplemented by that available to the FBI, it was learned that Mrs. Purdom, then known as Alicia Corning Clark, widow of Stephen Carlton Clark, a director of the Singer Manufacturing Company, had filed a 1.2 million dollar law suit against the "Clark Estate." She was said to have been married to Clark only 13 days before he died, September 17, 1960. A New York City private detective who used the name "Garden" had some papers in his possession, including a Photostat of a handwritten letter from the woman to an attorney in which, according to Senator Tower's aide, she stated that now that Kennedy had been elected President, "their" position was much better. "Garden" appeared to hope to receive money for the papers, and when the aide said he wanted nothing to do with such material, "Garden" suddenly broke off the contact. This was obviously an attempt on the part of "Garden" to get money, and the circumstances supposedly involving the Purdom-Clark woman raised questions concerning the validity of her claim. [30]

The foregoing information was provided to Attorney General Kennedy. Years later after his death, a reporter discussed with John Seigenthaler, who had been Robert Kennedy's administrative assistant, a claim by an unnamed New York City private detective that Bobby had paid $500,000 to quash the woman's law suit. Seigenthaler not only shared an office with him but lived at Bobby's house during the time this pay-off allegedly occurred. He had no knowledge of it, even though he said he was sure he would have known if it had taken place. This would certainly tend to give the lie also to this claim. [31]

Not infrequently people brought to Robert Kennedy's attention when he was attorney general allegations of indiscretions on the part of his brother, the President. Two representatives of the *New York Journal American* called on him July 1, 1963, to discuss what they had said to be information they desired to furnish that would be of interest to the Department of Justice. The attorney general asked a Bureau representative to sit in on the meeting. Just two days before, the newspaper had published an article containing a statement that a highly elected U.S. official was connected to the British sex scandal known as the John Profumo affair. [32]

John Profumo, British secretary of state for war, in 1963 was involved in an unsavory affair with a beautiful call girl named Christine Keeler, who was also romantically involved with Yevgeny Ivanov, naval attache at the Soviet Embassy in London. Since questions were raised about the possibility of a breach of security, a judicial inquiry was undertaken. While no such breach was found, the government was censured for failing to make a prompt and adequate investigation, and Prime Minister Harold Macmillan suffered acute embarrassment in the House of Commons. [33]

Robert Kennedy asked the two *Journal American* representatives to identify the highly elected U.S. official allegedly connected to the messy Profumo affair. In response he was advised that the U.S. official was the President. The *Journal* representatives also provided what they considered to be proof that, prior to his election, President Kennedy had been involved with a girl who had been identified in the article of June 29 as Suzy Chang, a Chinese-American.

One of the *Journal* representatives contended this involvement of a U.S. official was not what his paper was interested in but rather possible security implications of another case. He expected to get more information on this and, if he turned it over to the Justice Department, he wanted assurances he would get an exclusive story. He was not given any specific assurances by Bobby, who treated the two men at arms length. The meeting ended most coolly and there was almost an air of hostility between him and them. [34]

Through discreet investigation, the Bureau was able to prove that President Kennedy had no connection with the Profumo affair, and Robert Kennedy was so advised. He was appreciative, and said it seemed preposterous that such a story would circulate considering the scores of newspapermen who traveled with John Kennedy. [35]

ROBERT F. KENNEDY

Prior to Robert Kennedy's appointment as attorney general, his association with Hoover, although limited, was on a cordial basis. His father had previously told Hoover that Bobby was "enthusiastic" about the Director and the FBI.

Bobby called on Hoover in September 1959 to advise that he was resigning as chief counsel of the McClellan Labor-Management Committee in the senate and to express appreciation for the excellent cooperation the Bureau had extended to him. This was about the time John Kennedy decided to make a run for the presidency with Bobby as his campaign manager. In correspondence, Hoover addressed him as "Dear Bob."[36]

Two days before the election of John as President, Bobby was interviewed on the TV program "Meet the Press." He acknowledged he would like to work for the government but it would be "very difficult" for him to be given a high place in the Kennedy administration because it might bring charges of nepotism. Shortly following his election, on the other hand, John Kennedy laid the groundwork for appointing Bobby his attorney general. He said he would not be deterred from giving him a government post if he wanted one. Since crime-prevention had been a major interest of Bobby's, the speculation was that he would be the choice for the attorney general position.[37]

When within 45 days of John's inauguration Joe Kennedy was advised there were growing rumors that the two brothers had a rift with Hoover, he said that nothing could be further from the truth. "Both Jack and Bob admire Hoover," he said. "They feel they're lucky to have him head the FBI.... . They've always admired him." [38]

It seems, nevertheless, that the seeds for a serious rift between Hoover and his boss, the attorney general, had already been planted. In this regard, Deke DeLoach reported that a writer once asked Hoover about his feud with Bobby. The Director told the writer that he had advised Jack Kennedy to appoint his brother as attorney general to have someone in his cabinet in whom he had confidence.

When recounting this to DeLoach, Hoover said, "Worst damn piece of advice I ever gave." [39]

Mark Felt, former acting associate director of the FBI, explained the treatment accorded Hoover by his new boss, which did much to alienate the Director from him. Bobby Kennedy was described as brash, ruthless, and politically motivated. He resented the FBI's independent status and saw it not as a law enforcement agency but as an arm of "his" administration. He and Jack regarded the Bureau as "a weapon for political warfare, an adjunct of the Kennedy wing of the Democratic Party rather than as a nonpolitical investigative force." Felt explained:

> ...It was made very clear that Attorney General Kennedy thought of the FBI as a kind of private police department, with Hoover its desk sergeant. Bobby would not only storm into Hoover's office unannounced, or summon the Director to his own palatial suite in the Justice Department building as if Hoover were an office boy, but he also struck directly at Hoover's authority by calling a Special Agent in Charge or an agent on a case directly, violating the traditional chain of command... .

Perhaps the most disturbing act of Bobby's was his circulation among high government officials of a memorandum prepared by Walter Reuther, president of the United Auto Workers, and his brother Victor. Titled "The Radical Right in America," it included a sharp attack on the FBI and Hoover, both lumped under "radical right," which consisted of everything from extremists to some members of the Republican Party. To the Reuthers and to Kennedy, the "right" posed a "far greater danger" to the United States than the communist movement. [40]

W. Mark Felt. (FBI)

It was obvious that Bobby, with the concurrence of Jack, had set out to demean Hoover to the point that he would resign his position. The Director had a four-hour meeting at the White House with President Kennedy on March 22, 1962. An aide to Kennedy, Kenneth O'Donnell, was present, and when he was asked years later about what transpired, he would say only that the president had "eventually lost patience" and "hissed" to O'Donnell, "Get rid of the bastard. He's the biggest bore." [41]

It was equally apparent that the Kennedy boys didn't have the guts to fire Hoover. Considering the Director's popularity in the country, it would have been politically unwise to do so, and these thoughts must have passed through Hoover's mind.

Early in 1961, in keeping with Robert Kennedy's wishes, Special Agent Courtney A. (Court) Evans was selected to serve as the FBI's principal liaison man with the Department of Justice. Court was then appointed assistant director to head a new division which was established, known as the Special Investigative Division. Among the first matters requiring close liaison was the interest expressed by Kennedy in wiretapping. [42]

He requested that this technique be utilized to gather intelligence which might be of value in developing U.S. foreign policy. The section to which I was assigned at the time had responsibilities relating to foreign counterintelligence, and it befell our lot to recommend areas in which technical surveillances might produce positive intelligence information. The use of this technique was expanded substantially to comply with Attorney General Kennedy's request.

He also seemed to have a regard for the value attached to the judicious use of microphones. In late 1961 and again in 1962 the Bureau installed microphones in his office at his specific request and recorded discussions which took place there. [43]

Upon assuming the position of attorney general, Kennedy made a move which was unprecedented. He created a permanent task force consisting of representatives of several federal investigative agencies for an intensified drive against organized crime. At a meeting within one month of his becoming attorney general, he outlined generally the program he had in mind for making inroads into the underworld, particularly in the field of racketeering. [44]

Court Evans in July pointed out to Kennedy that the Bureau had used microphones in certain cases and would do so in all instances where feasible and where valuable information might be expected, despite the fact that it was an expensive investigative step. Kennedy said he was pleased that the FBI was making use of microphone surveillances wherever possible in organized crime matters. [45]

Subsequently in 1963, while visiting the Chicago FBI office in March and the one in New York City in November, the attorney general listened to recordings made by means of microphones planted to cover activities of organized crime figures. He was very complimentary of the coverage the Chicago Office was affording racketeering activities in that area. [46]

When Mark Felt was assigned to the Kansas City Office as special agent in charge, Bobby visited there. Mark gave him a tour of the office, which included the "plant," a room where microphone surveillances were being monitored. Mark reported that although Kennedy was busy shaking every hand in sight, "I find it difficult to believe he did not hear what I explained to him," about the nature of the microphone coverage. Kansas City at the time was headquarters for one of the more important Mafia "families" in the United States. The leaders called themselves the "Clique," and it was their meeting place which was being monitored by microphone coverage when Kennedy visited the "plant." [47]

The knowledge Robert Kennedy had of the FBI's use of microphones, especially in organized crime cases, has been particularly documented. During a national television appearance in June 1966, Kennedy, then a senator from New York with an eye on the presidency, responded to a question whether electronic coverage had been used in certain criminal cases in Las Vegas by declaring he had not authorized the use of <u>wiretaps</u>. He neglected to point out that <u>microphones</u> had been authorized and utilized. The fact that microphones had been used in an investigation of one Fred B. Black had become public knowledge; therefore, the impression was conveyed to many persons that the FBI, which investigated the case, had engaged in unauthorized eavesdropping. [48]

Solicitor General Thurgood Marshall on July 13, 1966, presented a memorandum to the Supreme Court which corrected this impression, but his factual statement received far less notice than had the erroneous impression conveyed by Kennedy during the national telecast. An atmosphere rife with misinformation and confusion continued to prevail through the fall months of 1966. Hoover was falsely charged with freewheeling and highhandedness in installing electronic listening devices contrary to the will of the former attorney general. [49]

Matters were certainly not improved for Hoover when Kennedy made a further incorrect public statement about the Black case on December 11, 1966. He declared that he had been unaware of "bugging practices" such as what the press reported had been used in the case. "I promptly ordered them stopped," he maintained. [50]

No such order to cease the use of microphone surveillances was given to the FBI during Kennedy's tenure as attorney general. [51]

Hoover took advantage of a January 10, 1967, appearance before a Senate committee to acknowledge FBI use of both wiretaps and microphones in the past in line with Department of Justice policy and with attorney general authorization. He said:

> Let me explain my strong belief that every man has a right to privacy and that this right cannot arbitrarily be infringed upon or taken away from him. However, in a democracy such as ours, the rights of the individual must be tempered by respect for the welfare of society and the public safety. I fully respect, for example, the right of members of the Ku Klux Klan to hold their furtive meetings and engage in mumbo jumbo rituals. But when those meetings are held for the purpose of plotting murders or bombings or arsons, then I feel the Klan members' "right to privacy" ought to be forfeited by the gross malignancy of the purpose which their meetings serve.
>
> The same is true of organized criminal societies whose hired killers have claimed the lives of mounting numbers of innocent citizens — including, in one Midwestern bombing, the life of a defenseless 11-year-old boy. It is true also of the Communist Party, USA, and other nefarious organizations which would alter our form of Government and inflict their will upon the American people by force and violence.

Director Hoover pointed out that these views were not inconsistent with those expressed by Attorney General Kennedy when he appeared on March 29, 1962, before the Senate Judiciary Committee.

On that occasion Kennedy urged prompt enactment of a federal wiretapping statute, saying,

I strongly believe that every citizen of the United States has a right not to have strangers listen in on his telephone conversations. But this right, like many other individual rights in our society, is not absolute or unqualified. Society also has a right to use effective means of law enforcement to protect itself from espionage and subversion, from murder and kidnapping, and from organized crime and racketeering. [52]

Mark Felt described Bobby Kennedy as ruthless and politically motivated. These traits seem to have surfaced during this controversy over the use of technical surveillances which arose between the former FBI Director and the former attorney general under whom Hoover served from January 1961 to September 1964.

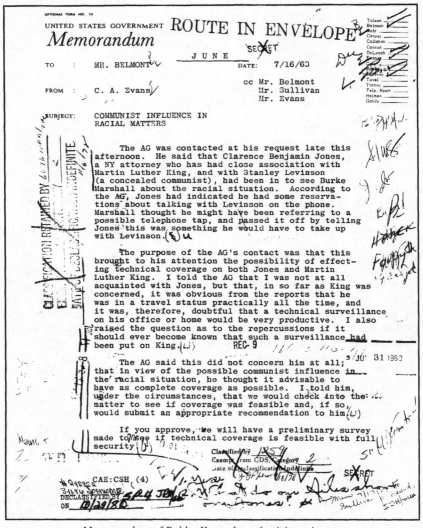

Memorandum of Bobby Kennedy authorizing wiretaps.

THOSE ALLEGATIONS OF PERVERSION

Some of the most egregious and damaging allegations made against J. Edgar Hoover, seemingly widely accepted despite the lack of supporting evidence, were the charges that he was a homosexual and engaged in cross-dressing. To believe these things, one must ignore the fact that for nearly a half century the Washington newspaper corps, consisting of the very cream of the country's investigative reporters, developed nothing to confirm rumors of this nature which cropped up occasionally during Hoover's lifetime, usually tied to his status as an avowed bachelor.

The media hounds vigorously pursued the slightest bit of gossip regarding his sexual orientation. Jack Anderson, one of the better-known scandal mongers, had his leg man, Charles Elliott, a rookie reporter for *The Washington Post*, regularly pick up the trash which Hoover discarded at his 30th street home. It was found to contain no information which, by any stretch of the imagination, might substantiate the myth that Hoover was homosexual. Upon learning of Anderson's forays against his trash can, Hoover called him "the top scavenger of all columnists." [1]

After conducting an investigation into the Director's private life, Anderson exploded the other myth, that of cross-dressing, by impugning him from another direction: "Hoover was so concerned about his image that he probably wouldn't have put on a dress in his own home, for fear someone might see him. So there was no way he would have appeared in a dress in public." With regard to the homosexual allegation, Anderson in a cable TV presentation concluded Hoover was not gay, pointing out that when he spoke of homosexuals, "his words were venomous." [2]

Ralph de Toledano, syndicated columnist and author of more than 20 books, stated that the *New York Post* spent a reported $500,000 trying to prove that Hoover was homosexual, and finally gave up in despair. [3]

During my years in the FBI, I, like all agents, was required to pass an annual physical examination, usually given at a military hospital facility. When I retired, I desired to continue annual physicals, and asked the Bureau's head nurse, Valeria Stewart, to recommend a good doctor. She said that Dr. Robert V. Choisser had been Director Hoover's physician during the last years of his life and was, in fact, the one summoned the day he died. He issued the death certificate.

Dr. Choisser became our family doctor, and for more than 15 years, until he passed away, gave annual physical examinations to both my wife and me. I often talked with him about Hoover. When I was preparing an article about the Director in 1993, Dr. Choisser approved the following statement for use:

> Dr. Robert V. Choisser of Bethesda, Maryland, stated on February 27, 1993, that he knew J. Edgar Hoover and treated him as his doctor for 20 years. Mr. Hoover's principal problem was of a digestive nature. He had no heart condition, no angina as has been alleged. Based on Dr. Choisser's knowledge and his

and his partner's medical records, there is no information to indicate that Mr. Hoover had any homosexual tendencies.

Long after Hoover passed away, British author Anthony Summers set out with the obvious purpose of disposing of J. Edgar Hoover in the dustbin of history. His track record for veracity and integrity was not without pitfalls.

In 1960 he wrote a book, *Conspiracy*, concerning the death of President Kennedy. In commenting on it, former Congressman Sam Devine stated that it was "typical of the tired, archaic, distorted, 'quick-buck' type books that are rapidly thrown together in order to promote sensationalized sales and make a dollar — regardless of the deliberate falsities shown therein."

In his book Summers wrongly accused the CIA of involvement in Kennedy's assassination, and CIA officer David Atlee Phillips of being assassin Lee Harvey Oswald's contact man. Excerpts from this book were carried in the British newspaper *The Observer* and the allegations regarding CIA and Phillips were picked up and repeated in the book *Death in Washington*.

Phillips instituted a libel action and as a result, the author and publishers of *Death in Washington* were forced to make a retraction, and they agreed to make a financial settlement. Summers' claims were proven to be false. Further, the High Court in London on October 7, 1986, announced the resolution of a libel action against *The Observer*. The paper agreed to retract the allegation that Phillips had been Oswald's contact man and to pay a specified sum in damages. [4]

When reviewing Summers' portrayal of Hoover as set forth in a 1993 book he wrote, *Official and Confidential: The Secret Life of J. Edgar Hoover,* I judged him to have been grubbing for financial gain and media attention, and not averse to engaging in measured hyperbole to attain his objective. He demonstrated a bias not only against Hoover but also against the United States.

With regard to the nation, reporting on an event involving the March 1913 inaugural parade for President Woodrow Wilson, he postulated, "Labor unrest had become a major issue.... . The United States was about to experience a wave of strikes, and a million American socialists would demand the overthrow of capitalism." [5]

This was such a frightening charge against the country that I spent some research time in an effort to verify it. The nearest information I was able to develop in this regard was in the Encyclopaedia Britannica to the effect that the Socialist Party — then housing the embryonic Socialist Workers Party — with a reported membership of 150,000, ran a candidate for President in the November 1912 elections. He polled 897,000 votes, less than 6% of the national total. This comment was included: "Socialism never became as influential in the United States as it did in Europe," and the Party declined after World War I, its last well-known leader being Norman Thomas. [6]

Writing in his hyperbolic vein, Summers, exhibiting an evident obsession with homosexuality, also made flagrant and damaging charges against Hoover's character. Demonstrating at the very outset that he was of a contentious nature and despised Hoover, he refrained from according the Director even the very slightest dignity, writing, "To bring him into mortal perspective, J. Edgar Hoover — the child and the man — will remain 'Edgar' throughout this book." Yet, he seems to have convinced a lot of people that Hoover was a homosexual and engaged in cross-dressing. Without checking the facts or the source of such charges, many obviously take delight in seeing the colossus crumble. [7]

Summers delved into various aspects of Hoovers life, but he is best known for his accusations of homosexuality and cross-dressing. Referring to this he said, "Dressing as a woman thing is a very small part of the book. I think it has been blown out of all proportions." Stating, also, that the "sexual part" of the book was extremely small, he commented, "Were talking about a few pages here."

Claiming to be unbiased in his feelings toward Hoover, he said, "He didn't mean anything to me in the way that he means something to most Americans, and certainly to anybody over 25 or 30." He resorted to using unsubstantiated information, and admitted to doing so.

With references to the reliability of information he received from sources he used, Summers was asked, "If in doubt, do you not print?"

After waffling, he came up with a convoluted answer:

> If I can't get any corroboration of any kind at all or if it doesn't fit into a pattern — I think, you know, sometimes when you are working on a newspaper, which I did use to at the BBC, you sometimes have to go to your editor and your editor says, "Why, why should we put this man on the air?" or "Why should we print this?" And in the end that is one of the reasons he hired you. You have to say, "Well, because I'm telling you that you should because that's my judgment after so long on the road." [8]

The Washington Times of March 7, 1992, carried a "Commentary" about Summers' slandering of a deceased CIA official. It was stated, "Irresponsibility isn't quite the word we would use to describe Mr. Summers' conduct. Another word better fits him: He is a coward who slandered a man who can no longer defend himself."

Reviewing his book for The Washington Post, Stephen E. Ambrose took note of Summers' bias against both Hoover and the United States:

> Drawing on anonymous and hostile sources, making extensive use of the Freedom of Information Act and other techniques of investigative reporting, and relying heavily on innuendo, rumor, hearsay and his own speculations, Irish-based author Anthony Summers depicts FBI Director J. Edgar Hoover as a moral and political monster without a single redeeming feature... .
>
> [It is not] possible to believe his contention that this country, from the 1920s to the 1970s, was corrupt to its core, or that the connections between the top criminals, politicians and businessmen are as intimate as he suggests. [9]

Summers' career as an author has been suffused with criticism. Reviewers of his previous books said that at times he overreached his evidence, apparently in the spirit of sensationalism and better sales. One reviewer of his book on Hoover, Steve Weinberg, wrote:

> *The book reeks with so much slime that I felt like bathing after each chapter. All that slime has meant plenty of publicity... .*
>
> *Most of the reviews emphasize the homosexuality angle; potential readers are bound to be curious when presented with so much titillation.*

Weinberg noted, as I did, that Summers' book contains 60 pages of documentation in type compressed and difficult to read. He said that in checking the book's alleged revelations against the source notes, "much of the time I found documentation that could most charitably be called iffy." [10]

Reviewer Christopher Lehmann-Haupt had the same difficulty with the source notes, finding his documentation unsatisfactory, "leaving us to figure out from ill-organized and impenetrable source notes whether his findings are first or secondhand." He thought that the case made by the book had to be acknowledged as "an impressive swamp of negativity about J. Edgar Hoover." [11]

Sam Devine, who served 22 years in the House of Representatives and was personally acquainted with Hoover, acknowledged having always been somewhat of a history buff, enjoying and knowing about the heroes of our country. "Consequently," he stated, "I grow a little suspicious when authors, particularly from foreign countries, constantly defame Americans who have devoted their lives to protecting and defending the United States." He was especially critical of Summers' sources:

> *Who are the sources used by Summers? And what are their backgrounds? A careful check reflects that Summers used convicted perjurers, mobsters, illegal wiretappers and, in rare instances, disgruntled FBI personnel who were either dismissed with prejudice or could not stand up to the FBI discipline and left the organization under a cloud. And customarily, with Summers' writing, a collection of deceased individuals who can no longer be called upon to testify. Innuendo, hearsay and third-handed gossip is rampant.*

Devine noted that hundreds of FBI agents had worked side by side with Hoover for years. These had included Devine himself and some former personnel who later became members of Congress, such as H. Allen Smith of California, Paul Kitchen of North Carolina, and Eldon Rudd of Arizona. Hoover was known to all of them as a straight, tough, well-disciplined, deeply religious man who was married to his job — leading the FBI. There was no hint of homosexuality noted at any time.

The PBS television network on February 3, 1993, afforded Anthony Summers millions of dollars free publicity for his tirade against Hoover by using him as a consultant and airing the principal points of sleaze in his book in a one-hour presentation "Frontline: The Secret File on J. Edgar Hoover." Jerry Seper of *The Washington Times* previewed the show and concluded that the presentation offered no compelling evidence to support the allegations against Hoover, certainly nothing bordering on "overwhelming," as claimed by producer William Cran. Seper reported:

Hoover biographer Curt Gentry has told reporters that rumors about the director's private life abounded within the bureau for more than 20 years. But he declined in his 1991 book, *J. Edgar Hoover: The Man and the Secrets,* to include the rumors because there was no evidence. He spent 15 years researching the director. [12]

Despite Summers' statement that the cross-dressing and "sexual part" of his book were very small, only a few pages, I counted 45 instances where he accused Hoover of homosexuality or homosexual acts; ten in which he cited things to try to show that Hoover and Associate Director Clyde Tolson were "lovers;" four where he accused Hoover of transvestitism; and three where he reported that Hoover had been arrested on a sex charge — just one alleged arrest but after its first mention, brought up again for emphasis 158 pages later, then 90 pages further along. [13]

This repetition was a standard practice. He followed it in claiming the widow of psychiatrist Marshall de G. Ruffin said her husband's destroyed notes would have proved Hoover was "troubled by homosexuality," and to cite instances when Hoover and Tolson allegedly held hands. I acknowledge that in this book running over 500 pages, I may have missed some instances. In wading through these diatribes, I was reminded of Adolph Hitler's "big lie" theory: if you repeat a lie often enough, sooner or later people will begin to believe it. [14]

The reported arrest of Hoover on a sex charge was described by a former police inspector, Joseph Shimon, as a second-hand bit of information. Shimon said that one Jimmy G. C. Corcoran, an FBI inspector in the twenties, became very powerful after leaving the Bureau, and as a lobbyist, for a $75,000 fee, sought congressional help for a business group to open a factory. Shimon said this was illegal during World War II, and "we" got a tip that the FBI was going to set up Jimmy when he went to pick up his fee.

Jimmy, angry, supposedly confronted Hoover and said, "This is what I get for doing you a favor, you dirty S.O.B.... ." Hoover allegedly backed away and Jimmy got his $75,000.

Shimon claimed that Corcoran told him what the "favor" had been. As Summers reported it: "Edgar had been arrested in the late twenties in New Orleans, on sex charges involving a young man. Corcoran, who had by then left the FBI and had powerful contacts in Louisiana, said he had intervened to prevent prosecution." [15]

Shimon talked about this alleged arrest on the Frontline PBS show and made no mention of Corcoran. In fact, when the narrator introduced the subject of the claimed arrest, he said that Shimon had *heard* of the arrest. In talking about it, Shimon, himself, said, "I don't know the details of the arrest. I never got it, other than he was arrested and charged. He was charged with a sex offense and the arrest was washed out."

In "confirmation" of the arrest, Summers quoted Jimmy "The Weasel" Fratianno, high ranking mobster, who named as his source for the information Johnny Roselli, the West Coast representative of the Chicago mob. This is quite representative of the kind of proof upon which Summers based his sleaze. [16]

When reporting the information attributed to Dr. Ruffin's widow about Hoover's being "troubled by homosexuality," Summers introduced this by saying Hoover first consulted the doctor "in the wake of continuing rumors that he was a homosexual." This can be considered as nothing less than the author's opinion. Some 300 pages later, he revealed that columnist Jack Anderson, who conducted an intensive investigation of the Director and concluded he was not homosexual, was told by competent sources that Hoover had consulted Ruffin about "his nightmares." This being contrary to Summers' preconceived ideas, he dismissed it by allowing as how Anderson was "perilously close to one of Edgar's most sensitive secrets, for it was Ruffin whom Edgar had consulted years earlier about his homosexuality." [17]

Summers must have recognized that the psychiatric appraisal of his subject, based on the recollection of Mrs. Ruffin, itself based on the destroyed notes of her deceased husband, could not be considered professional, or even valid. He shopped around for psychiatric support for his preconceived premise. Dr. Harold Lief, professor emeritus of psychiatry at the University of Pennsylvania, and Dr. John Money, professor of medical psychology at Johns Hopkins University, obliged him. Prior to rendering an opinion, neither doctor had the opportunity to examine, question, or test Hoover, since he had been dead for several years, and neither interviewed any person who was acquainted with him. Each of them gave his opinion based solely on information provided by Summers as gospel truth, information as it appears in his book, with no question raised by the doctors as to the validity or the integrity of the author's sources. This being true, it is highly questionable that *their* opinions had any validity.

Dr. Lief concluded:

There is no doubt that Hoover had a personality disorder, a narcissistic disorder with mixed obsessive features. I picked up some paranoid elements, undue suspiciousness and some sadism. A combination of narcissism and paranoia produces what is known as an Authoritarian Personality. Hoover would have made a high-level Nazi.

His basic problem seems to me to have been that he was both attracted and repelled by women. Because he separated lust and love it's likely that he idealized mother figures and lusted after the degraded woman.... . If I hadn't known anything about his alleged homosexual tendencies, my guess would have been that his primary adaptation was to transvestism, which indeed turns out to have been part of the picture.

Dr. Money's conclusion was that Hoover's "sexual conflicts" fit a pattern often seen in policemen:

You find this sort of thing in officers who work for the Vice Squad. They may hang out in men's toilets in order to arrest other men, but they make sure they get themselves serviced first. They may look like knights in shining armor, but they're undercover agents psychologically as much as by profession.

Hoover's whole life was one of haunting and hounding people over their sexuality, brutalizing them one way or another be-

cause of it. He took on the role of being the paragon, keeping the country morally clean, yet hid his own sexual side. His terrible thing was that he needed constantly to destroy other people in order to maintain himself. Many people like that break down and end up needing medical help. Hoover managed to live with his conflict — by making others pay the price... .

He had what I call "malignant bisexuality," and I suggest quite seriously that his condition should henceforth be called "J. Edgar Hoover Syndrome." [18]

While the opinions of only these two doctors were reported, it appears that Summers may have sought others. He stated, "Leading psychologists and psychiatrists ... asked to study the information gathered for this book, *all* recognize a distinct pattern in Edgar's makeup... ." He leaves unanswered the question: did he have to shop around to get two opinions to support his conclusion? [19]

A *holding-hands* report was said to have been made by a fashion model, Luisa Stuart, when interviewed in 1989 about an incident she claimed to have witnessed more than half a century before, New Year's Eve, 1936. She was at a party sponsored by Walter Winchell at the Stork Club in New York City and also among the guests were Hoover and Tolson. The latter, she claimed, had been "getting drunk." From a photograph of the party included in Summers' book, it is evident the crowd had been drinking and Tolson may not have been the only one "getting drunk." The revelers decided to move on to the Cotton Club and Stuart rode in a limousine with both FBI officials. There, she was said to have told Summers, she saw the two men holding hands. He thought enough of the validity of the report, despite the imbibing and the 53 years before it was dredged up, to present it as evidence of a "lover" relationship between the men. [20]

Summers saw fit to back up the idea that Hoover and Tolson were "lovers," but the integrity of his sources left something to be desired. One was Gordon Novel, an electronics expert. The others consisted of Joseph Shimon; Seymour Pollock, an associate of mobster Meyer Lansky; Irving "Ash" Resnick, Nevada representative of the Patriarcha family mob; and a British official who, upon first meeting Hoover in the company of Tolson, supposedly demonstrating a remarkable degree of clairvoyance "recognize(d) them as a homosexual couple." The four remaining references to the two men being "lovers" were based on their long, close friendship and, in one instance, on hints said to have been dropped by journalists. [21]

Aside from the basic allegation that Hoover was a homosexual, the one seemingly most widely accepted is that he was a cross-dresser. This has been made the subject of crude jokes by comics reaching for a laugh and rude drawings by cartoonists struggling for acknowledgment — a bull-dog-faced man needing a shave, decked out in a flowing dress, black lace stockings, and high heels.

Laying the groundwork for his piece de resistance, a raunchy portrayal by one Susan Rosenstiel of a homosexual bash at the New York Hotel Plaza, Summers tried to establish that there was a photo of Hoover and Tolson flagrante delicto.

As related by Summers, John Weitz, a clothes designer who had served in the Office of Strategic Services (OSS), recalled a curious episode at a dinner party in the fifties. He said his host, whom he would not name, exhibited a photograph of two men apparently engaged in homosexual activity, and said they were Hoover and Tolson. Another source, Gordon Novel — the electronics expert, who had links to the Central Intelligence Agency — claimed he was shown similar pictures by another OSS veteran, CIA counterintelligence chief James Angleton, and Hoover "was totally recognizable."

When questioned about this later by a friend, John Weitz said he had seen a photograph of "two men humping on a beach" and that the photo "was very, very blurry.... Perhaps it was Hoover, perhaps not. I didn't give it much import." He acknowledged this occurred at a private dinner party in the fifties and his host was James Angleton. [22]

Obviously, Weitz and Novel were shown the photograph at the same party. The reason why Weitz, according to Summers' claim, did not reveal the identity of Angleton is open to speculation that author Summers desired to present two independent sources who allegedly saw compromising photos at separate functions, or he wished to butress Novel's positive identification. In reporting the incident, he concluded: "While Novel is a controversial figure, his account of seeing compromising pictures must be considered in light of other such references — not least that of former OSS officer John Weitz." [23]

Susan Rosenstiel was the source of transvestite charges against Hoover. She was 28 years the junior of liquor tycoon Lewis Rosenstiel when they were married in 1956, and was his fourth wife. After five years of marriage, they plunged into an acrimonious divorce action. Lewis for most of this period was represented by Roy Cohn, an acquaintance of Hoover's.

After the separation, Susan charged expensive jewelry to her husband. Sued by 22 merchants, she was ordered to pay more than $100,000 of these bills. In hearing the case, New York Supreme Court Judge David Fink described Susan in this manner:

A woman with an insatiable desire and hunger for money, with an appetite that could not be satisfied or appeased.... In telling her story, the wife stooped to everything and stopped at nothing. There is no doubt that the wife was completely guilty of cruel and inhuman treatment.

Stories of Judge Fink's decision ran in New York newspapers in September 1966. So did accounts of a proceeding at which Susan Rosenstiel pleaded guilty to attempted perjury in Manhattan Criminal Court for her testimony in the jewelry case and paid a $500 fine. This public record strikes directly at the honesty and integrity of this source Summers presented as a major witness against Hoover. [24]

And this was Susan's story, as related by Summers: Her husband Lewis and Roy Cohn involved Hoover in a sex orgy. She claimed that Lewis enjoyed sex with men and that Cardinal Spellman was homosexual. Sometime in 1958, her husband asked if she had ever witnessed a sex orgy. A few weeks later he and Roy Cohn asked how she would like to go to a party at the Hotel Plaza. She went and it was in a large suite. Cohn admitted her and her husband and "Hoover was already there, and I couldn't believe what I saw." Summers wrote, "Edgar was dressed up as a woman, in full drag. He was wearing a fluffy black dress, very fluffy, with flounces, and lace stockings and high heels, and a black curly wig. He had makeup on and false eyelashes." He was introduced by Cohn as "Mary." In addition to the description of the costume, Susan Rosenstiel added more of her vitriolic charges, not only against Hoover but her husband and Roy Cohn as well. She claimed that homosexual activities went on in a bedroom of the suite. She further alleged that there was a repeat of this activity a year later at the Plaza involving her husband, Cohn, and Hoover decked out "like an old flapper" in a red dress and with a black feather boa around his neck.

In an effort to lend credence to the report of cross-dressing by Hoover, Summers added an anticlimax to Susan's recital. He said that two men who requested anonymity claimed to have seen photos in 1948 of Hoover lying across a bed in an evening gown and wearing a light-colored or blond wig. [25]

This whole story didn't impress columnist William F. Buckley, Jr., who had a couple of crisp comments:

Excuse me, but there are those of us who simply will not believe this, on the basis of testimony by a mobster's fourth wife and two gentlemen who insist on anonymity. [26]

That he [Hoover] sashayed into the Plaza Hotel dressed like Hermione Gingold violates Rusher's Second Law. (That law says: If someone calls and tells you that your best friend is parading nude in Times Square with a sandwich board denouncing you, doubt the witness before you doubt your friend.) [27]

Upon reading Summers' account of Susan Rosenstiel's revelations, author and investigative journalist Peter Maas included the following in an interesting article for *Esquire* magazine:

The trouble is that the sole source for this is Susan Rosenstiel. The trouble also is that she'd been trying to peddle this story for years. Among those she had approached was Robert Morgenthau, a former US attorney in New York and current Manhattan D. A. On paper, she couldn't have made a better choice. Morganthau had tried, unsuccessfully, to convict Cohn three times for various transgressions. He and Hoover were not on speaking terms. Morgenthau discovered that Rosenstiel — no paragon of civic virtue — had dumped Susan and an ugly divorce ensued. She hated Hoover, convinced he put FBI agents on her to help her husband's cause. "I didn't believe her then," Morgenthau told me, "and I don't now."

... (A) book like this, published by a reputable house — with an ad headline that screams, "At last, the truth about J. Edgar Hoover" — does grievous harm to serious investigative journalism. [28]

It did more to harm than just that. It has been the foundation for slanted television reporting. In a May 3, 1999, biography of Hoover presented on the A&E cable channel, the weight given to allegations of sources proven to be biased against him obviously suited the producers in accomplishing a previously decided-upon agenda. At the outset of the program, Summers was shown and identified as the conveyer of the hands-holding allegation while the commentator intoned, "When Anthony Summers put that and other sensational material in a 1993 book, the image of the legendary FBI Director was shattered overnight." This was A&E's conclusion and nothing presented thereafter detracted from it.

With a minimum of research the producers could have discovered the reviews of Summer's book in three Washington newspapers and *The New York Times*, which labeled it in such terms as "slime" and "an impressive swamp of negativity." They could also have learned of numerous reputable people who refuted the integrity and reliability of Summers and his principal sources who alleged Hoover was homosexual and a cross-dresser, prominent people such as Congressman Sam Devine; Judge David Fink; former U.S. Attorney Robert Morgenthau; columnist William F. Buckley, Jr.; George E. Allen, a friend of Hoover's and of at least three U.S presidents; and two of the Director's top officials who dealt with him daily, Deke DeLoach and Mark Felt.

The wholesale rejection of Summers' most vilifying charges and the fact that he had libeled another former government official, David Atlee Phillips, were omitted from the TV presentation. There appeared to be no particular effort on the part of A&E to establish the degree of integrity of Summers and some of his more important sources.

When this author called this to the attention of A&E's producer, Towers Productions of Chicago, the president, Jonathan Towers, assured him that, almost without exception, the biography met with universal acclaim. The power of the electronic media in contributing to the destruction of a man cannot be denied.

In the wake of Summers' book, Hoover's homosexuality was accepted by some as undeniable truth. "I think it's significant to note," Deke DeLoach commented, "that no one who knew Hoover and Tolson well has even hinted at such a charge." Tolson was the Director's second-in-command and had his complete trust. The two were personal friends as well as co-workers; however at Bureau headquarters, Tolson was "almost indispensable, but not quite a friend." The two men spent many off-duty hours together going to races and sporting events and eating at restaurants. A bachelor who devotes his entire life to a job has to have at least one male acquaintance. For Hoover, that companion was Tolson.

DeLoach from 1965 to 1970 was the third-in-command of the FBI and saw Tolson and Hoover practically every business day. As he stated, "I was in the thick of some of the greatest — and most terrible — events of our time. And yet even to me Hoover remained an enigma." In his opinion:

> *Clyde Tolson could have written the most accurate and detailed sketch of Hoover, but I'm convinced that even Tolson would have failed to capture the essence of this obsessively private man. He was too elusive, too contradictory, too defensive to sit still for a formal portrait... .* [29]

Mark Felt, as Tolson's deputy during the last 10 months of Hoover's life, like DeLoach also had almost daily contact with both men and offered this appraisal:

I never saw any indication of homosexual tendencies in Hoover. To my knowledge, neither did any of my colleagues in the FBI. Hoover was married to his job — the FBI and his home were his all-consuming interests. He could have retired on full pay but he chose to remain. He did have a close association with Tolson. They conferred frequently during the day and they invariably ate lunch together, most often at the Mayflower Hotel. On Wednesday they had dinner at Tolson's apartment, on Friday at Hoover's house... .

That association was not without its rifts. As he did with all other high-level subordinates from time to time, Hoover occasionally became displeased with Tolson. Other officials in the Hoover "dog house" had to put up with being bypassed in the daily business of the Bureau until he cooled off. With Tolson the strain was much more severe because he was constantly in direct contact with Hoover "letting off steam."

I know from my talks with Hoover that he was genuinely fond of Tolson, as an older brother might be. He looked after him and worried about his precarious state of health. [30]

George Allen, an intimate of presidents from Franklin Roosevelt to Dwight Eisenhower and a good friend of Hoover's, was once asked if Hoover and Tolson had been "homosexual lovers." He said, "That's ridiculous. Clyde was sort of an alter ego... and could speak for Hoover on anything. You can't take it much further than that. They were very, very close because he needed Clyde so much." [31]

In a confrontation with Anthony Summers on TV, Deke DeLoach was asked, "Was Hoover homosexual?" His response: "No he was not. Absolutely not." He said that he was in Hoover's home and Hoover was in his occasionally. He traveled with the Director and stayed in the same suite with him. During the 28 years that he worked in the Bureau, DeLoach saw no indication that either Hoover or Tolson was homosexual. He was just as positive, even brutal, in telling Summers what he thought of his book on Hoover, describing it as:

A pile of garbage, sleaze built upon sleaze, and you have one fast-buck book artist trying to build upon another fast-buck book artist, and sleaze keeps building up. And this is the biggest pile of garbage, so big that it smells.

Peter Maas acknowledged having been "a Hoover foe from the first," declaring that he, himself, was the subject of numerous FBI investigations "while working on stories that Hoover found irksome." Prepared to read and believe anything about Hoover, whom he described as "a fatuous, personally corrupt, evil ass," he still had this reaction upon reading the book authored by Summers: "Alas, it turns out to be all garbage without even a presentable trash can to contain it." [32]

HOOVER AND ORGANIZED CRIME

There were no statutes prior to the early 1960s which declared racketeering, gambling, and related activities violated federal law. Americans, concerned about the increasing influence on our national economy of businesses controlled by La Cosa Nostra and the Mafia, as well as illegal activities like bootlegging, prostitution, and "protection rackets," began seeking a scapegoat on which to place blame. La Cosa Nostra, "Our Thing," was the name the Eastern establishment of organized crime in the United States gave itself, and the term "Mafia" came from the underworld membership that originated in Sicily. Being the principal federal investigative agency, the FBI came in for a share of the blame. Learning of this through his extensive research, Anthony Summers seized upon it and developed a scenario to support a conclusion which he knew would attract attention and sell books, a real blockbuster.

He first referred to Bureau investigations of gangsters and hoodlums in the late 20s and early 30s. Next, he alleged that near the end of the 30s decade, the FBI discontinued investigating them because a famous gangster had acquired compromising photographs of Hoover to be used to blackmail him should he continue such investigations — a premise not supported by facts. According to him, Hoover closed his eyes to organized crime until forced to investigate it in the 1960s by Attorney General Bobby Kennedy, thus rounding out Summers' preconception.

When weaving a myth, it is well to include actual facts which can be verified, and Summers drew on a few of these to lay the groundwork for his scenario. He neglected to highlight two things which very much limited the FBI's authority, on the one hand, and its capacity on the other, to wage an all-out war on the criminal element: (1) The FBI was powerless to move against the underworld empire unless and until the gangs violated a federal law, such as the Antitrust Act, which forbids restraint of interstate commerce; and (2) During the 1920s under Hoover, the FBI had a total of only 326 investigators to cover the entire United States, and this number remained at about this level into 1933.

Nevertheless, Hoover made the best with what was available. For instance, Alphonse "Scarface Al" Capone, who seized full command of the Chicago underworld in the 1920s, was cited for contempt of court based on an FBI investigation in 1929. He had failed to answer a subpoena to appear as a witness in a federal prohibition case. Investigations under the prohibition statutes were within the jurisdiction of the Prohibition Enforcement Bureau; however, Capone's ignoring a summons to appear as a witness in the case made it possible for the FBI to undertake investigation to determine if his claim that his failure was caused by the fact that he had been bed-ridden for six weeks was valid. The Bureau proved that during that period, Capone had gone to the horse races, taken a boat trip, flown to the Bahama Islands, and visited public places "with a glow of health on his cheeks." He was convicted on the contempt charge and sentenced to six months in jail. While he was serving this time, Internal Revenue Bureau agents were able to work up an income tax case against him which resulted in a 10-year prison term. [1]

John Dillinger in 1933-34 murdered ten men, wounded seven others, and robbed four banks... not a single one of these acts being a federal offense. However, he slipped into a situation which, without his meaning to do so, brought him within the scope of FBI investigative authority, and the Bureau was swift to seize the opportunity to accommodate him.[2]

In January 1934 he was arrested in Tucson, Arizona, and extradited to Indiana, being first flown to Chicago then taken in a 13-car caravan, escorted by armed lawmen, to a jail at Crown Point, Indiana, which was reputed to be escape-proof. There he was charged on January 15, 1934, with the murder of police officer Patrick O'Malley in a previous holdup of the First National Bank of East Chicago, Indiana.

On March 4 when the sheriff and the jailer walked into the cell block, Dillinger greeted them with a pistol in his hand, saying, "I don't want to kill anybody. Just do as I tell you." He locked them and other guards present in the cell block and seized two Tommy guns from the sheriff's office. [3]

Dillinger offered to take along with him any of the other 15 or 20 prisoners incarcerated there, but only one took up the offer, a man awaiting trial for murder. They then forced a deputy sheriff and a mechanic to accompany them and set off in the sheriff's Ford V-8 in a northwesterly direction, apparently headed for Chicago. Fifty miles west of Crown Point, near Peotone, Illinois, Dillinger released the two hostages along a deserted stretch of road.

Word got out that Dillinger claimed he had pulled off the breakout by using a razor blade to carve a crude-looking wooden pistol from the top of a washboard, then darkening it with bootblack provided to him earlier by accommodating guards impressed with his friendliness and national renown. His spectacular breakout from the "escape-proof" Crown Point jail triggered a rash of blaring headlines, and Dillinger became even more renowned. He emerged as a kind of Robin Hood folk hero among many Americans who followed his escapades and trail of crimes as a diversion from the Great Depression which had them impoverished and embittered. He projected an image of swashbuckling glamour, which resulted in a number of people overlooking the widows and young children of law officers gunned down by him and his gang. [4]

Shortly after Dillinger had released his two hostages near Peotone, Illinois, the sheriff's car which he had stolen in Indiana got stuck in a roadside ditch and had to be abandoned. When it was discovered, Hoover, who was outraged by the mood of much of the public, was openly able to order his agents into the pursuit of the itinerant gangster, whose escapades they had been watching from a distance as he pursued his criminal spree. By transporting the stolen Ford of the sheriff across the state line between Indiana and Illinois, the criminal had violated the National Motor Vehicle Theft Act, commonly known as the Dyer Act. In 20 weeks the FBI was able to end his rampage of crime and murder.[5]

Two days after he escaped from the Crown Point jail, Dillinger formed a new gang which included Lester Gillis, who preferred to be known as "Big George" Nelson. Since he was only 5 feet, four inches tall and tipped the scales at 133 pounds, his associates, behind his back, dubbed him "Baby Face" Nelson. They dared not address him in this manner since he was brutal and had a violent temper. The same day Dillinger recruited him for his gang, Nelson's car collided with another vehicle whose driver leaped out and accosted him.

"Are you blind?" the other driver screamed. "You ran a stop sign."

Baby Face's reply was a slug from his already drawn gun aimed and striking true, squarely between the driver's eyes, killing him instantly.[6]

During the course of the Bureau's efforts to apprehend Dillinger, an FBI agent was killed, three others were injured, and Dillinger, himself, was shot in the leg when he managed to slip out the back door by spraying a hallway with Tommy gun bullets while agents were laying siege to an apartment where he was holed up. It was not long before newspaper headlines proclaimed him to be Public Enemy Number 1.[7]

President Roosevelt took a big step toward bringing about Dillinger's apprehension. On June 7, 1934, he signed a bill authorizing the Department of Justice to offer up to a $25,000 reward for the capture of criminals, such as John Dillinger, and other "public enemies."[8]

Anna Sage, a working girl at a Gary, Indiana, brothel, was picked up at a Chicago diner by a man who gave his name as Jack Lawrence, but whom she soon realized was Dillinger. Through East Chicago police officers, she arranged to meet with FBI agents, and told them that with Polly Hamilton, madam of the brothel, she had gone to see moving pictures a few times with Dillinger, who especially loved gangster films. Since the three of them planned to make another trip to a theater in the near future, she offered to notify the FBI when and where they would go. In return, she wanted a substantial reward and assistance in her effort to remain in the United States, she being an alien subject to deportation.[9]

On Sunday, July 22, 1934, Anna Sage established her 15 minutes of fame in history by providing the information which permitted Hoover's special agents, after working thousands of hours to capture him, to bring his life of crime to a sudden end. As he left the Chicago Biograph Theater accompanied by Polly Hamilton and Anna Sage, who was dressed in a bright red dress and forever afterward known as the "Lady in Red," an agent approached him from behind.

"Stick 'em up, Johnny," the agent called out. "We've got you covered."

He was, indeed, well covered. Giving no heed to the challenge, Dillinger clawed in his pocket for a Colt automatic. Three agents fired five shots at him with three finding their mark. His criminal career and life came to an end on the sidewalk outside the Biograph Theater. [10]

Developing his theory that Hoover was active against organized crime figures in the thirties but then turned away from them because of possible blackmail by the mob, Summers himself cited a few things to bolster his case.

He noted that in 1935 the Director declared Dutch Schultz, prohibition days nabob, "Public Enemy Number One." Early the next year Hoover called racketeering a problem which, if not solved, would eventually destroy the security of American industrial life and the faith of people in American institutions.

In 1937 Hoover personally led a raid against Baltimore brothels operated by gangsters. In August that same year, the FBI arrested several mobsters, one of whom was running prostitution rackets for Charles "Lucky" Luciano, father of organized crime in America and founder with Meyer Lansky of the national crime syndicate. Summers went so far as to acknowledge, "In targeting the Luciano network, Edgar was threatening the heartland of the Mafia."

He also endeavored to establish in his readers' minds that in the forties there was a 180 degree turn away from hot pursuit of the mob on the part of the FBI Director by recording that in the previous decade Hoover set up a Hoodlum Watch. This required all FBI field offices to collate information on local crime bosses, and Hoover announced a national drive against racketeers, or "organized business criminals." [11]

In each of the cases mentioned where the FBI was able to move against a racketeer or mobster, it was on the basis of an actual or possible violation of a federal statute. This is what Hoover was held to in the burgeoning growth of organized criminal activities in America. He and Homer S. Cummings, attorney general from 1933 to 1939 and as such Hoover's superior, had shared the viewpoint that primary responsibility for the suppression of crime rested with local law enforcement agencies. This should not come as a surprise to anyone as far as Hoover is concerned. All his life he opposed and spoke out against a national police force, holding to the view that the cop on the street was best qualified to know what was developing on his beat. However, the tentacles of the "organized business criminals" following the repeal of prohibition laws in 1933 snaked their way into legitimate enterprises and endeavors, causing Cummings and Hoover to reevaluate their thinking. Accordingly, both began advocating expansion of federal penal statutes to include control over the unlawful activities of those who deliberately took advantage of the protection afforded them by state lines in perpetration of their crimes.

At the urging of Cummings, in 1934 legislation was signed into law making it a federal crime to:
- Assault or kill a federal officer.
- Rob a federal bank.
- Flee from one state to another to avoid prosecution or giving testimony in certain cases.
- Carry stolen property worth $5000 or more across a state line.
- Use interstate communications, such as the telephone and the telegraph, in criminal endeavors.
- Abduct kidnapping victims interstate even though ransom or reward was not the motive.

By the end of the thirties the "G-Men," so christened by "Machine

Gun" Kelly when arrested September 26, 1933, were glamorized by a wave of favorable publicity. However, Hoover also became a special target for attack by some, being assailed as a headline hunter. One writer said, "We Americans no sooner set up a hero than we prepare to knock him down... . It's working that way with J. Edgar Hoover." Larry Heim put it this way, "Unfortunately, there has always been a penchant in our country to belittle the nation and dethrone our national heroes." [12]

The attacks on Hoover fit so perfectly into Summers' scheme of things that he could not help but gloat, "From the late thirties on, the FBI's war with organized crime became a nominal affair, a thing of occasional sound but no fury at all." [13]

When he made a similar statement on a February 12, 1993, TV talk show and charged that Hoover was a homosexual, a transvestite, and a pawn of the Mafia, Deke DeLoach turned to the host, Larry King, and said, "Tony knows its false and he should know his charge Hoover never moved against the Mafia was false." And this is substantiated by the facts. The same sort of actions were taken against hoodlums after the thirties as had been taken in prior years, based on federal laws then in existence.

I have a personal recollection of one of these which, because of a quirk of fate, resulted in the capture of a notorious kidnapper and a bank robber. It happened shortly after I arrived on October 23, 1942, at the FBI field office in Oklahoma City, my first assignment fresh out of the FBI Academy in Quantico, Virginia.

The case involved two hoodlums, Roger "The Terrible" Touhy, a Detroit gangster who was serving time in the Illinois State Prison for the kidnapping in Chicago of Jake "The Barber" Factor, and Basil Banghart, a convicted bank robber also incarcerated there. Both were serving long sentences. Having little to lose, they attempted and made good their escape. Legally, the escape was strictly a local matter for the State of Illinois, which had few resources for tracking down such desperate men. Hoover was interested in giving the Illinois authorities a hand, but was insistent that there had to be a legitimate basis for a federal presence in the search for the fugitives. Finally, someone hit on the solution Hoover sought – a violation of the Selective Service Act. Under its provisions, both men had been required to register for the draft on October 16, 1940. They were also required after registration to notify their draft boards when they changed addresses, which they had failed to do when they escaped from prison. The Bureau entered the chase, caught up with, and recaptured the culprits. This was especially satisfying to the FBI Director, who personally led the raid which resulted in their apprehension. He considered Touhy to be one of the most vicious and dangerous criminals in America.

Where federal laws could by utilized to fight organized crime they were applied, at times in unusual ways, as in the apprehension of Touhy and Banghart. In 1947, utilizing the hijacking statute, 15 members of a Brooklyn gang were netted.

A major criminal, Larry Gallo, was nabbed for filing with the Federal Government a fraudulent mortgage application in which he claimed to have a substantial income, while listing on his income tax return only a fraction of that figure.

Shortly after World War II, the Bureau began a major initiative against racketeering. It was code-named CAPGA. Agents across the country were ordered to investigate organized crime and to gather information on all known criminals. One of those targeted was Benjamin "Bugsy" Siegel, a key associate of Meyer Lansky, who was negotiating a loan in New York to build a casino in Las Vegas. Suddenly, Attorney General Tom C. Clark, who served as Hoover's boss from 1945 to 1949 before becoming a Supreme Court justice, pulled the Director's chain. He ordered Hoover to discontinue the CAPGA program. He pointed out that the FBI had no business investigating activities that could not be construed as violating federal law. Later it was learned that Senator Pat McCarran of Nevada had complained that the FBI activities were "designed to damage the economy of his state." [14]

Indicative of the success of the program before its ordered discontinuance was the fact that in 1948, Bureau files contained 600 pages of information on racketeer Longy Zwillman. Summers acknowledged this but placed the information in the confusion of "Author's Notes" at the end of his book where it was less likely to be found. [15]

Entering the 1950s, the Bureau's sights were leveled again at individual crime figures or entities which were skirting federal law. When the mob took control of some unions in the motion picture industry, Hoover was able to move under the labor racketeering statutes. When Johnny Dioguardia, a La Cosa Nostra member, arranged for an attacker to blind syndicated columnist Victor Riesel on April 5, 1956, by throwing acid in his face, the Bureau was able to enter the case under two statutes: Labor Racketeering and Obstruction of Justice.

The mounting intensity of criminal activities on an organized basis prompted Hoover once again to approach the problem under a program, as he had with the Hoodlum Watch in the thirties and the CAPGA after World War II. In 1957 the Top Hoodlum Intelligence Program was instituted with the goal of identifying and tracking the movements of every mob leader in the United States, and the first comprehensive picture of the operations of organized crime began to form. The program was established just months before a New York State police officer investigating a bad-check complaint at a motel in Apalachin in November 1957, overheard the front desk clerk confirm a reservation for an unusually large number of rooms. It was made for a man named Joseph M. Barbara, a suspected bootlegger, who was also a suspect in connection with two unsolved murders in Pennsylvania. As rumor had it, he had hosted a meeting of mobsters in Binghamton, New York, just a year earlier. The state trooper returned the next day with two Treasury Department agents who had an interest in the possible bootlegging aspects of Mr. Barbara's operations. The law enforcement officers observed a frantic exodus of hordes of men, alarmed at the arrival of the three observers in a marked state patrol car. At barriers quickly established by police, more than 60 mobsters from various parts of the country were identified as having been at this convention of gangsters in Apalachin, New York. Forty more slipped through the net.[16]

In the face of all the foregoing, Summers' "bombshell news" was that since the mid-nineteen thirties the mob had pictures of Hoover and Clyde Tolson, proof that they were homosexual, and that the pictures were in the hands of famous gangster Meyer Lansky. [17]

Summers approached this subject very gingerly, lacing his report with hedging terms and phrases, e.g. *"if this occurred," "it is likely," "information suggests,"* specifically:

> *If the homosexual arrest [of Hoover in new Orleans] occurred, it is likely the local mobsters quickly learned of it.*
>
> *Other information suggests Meyer Lansky obtained hard proof of Edgar's homosexuality and used it to neutralize the FBI as a threat to his own operations. The first hint came from Irving "Ash" Resnick, the Nevada representative of the Patriarcha family from New England, and an original owner-builder of Caesars Palace in Las Vegas. As a high-level mob courier, he traveled extensively. In Miami Beach, his Christmas destination in the fifties, he stayed at the Gulfstream, in a bungalow next to one used by Edgar and Clyde. "I'd sit with him on the beach every day," Resnick remembered. "We were friendly."*
>
> *In 1971 Resnick and an associate talked with the writer Pete Hamill in the Galeria Bar at Caesars Palace. They spoke of Meyer Lansky as a genius, the man who "put everything together" — and as the man who "nailed J. Edgar Hoover." "When I asked what they meant," Hamill recalled, "they told me Lansky had some pictures — pictures of Hoover in some kind of gay situation with Clyde Tolson. Lansky was the guy who controlled the pictures, and he made his deal with Hoover — to lay off. That was the reason, they said, that for a long time they had nothing to fear from the FBI." [18]*

This was the principal bit of information upon which Summers anointed Hoover a homosexual, a bit of gossip which converted a myth into reality for some people, including media types, who welcomed a scandal and did not bother to check into it before spreading it abroad and demolishing the reputation of a dead man who could not defend himself. Some, with a regard for truth and fairness, even though not enamored of Hoover, were dedicated to honesty in reporting and did sufficient checking to verify that an injustice had been done to J. Edgar Hoover by Anthony Summers. One of these was Peter Maas:

> *One of the main pillars to support the blackmail charge is a quote Summers attributes to the editor and columnist Peter Hamill. It's presented as if Hamill had been personally interviewed, with lines like, "Hamill recalled." But, it turns out, Hamill was never interviewed. Pete told me the quote must have come from a column he'd written right after Hoover's death. In it, two Las Vegas gambling figures tell him that Lansky had pictures of Hoover and Tolson in some gay situation. "It was strictly anecdotal stuff and written in that context," Hamill said. "You know how mob guys gossip like old women. It was*

the sheerest hearsay. The fact is that I don't even know if Hoover was gay."

Two or three other alleged Lansky associates were also quoted — at what hand, first, second, or third, is hard to say — about the photographic "proof" on Hoover. But one man, universally recognized as the person closest to Lansky, who was at his side for nearly fifty years — from the late 1920s in New York, through the opening and flourishing of the Las Vegas casinos, on to the pre-Castro casinos in Havana and beyond — is notably absent from the book. He is the legendary Vincent "Jimmy Blue Eyes" Alo. Lansky and Alo went together, as one Mafioso put it to me, like "ham and eggs. Like the song goes, you can't have one without the other."

Hoover is dead. Lansky is dead. Alo, while still remarkably alert, is pushing ninety years of age. Now long out of the business, he's spent time in a federal slammer. Throughout a good deal of his life, he was constantly harassed, bugged, and surveilled by Hoover's FBI. I got to Jimmy about the pictures that Lansky allegedly had of Hoover and Tolson. He said, "Are you nuts?"

The thought of Hoover becoming a nervous wreck because of Lansky's sinister hold over him becomes even more ludicrous upon examining FBI files....

Here is one example. The FBI field office in Miami, where Lansky was residing, complained to headquarters that too many agents were expending too much time and energy monitoring Lansky. At the time, it said, "There are more important and active top hoodlums in the Miami area."

Maas developed additional evidence from William Hundley, a source who could hardly be impeached, that Summers ignored information indicating that there were no compromising photos of Hoover. Hundley, who was quoted a number of times in the book, was chief of the organized crime section in the Kennedy Justice Department and probably unrivaled in his knowledge about the nation's crime syndicates. When asked by Maas whether Summers had inquired of him about such photographs, he replied that the author had, indeed. Hundley said, "I told him that it was baloney. I guess he didn't use it because it didn't fit with what he wanted to hear." [19]

Although the "brains" and chief treasurer of the Mafia, Meyer Lansky was never indicted, lived to an old age, and died in bed, probably because he was not involved in day-to-day activities of the hoodlums. He was hounded unmercifully by the FBI through close tactics that lasted for many years. When Deke DeLoach commented to this effect on the Larry King TV program, King confirmed this, saying, "They drove him nuts."

Lansky used to complain bitterly that he could not "even enjoy visits from my son because of the FBI." The prevention of visits by family members was not the purpose of the FBI, but rather it was to identify the steady stream of mobster visitors, all of whom were observed then tailed to establish who they were, making it possible for the Bureau to compile a "Who's Who in the Mob." [20]

There is little doubt that Lansky would have used any means available to have prevented the intense interest in him by the FBI, including, or especially, a compromising photograph of its Director.

Summers had to admit that Lansky came under heavy FBI surveillance but again used the disorganized "Author's Notes" at the end of his book to bury the fact, claiming that this was in 1961, and dismissing it as part of a push against organized crime under Attorney General Kennedy. [21]

Sources Summers relied upon to bolster his "proof" that Hoover was homosexual, that the mobsters' "insurance policy" was the photographic evidence of Hoover's homosexual activities, were: Carmine "The Doctor" Lombardozzi, one of the last Mafia bosses; Seymour Pollock, Meyer Lansky's associate; Irving "Ash" Resnick, Patriarcha family representative in Nevada; Jimmy "The Weasel" Fratiano, highest-ranking mobster ever to turn against the mob; Frank Bompensiero, notorious West Coast Mafioso; Jack and Louis Dragna, Los Angeles mobsters; and Johnny Roselli, West Coast representative of the Chicago mob. They were quoted, to adopt Peter Maas' phrase, "at what hand, first, second, or third, is hard to say." [22]

Referring to this so-called mobsters' insurance, and using hedging terms again, Summers claimed, "The evidence *suggests* that in the late fifties, at a difficult time for the mob, the episode at the Plaza *may* have renewed that insurance." The evidence, of course, was the story invented by Susan Rosenstiel who was completely discredited. It was in the late fifties, furthermore, before the Apalachin convention of top mobsters, that Hoover began the Top Hoodlum Intelligence Program.

When DeLoach challenged Summer's statement on the Larry King show that Hoover was a pawn of the Mafia, he reminded the author of something he obviously already knew – that before 1961, the FBI had no jurisdiction regarding organized crime as such. That did not keep the Bureau from getting into cases where it was possible, even by such far-fetched means as apprehending escaped criminals for failing to let their draft boards know they had moved from prison. The Top Hoodlum Intelligence Program which permitted the FBI to identify mob leaders across the country placed the FBI in a strong position to move against them once the 1961 statutes were adopted outlawing interstate transportation of gambling paraphernalia and wagering information. DeLoach cited statistics on the Larry King program showing that the very next year after the passage of these laws, there were 80 arrests of organized crime subjects, 72 based on FBI evidence. Between 1961 and 1972, the year of Hoover's death, there were 1783 convictions of such subjects, including Sam Giancana, Johnny Dioguardia, Raymond Patriarcha, Carlos Marcello, and Stefano Magaddino.

During the 1971 fiscal year when Hoover was still alive, over 340,000 items of criminal intelligence data were furnished to local, state, and other federal agencies by the FBI field offices throughout the United States. Included among this was information which led to the arrest of nearly 4,000 rackets and gambling figures by other agencies and the seizure of more than $2,000,000 in currency, contraband and gambling paraphernalia. [23]

No photograph of Hoover in a compromising position was ever exhibited by any organized crime figure or anyone else in support of Summers' malodorous allegation. The facts speak for themselves. No such photograph existed for it surely would have surfaced when Mafia bosses and other hoodlums were being rounded up and convicted.

Throughout his slanted biography of J. Edgar Hoover, author Anthony Summers played fast and loose with the facts. Another prime example of this was his accusation of Hoover's "trying to get Robert Kennedy to authorize wiretaps not just against close colleagues but against [Martin Luther] King himself." Since elsewhere in his book, he made it clear that he had access to the so-called Official and Confidential files, to the extent, indeed, that he used their designated name to title the book, he knew that they contained clear information showing that this statement was false. He read, as I did, that on July 16, 1963, Kennedy told an assistant director of the FBI that in view of the possible communist influence on the racial situation, he desired that consideration be given to placing a wiretap on King. It was he who introduced the subject of wiretapping King, not Hoover or anyone else in the FBI. Summers coupled this misstatement about the wiretapping of the civil rights leader with other such statements about Hoover's "using the press to distort the facts on organized crime" and "bringing pressure to brand Martin Luther King a Communist." [24]

On March 26, 1993, in a lengthy editorial *The Washington Times* commented on Anthony Summers and his book. Excerpts from it are pertinent for they show how his portrayal of Hoover was received inside the Washington beltway where he was born, lived all his life, and reigned as Director of the FBI for 48 years:

> *Mr. Summers manages to lay the blame for nearly every scandal and disaster of 20th-century America at Hoover's long-deceased feet, including the Kennedy assassination itself, the Japanese attack on Pearl Harbor and the rise of organized crime. Just about the only bad things Hoover wasn't responsible for, in Mr. Summers' account, were the destruction of the Hindenburg and the stock market crash of '29, but give him time and another several hundred pages and he'll probably get to work on it.... .*

> *The problem with the Summers book, as The Washington Times' Jerry Seper pointed out several weeks ago, is that it relies on "a cast of questionable characters": former organized crime members or groupies, ladies of dubious reputation, former FBI agents who left the Bureau under a cloud and the usual gang of dolts and idiots, all of whom have gone to the Big House in the Sky.... .*

> *J. Edgar was a man who had many flaws. He was deeply prejudiced and imported his prejudices into his work. He was power-hungry and he may have misused his power to pressure presidents and congressmen into letting him keep and enhance his power. Despite those flaws and others, however, Hoover remains an American giant and one of the world's greatest cops. He lifted the FBI from scandal during the days of Teapot Dome[25]*

to what was at his death the foremost law-enforcement and counter-espionage agency in the world. That legacy, and Hoover's lifelong war against crime and subversion, will outlive the rumors, jokes and politically convenient double standards in which phony scholarship, scandalmongers and conspiracy freaks seek to dress his corpse.

The Official and Confidential Files

George Allen, the intimate of presidents and Hoover's good friend, referred to critics who maintained that the Director kept secret files of scandalous information about hundreds of officials and leaders in various walks of life. He commented, "It is interesting to note that no evidence that any such files exist or ever have existed has been discovered by his successor." He dismissed the whole idea of secret files by suggesting they were a myth deriving principally from the bad consciences of people who feared that Hoover's men had been peeking over their transoms or tapping their phones.[1]

L. Patrick Gray as acting director was Hoover's immediate successor, and he arrived at Mark Felt's office in the Bureau shortly after 3:00 P.M. the same day Hoover was buried, obviously with a mission. After greetings were exchanged, Gray told Mark, "We will have a lot of things to talk about later, but today, the first thing I want to know about is the 'secret' files."

Felt explained that there were no secret files, but there were thousands which contained derogatory information, some obtained through investigation of cases and some volunteered. There were files which contained extremely confidential and sensitive information about espionage investigations. Many files were classified "Top Secret" or "Confidential" under rules that governed all government agencies, Mark explained.

Gray replied, "Mark, I'm not talking about the regular files. Everybody knows that Hoover had his own secret files containing derogatory data on important people."

Mark went into detail explaining how the FBI had opened files on many important people, a few who reportedly had violated Federal statutes, but many more being investigated for high Federal offices. Some files on important people might contain information that was unsolicited by the FBI.

Gray interrupted, "I know all that, but what about the files that Hoover kept in his office?"

Felt acknowledged there were some files kept there which were so sensitive that Hoover felt they should be available only on a need-to-know basis and not to curious eyes of any agent or clerk who might come across them in the central filing system.

"Would he follow this practice," Gray interjected, "if the information involved a high-placed person?"

Despite Felt's assurances about the basis for Hoover's retaining tight control over such information, Gray obviously had some doubts. Thereupon, Mark offered to accompany him to the Director's office, which had been unoccupied by him for only three days, so Gray could look at the files there. Gray readily agreed.

Helen Gandy, whom he met when he entered the outer office, pointed to ten five-drawer file cabinets and said, "Well there they are."

She explained,

> Most of this material is Mr. Hoover's personal correspondence — some going back to when he first became Director. I am planning to pack up the personal correspondence in card-

board file boxes and ship it out to his house. Mr. Tolson in-
structed me to do that. He also said that all the Bureau files
should be sent to Mr. Felt.

After looking casually at one open file drawer, Gray made no further references to these files, and there was no indication that he was not completely satisfied with the explanations he had received. [2]

Subsequently, with Gray's knowledge, Miss Gandy shipped 34 boxes of personal files to Hoover's house and sent 12 boxes containing the Bureau files to Felt. He sent three of these 12 containing monographs, research material and other similar items to the general files. After three months of waiting for Gray to look at the remainder, which he failed to do, Felt had an inspector prepare a complete index and catalogue of them, a copy of which was sent to Gray. Despite frequent suggestions that he review the files, Gray never did so, apparently satisfied that there were no "secret files." He so stated this to the media. [3]

British author Anthony Summers dwelt on this matter of alleged secret files, pointing to the material Hoover maintained in cabinets in his outer office and designated "Official and Confidential Files" (O and C files). Referring to a description of the Director by his most deleterious adversary, William Sullivan, as "a master blackmailer," and identifying Sullivan simply as "Hoover's closest colleague," Summers proceeded by innuendo to try to prove that the contents of the O and C files were used for blackmail purposes.

Statements which he relied upon to prove his case:

...Many senators and congressmen lived in fear of the files
Hoover had on them — or that they feared he held.

Edgar saw to it that all information gathered, including that
collected on thousands of innocent citizens, was duly filed away
for future reference.

A senior aide to Francis Biddle felt that attorneys general
were cowed by Edgar's relationship with the President, and by
an "even deeper fear that he had files on everybody."

Gordon Liddy, Nixon's dirty-tricks specialist, [upon hearing
of Hoover's death, reportedly said,] "I called the White House
at once. I said, 'You've got to get those files. They are a source
of enormous power. You don't have much time. There's going
to be a race on. Get those files.' "

Martin Luther King's widow, Coretta... spoke of Edgar's "de-
plorable and dangerous" legacy and of a file system "replete
with lies and sordid material on some of the highest people in
government, including presidents." [4]

One statement he relied upon was attributed to columnist Igor Cassini who, in discussing President Kennedy, was said to have made the statement, "I didn't know then that Hoover was blackmailing him." No explanation of or basis for this alleged statement was offered by the author.

He claimed to have spent five years in preparing his presentation on Hoover, seeking, of course, specific examples of blackmail. During all that research he came up with what he presented as two examples. One was refuted by Deke DeLoach when he confronted Summers during a joint TV appearance. The other was termed "blackmail" by Judith Exner, nee Campbell, who in her 1977 book *My Story* admitted having shared her favors with Jack Kennedy and Sam "Mo Mo" Giancana, Chicago Mafia boss.

In the first instance, according to Summers, Senator Edward Long, head of the Subcommittee on Invasion of Privacy, was blackmailed to keep him from checking into FBI operations. Deke and another agent called on the senator and handed him a thin folder. He read its contents for a few minutes then handed it back. Summers quoted Long's Chief Counsel Bernard Fensterwald as saying, "The next thing I knew we had orders to skip over the FBI inquiries." The folder, Deke informed him and the television audience, contained information requested by Senator Long on the number of attorney general-authorized wire taps the FBI was conducting at that time and how many phone-monitorings the FBI was using on organized crime investigations. [5]

By way of background regarding the second incident of "blackmail" – Director Hoover, as a result of investigation by the FBI of Sam Giancana at the urging of Attorney General Robert Kennedy, had evidence that the President of the United States was intimate with a young woman, Judith Campbell, who was close to Giancana. The mobster was reportedly involved in a plot to assassinate Cuban dictator Fidel Castro, which Hoover had reason to believe the President had authorized. At the same time, Robert Kennedy's onslaught on organized crime not only included Giancana among its targets, but also singled him out for especially intensive harassment.[6]

On July 12, 1961, Giancana, when entering a waiting room at Chicago's O'Hare Airport, found a group of FBI Agents there anticipating his arrival. He became very angry and threatened, "I know all about the Kennedys and Phyllis [McGuire, his mistress] knows more about the Kennedys, and one of these days we're going to tell all... . One of these days it'll all come out." [7]

In the spring of 1960, Judith Campbell, had become Kennedy's lover. After his election to the presidency, she acted as a courier for him in delivering vast amounts of money to Sam Giancana. She said that the money had something to do with the West Virginia primary campaign which was won by Kennedy that year, that "someone was being paid off, something was being bought with this money." According to her, John Kennedy himself took outrageous risks to enlist Giancana's help.

As early as March 1960, the month Kennedy began discussing Giancana with Judith Campbell, money of the Kennedy dynasty along with contributions from mobsters, reportedly arranged by Joseph Kennedy, Sr., was used to buy votes during primary elections. [8]

Summers interviewed Campbell during 1990 to 1992. He related that she gave him the following version of what transpired at a four-hour meeting between President Kennedy and Hoover at the White House on March 22, 1962:

> Hoover had more or less tried to intimidate him with the information he had. He [Hoover] made it clear that he knew about my relationship with Jack, even that I'd been to the White

House, that I was a friend of Sam and Johnny Roselli [Sam's West Coast lieutenant], and that Jack knew Sam, too. Jack knew exactly what Hoover was doing. Knowing that Jack wanted him out of office, he was in a way ensuring his job — by letting Jack know he had this leverage over him.

While Judith was understandably distraught that her relationship with Kennedy was known to the Director of the FBI, and obviously outraged that he would face the President with the information, Hoover's concern was surely more logical and frightening. Through revelations of Giancana and Phyllis McGuire, the people of the United States, in fact, of the entire world, could learn that President Kennedy and the boss of the Chicago Mafia were sharing the same lover, a U.S. Profumo-type situation. They could also learn that Giancana, with apparent presidential sanction, was involved in a plot to kill the head of a foreign nation, and that the mobster had assisted Kennedy along the road to the presidency. Had this information come out, embarrassment would have been the least of Jack Kennedy's concerns – he could have faced impeachment – and his brother, Bobby, who all the while was doing his best to throw Giancana in jail, would not have looked exactly like the brightest star in the political firmament.

Even Anthony Summers put aside the conclusion that what Judith Campbell told him should be interpreted as blackmail, albeit he did so somewhat reluctantly. Noting the extent of Hoover's knowledge about these things, he said, "Any Director of the FBI would have been justified in bringing such a scenario to the President's attention." Revealing his prejudice against the man whose quintessential biographer he desired to be, he added, "With his malice toward the brothers and with the threat of dismissal hanging over him, Edgar must have relished doing so." [9]

With reference to the O and C files which attracted Summers' attention, DeLoach confirmed that they consisted of items too sensitive to place in the Bureau's central filing system, which was open virtually to the entire headquarters staff, many of whom were filing clerks. [10]

During research in preparing this book, I reviewed huge volumes of material, including 8566 pages of the O and C files, made available through a Freedom of Information Act request. Following are some representative examples, set forth by file numbers, illustrating the original reason for establishing these files and the type of information designated for them, beginning at least as far back as May 1940. The sensitive nature of the information and the reason for withholding it from the central filing system are obvious.

- 114: Background of authorization for use of microphones.
- 115: Surveys to accomplish security of attorney general's residence and Hoover's office.
- 127: Response by Hoover to a 1943 request from the secretary of war to recommend someone to undertake a highly secret mission.
- 140: A January 26, 1942, strictly confidential chart showing

coverage by the FBI in the Western Hemisphere at the outset of World War II.

- **145**: A memorandum Hoover prepared concerning a June 6, 1952, discussion with the attorney general, who authorized installations of microphones even when technical trespass was involved.
- **149**: A brief prepared January 20, 1956, for use by the Director in an appearance before a presidential board.
- **155**: A personnel situation in an FBI field office requiring headquarters' inquiries.
- **157**: A 1941 investigation undertaken at the request of the White House regarding alleged immoral activities on the part of a high-level state department official.
- **163**: A copy of a May 21, 1940, memorandum signed "F.D.R." authorizing the attorney general to approve the use by investigative agents of listening devices to cover "persons suspected of subversive activities against the Government of the United States, including suspected spies."

In subsequent years as information volunteered to the Bureau or developed through investigation included sensitive material on individuals, it was placed under lock and key in the Director's outer office. This included information regarding presidents and other prominent individuals. A person's conduct and/or his activity was not the only factor which was judged in deciding whether the material was of sufficient sensitivity to designate it for these files. Details concerning the Director's dealings with presidents and others, such as his June 6, 1952, discussion with the attorney general about the use of microphones, was retained in the O and C files. They also served as a repository for monographs prepared for the Director on subjects in which he had an interest, as well as booklets containing research results, and other similar material.

Authors writing about Hoover have refused to accept the fact that the files were set up and used for a valid and legitimate reason. They have circulated false information which has resulted in the files being considered by some as comparable to a witch's brew with ingredients concocted by Hoover for ulterior purposes. Even Curt Gentry, one of the less-biased chroniclers of Hoover's life and career, put a spin on O and C file number 142 which painted Hoover as having used an illegal wiretap and "probably" other techniques to spy on one of his officials.

When, during the summer of 1971, Bill Sullivan began openly opposing Hoover, Mark Felt was placed in a position over him because Hoover felt he had been the only one to curb Sullivan. Referring to this situation, Gentry, without documentation, made the bland statement that following Felt's appointment, "Sullivan's home telephones were tapped." He footnoted this statement:

It is probable that still other techniques were used to spy on Sullivan. Among the still-classified folders in J. Edgar Hoover's Official/Confidential file is OC no. 142. Headed "Specialized Mail Coverage" and categorized "Investigative," it is five pages in length, covers the period July 2-7, 1971, and contains two

> memos "re highly sensitive information concerning two types
> of security coverage on _____." Although the name has
> been excised in the OC summary, it is approximately fifteen to
> seventeen letters in length. "William Sullivan" would fit. As
> would the date, July 2 being the day after Mark Felt's appoint-
> ment. [11]

The O and C file, as stated by Gentry, contains two memoranda. One, dated July 2, 1971, was addressed to Sullivan by Charles Brennan, the official heading the intelligence division; the other was addressed to Clyde Tolson by Mark Felt on July 7 the same year. Sullivan placed his initials on both memoranda signifying his approval. This is not surprising since the memos represented an attempt to get the Director's concurrence for the use of a covert investigative technique Sullivan had tried, through the Huston Plan, to have approved, to which the Director took exception on the grounds that it was illegal. The fact alone that Sullivan placed his initials on both memos should be sufficient to refute any thought that the memos had anything to do with a technical surveillance or any other type of techniques applied to "spy on Sullivan."

When agents and officials had reason to review material in the O and C files in connection with official matters they were handling, they were made available by Helen Gandy, the Director's administrative assistant. They simply were not maintained as a seedbed for blackmail or for any other devious or illegal purpose.

I recall having to revise material in them on a twice-weekly basis in 1956 and was granted full access. President Eisenhower ordered Hoover to brief the National Security Council in January that year. I had the assignment to prepare the briefing paper and have it ready by the 8th of the month, which I did. Unfortunately, the President suffered an attack of ileitis, causing the briefing to be postponed to an unspecified later date. The briefing paper contained the Bureau's most sensitive, top secret information regarding its national security intelligence operations. Hoover had it placed in his O and C files and ordered that it be revised twice each week so it would be immediately available in an updated form if the president requested the presentation on short notice. The briefing finally took place March 8, and until that time I had to get the briefing paper from the confidential files and insert corrected pages to update it. Other headquarters agents and officials had similar access to the files on a need basis.

My own research into the life and times of J. Edgar Hoover proved to be more successful than that of Anthony Summers insofar as recognizing an example of blackmail by the FBI Director. It involved his good friend Julius Lulley, the proprietor of Harveys Restaurant.

Julius and his wife were engaged in a test of wills. She was trying to convince her husband to buy her a fur coat, "like all the girls have." Hoover, who was very fond of her, sympathized but would not become openly involved in the dispute. He did, however, needle Lulley about it.

"Julie," he said, "your wife wants a fur coat and you are too damn cheap to buy it."

Lulley stood pat, his stock answer being, "Edgar, I just can't afford it."

Hoover, well aware that Julie was not poverty-stricken, watched for an opportunity to cure him of his falsely claimed money problem. When Lulley made a trip to New York, sans Mrs. Lulley, a mutual friend took a picture of him in a prominent night spot. He snapped the photograph when he was able to include in the foreground a very attractive, buxom blonde. This offered Hoover the opportunity to give Mrs. Lulley an assist while playing a practical joke he just couldn't resist. Putting a copy of the photo in his pocket, he arranged a dinner date with the Lulleys.

During the course of the dinner conversation, he casually introduced the subject of fur coats. It was not long before Mrs. Lulley decided that was not a subject she desired to discuss. Excusing herself she headed for the powder room.

Hoover pulled the photograph from his pocket and showed it to Julie, remarking, "Don't you think that your wife should have a fur coat?"

The perpetrator of the practical joke and the perpetratee got a laugh from it. Mrs. Lulley got a fur coat. I suppose it is correct to say that Julie Lulley was blackmailed by the Director of the FBI. [12]

Anthony Summers knew that Hoover was a practical joker, was even aware of the fur coat incident, but was not interested in portraying his lighter side. [13]

THE ENIGMATIC DIRECTOR

No doubt the best and most objective characterization of J. Edgar Hoover has been made by the special agents who served under him. In 1982, Arizona Congressman Eldon Rudd, who had been an agent for 20 years, inserted the following in the *Congressional Record:*

J. Edgar Hoover was born, he lived, and he died — the same chronology for all mortals. Like all mortals, he had his virtues and vices, his strong characteristics and his weaknesses, his likes and his dislikes. He could be dictatorial and dogmatic in business matters, compassionate to a friend in need, relentless against malicious attacks [against the FBI], austere in adminis-tration, humorous and personable in social affairs. The vast majority of FBI Agents who served under him recognized him as a leader who demanded no more than he was willing to give, and one who would support them in any honest effort in the fulfillment of duty. And yet, it is safe to say that at one time or another, every agent grumbled about some idiosyn-crasy or rule of the late Director.

Former FBI official W. Mark Felt, in his book The FBI Pyra-mid, said of Mr. Hoover:

Charismatic, feisty, charming, petty, giant, grandiose, bril-liant, egotistical, industrious, formidable, compassionate, domi-neering — all these adjectives were applied to Hoover and, to a degree, they all fitted him. He had both wide recognition and detraction — and he accepted this. He was a human being.

In an editorial in the Tucson Citizen of July 8, 1982, chief editorial writer Asa Bushnell, a former FBI Agent, stated:

He made mistakes, who doesn't? — as he tried too hard to protect America by the old-fashioned book. But the man did not deserve the totally unfair and unbalanced treatment he received... .

In America the record of an individual and his place in his-tory is based on the 'bottom line.' None of our 'founding fa-thers,' illustrious Presidents, or other giants of American his-tory has ever been an unanimous selection to fame without some dissenting opinion. However, it is customary to judge a person on the overall performance of his short-comings and achievements. [1]

Hoover divorced his public and business life from his private one. When attending social functions at which he also was present, I certainly observed a side of him not apparent around the office.

At one of these functions (in the Rotunda of the British Embassy) as I glanced across the room, I saw that my wife, Trudie, was in a one-on-one conversation with my boss. If not apprehensive, I was at least curious to know what topics they were discussing that seemed so absorbing, hopefully not her husband. On the way home, Trudie commented that they touched upon various subjects, one being Shirley Temple, of whom the Director seemed to be very fond. Trudie said that she had been completely charmed by Hoover. As she put it, "He is one of those rare men who can make a woman feel that she is the only female in the room that he wanted to talk to."

To the very end, his charm and graciousness with women remained with him. Wives left his office all aglow when they were received with agent husbands who had been congratulated by the Director for an anniversary or for a job well done. [2]

Chief Nurse Valeria Stewart remarked about how pleasant and happy these occasions were. An agent with his wife and family would arrive in the Director's office at 8:30 A.M. and the meeting would last perhaps not more than 10 minutes. He was outgoing, friendly, and especially gracious. Frequently, he would compliment the wife

Mr. and Mrs. Ray Wannal with J. Edgar Hoover at the author's 25th anniversary with the FBI.

on how nice she looked, and if there was a child with the couple, he'd ask that the youngster stand next to him while a picture of the group was taken to commemorate the occasion. As the family left, some member would often comment that the time he spent with them was memorable and seemed longer than the comparatively few minutes it covered. And true enough, the wives usually left all aglow. [3]

One of those captivated by the Hoover charm was Martha Mitchell, wife of Attorney General John Mitchell. Their relationship was one of mutual admiration.[4]

According to Anthony Summers, Hoover considered marriage in the closing months of World War I with a young lady named Alice, the daughter of a prominent Washington attorney, but she turned to a young officer. Helen Gandy was said to have commented that this may have been part of why Hoover never really trusted women, why he never married. Summers hypothesized, "The episode proved a devastating emotional setback, one that may have played a key role in triggering his sexual ambivalence." [5]

Summers' brash statement about Hoover's experiencing a "sexual ambivalence" was discounted by his recital of the Director's associations with Lela Rogers, Frances Marion, and Dorothy Lamour. Contradicting his statement that Hoover suffered "a devastating emotional setback" was his own reporting:

> Hoover began seeing women immediately after his mother's [Annie Hoover's] death in 1938 following a long battle with cancer... .

> Edgar was seen dining out with older women within weeks of Annie's death. His new "favorite person," as Walter Winchell put it, was Lela Rogers, mother of Ginger, and a formidable figure on her own.

> There were soon rumors that Rogers and Edgar were planning marriage.

> In New York to promote a play she had written, she received the press standing in front of his silver-framed photograph... . "Are you going to get married, or are you just interested in detective work?" asked a reporter. "That," she beamed, "is up to him... ."

> "He was really smitten with her," recalled Effie Cain, a wealthy Texan who met Edgar in the forties. Edgar said as much to Leo McClairen, the trusted black Agent who chauffeured him in Florida. "Mr. Hoover told me one time," McClairen remembered, "he was in love with Ginger Roger's mother. He told me she was thinking of getting married to him, but something came up... ."

> Richard Auerbach, a top Bureau official, ... said, "I brought the news to her one day [when both Lela Rogers and Hoover were in Florida] that the President wanted him back in Washington the next morning. And his lady love said, 'This just isn't going to work. I'm going back to L.A... .' She turned around and left the room with tears streaming down her face... ."

Summers reported on what he referred to as "two other women

in Edgar's life." One was Oscar-winner, screenwriter Frances Marion, who "wouldn't marry him because of the boys, her sons, ... and perhaps [the] most important liaison was with the actress Dorothy Lamour." He revealed:

> In her autobiography, Lamour wrote only that Edgar was "a lifelong friend." In private, in the seventies, she spoke of deeper feelings. "She just started to glow when his name was mentioned," said acquaintances of hers in California. "But she told us she knew marriage would not have worked. They were both too involved in their careers. They were heartbroken, though. It was really a sad story."

After playing it straight about the Director's interest in women, Summers tossed away the impact of this and, immediately after reporting on the man's association with Dorothy Lamour, lapsed into such allegations as: "Edgar's sexual torment had effects far beyond his personal life," and "Edgar often behaved viciously toward fellow homosexuals." [6]

Being a bachelor, when he entertained, Hoover called upon close friends to be hostess to his guests. Armand (Art) Cammarota, an FBI agent who had played a significant role in the trial and conviction of Soviet spies Julius and Ethel Rosenberg, was selected by the Director to serve in the Bureau's foreign liaison post in the U.S. Embassy in Rome, Italy, a country of which Hoover was very fond and whose history and culture he enjoyed discussing with Art whenever the latter called on him. On one such occasion, he talked about his friendship with Clinton Murchison, the well-known Texas oil magnate. He commented that since he had never married, Mrs. Murchison had acted as hostess for him many times during both formal and informal gatherings. He also mentioned having often met socially with the mother of movie actress Ginger Rogers, Lela, of whom he was very fond. [7]

Besides maintaining his health with a daily allergy shot, Hoover took advantage of his frequent trips to Atlantic City to unwind and soak up the sun. When Chief Nurse Val Stewart arrived at his office one morning following a week she had spent in Atlantic City, Clyde Tolson was there discussing with the Director one of the cases under investigation.

Interrupting the discussion, Hoover turned to her and remarked, "Welcome back. We missed you. I see you have a great suntan."

When Val told him where she had been, he said, "Come here, child, and let Tolson and me look you over. I love to go to Atlantic City myself, sit in the sun and in my cabana, watch the ocean, and feel the nice breezes. It is so restful. And besides, they have a great racetrack there."

Horse racing was a favorite source of relaxation for him, and a welcome diversion from the enormous pressure exerted by his responsibilities as head of the FBI.

He also showed considerable concern for the health and well-being of others, as in the case of Roger Vincent, the young polio victim, and James Crawford, his chauffeur and bodyguard. Whenever his birthday or Bureau anniversary rolled around, his office would be flooded with flowers sent by well-wishers. He told Val that he enjoyed flowers, something he inherited from his mother who treasured working in her rose garden. On these occasions he would have Val prepare a list of sick Bureau employees and give it to Helen Gandy so she could arrange to have the flowers sent to them. At Christmas time, toy manufacturers sent him many toys, all of which were sent to organizations which helped needy children.

At Valeria Stewart's suggestion he approved many preventive measures to enhance the health of Bureau employees. The flu vaccine program was one of these. He followed this closely until Val was able to report to him that drug companies had supplied sufficient vaccine to permit the program to be carried out not only at FBI headquarters but in every one of the 59 field offices. [8]

On occasion the Director became emotionally involved in a case where an innocent life was at risk. This was true of the Mackle kidnapping.

Eight days before Christmas 1968 Barbara Jane Mackle, the twenty-year-old daughter of a prominent Florida real estate developer and part owner of the Key Biscane Hotel, was kidnapped from a motel room she shared with her mother in Decatur, Georgia. Mrs. Mackle was left bound hand and foot and with tape over her mouth.

Later that day, a ransom of a half million dollars was demanded and the Mackles were advised that Barbara was "inside a small capsule buried in a remote piece of soil" with enough water, food, and air to last seven days, when "the life-supporting batteries will

Tolson and Hoover present Helen Gandy with a Service Award. (FBI)

be discharged and the air supply will be cut off." Without hesitation, the Mackles decided to pay the ransom.

Deke DeLoach was directing the investigation to locate and release the girl who was buried alive. Hoover called him several times a day for a report on progress being made, as nervous as his men who were working desperately to find her.

One of the most extensive and intensive investigations ever conducted was pursued. On December 21, after an attempt to pay the ransom went awry, a second attempt was made and was successful. The next day a man called the operator on the switchboard of the Atlanta, Georgia, FBI office and gave directions to Barbara's burial site and she was found, still alive. Notified immediately of this, Hoover, after expressing great relief, called her parents personally to let them know.

Two kidnappers were identified, the first, Gary Steven Krist, aged 23 years, who had a criminal record beginning when he was 15 years old and who was on the FBI's "wanted list" for unlawful flight to avoid confinement. He had escaped two years before from the Deuel Vocation Institution at Tracy, California, where he had been confined for stealing an automobile. His last employment had been with the Marine Science Institute at the University of Miami. He masterminded the kidnapping, having planned and built the capsule.

The second was a 26-year old woman, Ruth Eismann-Schier, who was born in Honduras, had a degree in chemistry from the National University of Mexico, and had worked as a biology researcher in Washington, DC. She had met Krist at the Marine Science Institute in the fall of 1968.

Within three days after the ransom pay-off, Gary Krist was captured in Florida in a mangrove swamp in a stream that ran from the Myakka River through portions of Hog Island. Of the $500,000 ransom, $479,000 of it was recovered. Following presentation of the case against him at his March 7, 1969, trial, he changed his plea from "not guilty" to "guilty" and was sentenced to life in prison. He was eligible for parole in just ten years. He was out in eleven.

Ruth Eismann-Schier was apprehended March 5, 1969, in Norman, Oklahoma, where she was working as a waitress at a drive-in restaurant. Charged with the crime of kidnapping for ransom, she entered a plea of "not guilty." In exchange for a reduced charge of kidnapping she changed her plea to "guilty" and received a sentence of seven years.

Despite the extensive and successful FBI investigation, both kidnappers were tried by state courts. Since Barbara Jane Mackle was not transported across a state line, no federal offense was involved. [9]

Several days after Barbara Mackle had been found, Hoover talked about the case with Val Stewart when she arrived to give him his allergy treatment.

"I've just come back from our laboratory," he said. "I saw the long box-like casket that the kidnappers had buried the young lady in. It was incredulous that anyone would build anything like that. It was put together with long screw-like nails that were very strong. I just don't know how anyone could have come through an ordeal like

Barbara did. Thank God that our agents were able to find her in time." [10]

The capsule was eight feet long and two feet in both width and depth. Barbara had spent 83 torturous hours in it under ground, maintaining her spirits by singing songs, going over college homework in her mind, reciting passages from the Bible, and praying. As she was released, she was sobbing, tears of joy and relief streaming down her face.

But in a voice barely audible she told the agents, "I knew you'd find me. I knew it." [11]

Hoover told Val, "Mrs. Stewart, You must go over to the lab and see that box when you leave here. I have seen Mr. Mackle since his daughter's miraculous recovery. He couldn't thank the FBI enough. He also said, 'J. Edgar, name anything and it is yours.' I told him I didn't want anything.

" 'I'm just happy that our agents found your daughter and that she is OK,' I assured him. But he kept insisting, 'Can't I give you a condo, a house, anything?' I just kept telling him no."

Val asked if the Director had seen Mr. Mackle's daughter, and he said that he had.

"Yes," he responded. "I met Barbara. She's a lovely young lady, and she just seems to have come through that terrible ordeal so very well."

During another conversation with Valeria Stewart, Hoover revealed why he became disturbed at times over newspaper stories. He asked her if she had seen an article in the morning edition of *The Washington Post*. It was about an agent who had shot and killed a gunman who attempted to hijack a plane in New York. Val said she had seen it; she had noted that it indicated the agent had been disciplined by Hoover by being transferred.

Hoover said, "The article is completely wrong. You can't trust the press. I did, in fact, transfer the agent and his family out of New York because not only the agent but his family, also, were being harassed and were receiving threats. Mrs. Stewart, I gave him a meritorious award and put his name at the top of the list for transfer to our Academy in Quantico when there is an opening. That is his office of preference, where he wants to work."

Val, expressing the opinion that it was a wonderful thing Hoover had done for the agent and his family, asked, "Why don't you tell the press?"

He replied, "I just don't hang out my wash to any newspaper."

While accusations have been heard that the Director courted presidents to stay in office, if true, the courting was a two-way street. There were genuine feelings of neighborliness and friendship between him and some of the eight presidents under whom he served, such as Lyndon Johnson and Richard Nixon who actually were his neighbors before being elected to their high office. But in many cases, while Hoover didn't hang out his wash to newspapers, presidents did hang out their FBI Director when it served purposes of their own — especially during photo opportunities.

When telling Valeria Stewart one Monday morning of "a big

weekend" he and Clyde Tolson had spent as guests of the President at the Camp David retreat, he poked a little fun at Clyde.

He urged Val, "Ask Mr. Tolson what he forgot to bring home."

Tolson quickly said, "It was nothing."

"He left his bathrobe," Hoover needled. "Of course, there are always bathrobes there, but Mr. Tolson has to take along everything with him."

He described Camp David to her, saying in was quite picturesque and the food was delicious. They'd had a "great" time, it was a restful place, "But of course, we did some work."

He greeted her one day with, "Guess whom I'm having for dinner tonight. The President." When she asked, "Whatever do you serve a president?" he took delight in telling her.

"I can tell you the entire menu. I will serve Omaha steak and everything that goes with it. President Nixon will take off his coat, roll up his sleeves, and make the drinks. He makes a mess but he has a good time. Everyone will enjoy it."

The next morning, on request, he gave a report, saying, "The evening was a success, the President was in a good mood, and the meal turned out fine." [12]

Hoover and Nixon were very close friends. The President referred to Hoover as his "crony," and the two men met socially at least a hundred times. [13]

For some reason unknown to Val, Hoover was studying about five large pictures on his desk when she saw him one day. He said he had to decide which one he should give to the President. Asked to help him decide, she chose a particular one, saying she liked it because it depicted him walking along and swinging his arms, making him "look good and very alert."

Hoover looked up and said, "OK, that's it," then , smiling, added, "You kissed that blarney stone again."

Quite often Hoover was given some assignment by the President which served some purpose not readily apparent. On one occasion he was "requested" to go to National Airport a particular evening and meet the secretary of state who was returning from a European trip. It rained cats and dogs that night, and when Val expressed the hope the next morning that he didn't have to make the trip because of the weather, he laughingly said, "Oh, I was there. When the President calls and tells you to be there, you go, rain or not — and believe me, it was wet."

The Director got marching orders again when Queen Elizabeth of England, after she had ascended to the throne in 1952, paid a visit to the United States with Prince Philip. The royal couple was greeted with a huge parade on Pennsylvania Avenue and honored the following night at a state dinner in the White House, to which Hoover was "invited." Upon learning the morning of the dinner that he would be there, Val had a request to make.

"Everyone says that the Queen has skin like peaches and cream. When you see her tonight will you please take a close look and let me know if she really does?"

As he did with presidential "requests," Hoover carried out this one with dispatch. "Mrs. Stewart," he advised her the next morning,

"I have a report for you. The Queen's skin is like peaches and cream and she is even more beautiful than she appears in her pictures. When she shakes your hand, her eye contact is intense and she is most gracious. And," he added, with a twinkle in his eye, "just incidentally, I had a grand time."

He was often invited to White House functions, both state dinners and informal parties. At one of these Lucy Johnson, LBJ's daughter, was there. She slipped up behind him and kissed him on the cheek. This world-shaking event made the pages of *The Washington Post* in a story in which it was reported that Hoover was really taken by surprise. When Val mentioned this, he acknowledged that it was true.

Smiling, he explained, "I was so surprised and it was so unexpected that I almost died. It was so nice to see her. I've always been fond of Lucy. She was a lovely child." She had, of course, been an across-the-street neighbor of Hoover's when she was quite young.

When Val arrived in his office on one occasion, she found that he and Tolson were in the midst of one of their discussions about a case; this particular one was drawing close media attention. Putting it aside for the moment, he greeted her in his usual, pleasant way.

"Mr. Tolson and I are off to an enjoyable afternoon later today," he said. "We're going to the racetrack. I love those horses, but I'm just a $2.00 bettor. It's the atmosphere I like so much. But ask Mr. Tolson, here, how much he bets."

Turning to Clyde Tolson, Val posed the question.

Looking her squarely in the eyes, Tolson responded, "No way!"

Hoover observed, "Don't mind him; he's just grumpy."

The next morning, Val asked how his previous afternoon had been.

"The horses were great," Hoover said, "but I didn't have much action. But just ask Mr. Tolson."

The latter looked at her and smiled — a fairly rare thing on his part, Val had to note — and merely said, "It was a good day." This brought a smile to Hoover's face as well. Obviously a loss at the track produced grumpiness in Tolson, whereas a win resulted in cheerfulness.

Val noted that there was a good relationship between the two men, something which the Director seemed to keep well in hand; but he did enjoy teasing Tolson. [14]

On the last Saturday of his life, April 29, 1972, Hoover with Clyde Tolson spent the day doing what they usually did on Saturdays when the horses were running at a race track anywhere within an hour's drive of Washington — placing bets at the $2.00 window. They were at a racetrack with raconteur and humorist George E. Allen. For some 40 years the three of them, he, Hoover, and Tolson, had attended the races together more or less regularly. For the previous 27 years, they had never missed a Preakness at Pimlico. [15]

Early Monday morning, May 2, Hoover's live-in housekeeper, Annie Fields, rose and prepared his breakfast. Hoover, himself, was an early riser, 6:30 on workday mornings. Soon Annie began to worry. She heard no shower running and no stirring around overhead.

Shortly after 8:00 o'clock, former Special Agent Jim Crawford arrived. After he had retired from the Bureau, Hoover hired him to supervise repairs to the house which Hoover had ordered, and to see that his yard and flower garden were kept in display shape.

Annie expressed concern to Jim about Hoover's not having come down yet for breakfast. It was near time for him to leave, stop by Clyde Tolson's residence, pick him up in the car driven by Tom Moton, Hoover's chauffeur, and proceed to work. The Director always kept his bedroom door locked at night, and Annie had no key to the lock. Crawford did; in fact he had ones that fit all the locks in the house so he could properly supervise

Clyde A. Tolson. (FBI)

repair jobs. At Annie's request, Jim went upstairs to Hoover's bedroom and, when there was no response to his knock on the door, unlocked it, entered, and found the Director dead in his bed.

Word was sent to Tolson immediately so he would not be left standing at the curb waiting for the car, then Helen Gandy and Val Stewart were advised. Val summoned Hoover's doctor, Robert Choisser, who proceeded to the house, confirmed Hoover's death and issued a death certificate. [16]

George Allen observed that Hoover's spirits and, to all appearances, his health were never better than on that last Saturday when they were at the racetrack together. Writing about this in an article titled "J. Edgar Hoover Off-Duty," Allen stated, "News of his death the following Monday was just short of unbelievable."

Over those long years of association, Allen observed that Hoover was, to quote him:

> ...neither a horse lover nor a gambler by inclination, much less by compulsion. He liked the crowd and the color as much as the sport itself. He didn't much care whether he won or lost. He liked to feel himself part of a human pack passionately sharing an enthusiasm.
>
> At the races the austere loner became a gregarious participant. There he was approachable by anyone and welcomed all comers. Every autograph seeker was cheerfully accommodated. He seldom spoke a serious word. He muttered wry imprecations against the horse he had bet on in the last race or the jockey who held him in. He insisted that I was the worst

handicapper it had ever been his misfortune to know. He once told President Eisenhower never to trust my judgment about a horse. [17]

As a result of his long association with J. Edgar Hoover, George Allen was able to present a candid and realistic picture of the man away from his desk, away from the responsibility of heading a world-renowned law enforcement and intelligence agency. Hoover was a regular guy to his neighbors on 30th Street in the Chevy Chase section of Washington where he lived in the house his old friend "HGM" — Harry Viner — had arranged to buy for him through a strawman because Hoover considered himself no businessman, but someone who "would be taken advantage of."

Among his neighbors, he was particularly close to the Calomaris and Wardrop families. John Calomaris was a retired Navy commander and William B. Wardrop a practicing physician.

A 20-year old Calomaris son, Anthony, whom Hoover watched grow up from babyhood, was considerably shocked at the sudden and unexpected death of the Director. He told Isabelle Shelton, a reporter for *The Evening Star,* that Hoover never married because he believed the frequent threats against his life would make life with him "sheer misery" for a woman. During one particularly tense time the threats were, in the young man's eyes, "running a thousand a day." [18]

The FBI Director didn't strike his neighbors as gruff or tough, as he was sometimes characterized. Mrs. Calomaris considered him:

A very generous, kind man, very warm, with a wonderful sense of humor; he was always sending us nice presents; and whenever we sent him anything — even flowers from our garden — he loved my peace roses — we got a beautiful thank you note the next day.

Mrs. Wardrop agreed: "A very generous man and very warm; he gave the appearance of being distant and cold, but he was anything but that."

Anthony's older brother, Louis, was impressed with Hoover's ethical standards, describing them as "fantastically high, even in little things." He said that whenever the government furnished a new, black, bullet-proof Cadillac to afford protection for the country's head G-man, Hoover would personally purchase an identical car, even to the bullet-proofing.

"He was scrupulous about never using the government car except to go to work and come home at night," Louis said. "He used his personal car for everything else." [19]

This was the friendly, intimate Hoover known to his neighbors. His public image was that of a person who was strongly for Americanism and patriotism, and equally strongly against crime and communism in all its forms.

For his continuous and active advocacy on behalf of these things, on several occasions he received the "George Washington Honor Medal" and other awards from the Freedoms Foundation at Valley Forge.

President Truman on March 8, 1946, awarded him the Medal for Merit acknowledging his outstanding World War II service, and commending him for his "able leadership" which made the Bureau "a powerful instrument of law enforcement in both war and peace."

On May 27, 1955, President Eisenhower presented to him the National Security Medal, for his outstanding service in the field of intelligence relating to National Security, and on January 27, 1958, the President's Award for Distinguished Civilian Service.

When on September 30, 1975, the J. Edgar Hoover FBI Building was dedicated in his honor, President Ford described him as a pioneering public servant who earned "praise and admiration from eight Presidents because, under his direction, the FBI became the superior professional organization it is today."

He was honored by the National Alumni Association of The Catholic University of America when, on November 13, 1954, he was presented the Cardinal Gibbons Medal for outstanding service to his country. [20]

Hoover was probably the only person in the world lauded by both the U.S. Senate and the U.S. Supreme Court.

On August 4, 1961, the Senate passed a resolution commending Hoover upon his 37 years of "distinguished service to the United States as Director of the FBI." [21]

In that landmark decision in the history of criminal justice, rendered in the 1966 Miranda Case, the Supreme Court declared that persons in custody must, immediately upon arrest, be advised of their right against self-incrimination and their right to counsel. The Court in its decision paid Hoover an honor by specifically lauding him for his "examplary record" in having had the FBI discharge these two requirements for several previous decades, which record, the Court stated, should be "emulated by state and local law enforcement agencies." [22]

Civil libertarians, minority activists, and even FBI detractors credit Hoover for this, as well as for his stand against the confinement in concentration camps of more than 100,000 Japanese-Americans, without due process of law, at the outset of World War II.

Throughout his life, Hoover received honorary degrees, awards, and acknowledgments for his distinguished service from educational, civic, and religious groups. They are listed in Appendix B.

James J. Angleton, when he headed CIA counterintelligence operations, worked with representatives of intelligence and security services of friendly Western nations throughout the world. He also had close dealings with the FBI on some of the most sensitive matters the U.S. intelligence community handled over a period of more than 20 years. He had ample opportunity to judge Hoover from the standpoint of both his ability and how he was regarded in the Western intelligence communities. When testifying before the Church Committee on September 24, 1975, he gave his appraisal of the man:

> I think that Mr. Hoover was conscious of all aspects of situations where the Bureau's interests were affected, whether it be professional, whether it be public relations. He was without question the number one law enforcement officer in the United States and probably the most respected individual outside the United States among all foreign intelligence and security services. [23]

There was a side of Hoover not well known to the general public, and certainly neglected by his detractors. He was very civic minded and a joiner or participant in numerous organizations.

He was a Mason, both Royal Arch and Scottish Rite, 33rd degree, and a Shriner. He was a member of Kappa Alpha Fraternity; Omicron Delta Kappa; Delta Theta Phi; Alpha Phi Omega; and Zeta Sigma Pi. He belonged to many national and statewide law enforcement associations, which might be expected. He served as an honorary trustee of the George Washington University, his alma mater; a member of the Board of Directors, Boys Clubs of America; a member of the National Court of Honor, and an honorary member, National Council, Boy Scouts of America; and a member of the National Advisory Council, Girl Scouts of the United States of America. He was also a member of The International Supreme Council of the Order of DeMolay. He held membership in the Columbia Country Club, Chevy Chase, Maryland. He authored four books, *Persons in Hiding,* 1938; *Masters of Deceit,* 1958; *A Study of Communism,* 1962; and *J. Edgar Hoover on Communism,* 1969. [24]

Hoover's support of youngsters' organizations — Boys Clubs, Boy Scouts of America, Girl Scouts of the United States, Order of the DeMolay — was indicative of his life-long interest in the welfare of young people and in measures and activities to prevent their getting caught up in crime. Referring to the spiraling crime wave of the 1930s, he had this message for parents:

> *Whether the infraction be the theft of a robe from your automobile or the invisible hand of the racketeer... its breeding place can be in the home of your next-door neighbor, or even your own.... If you are a parent, it might be well to study yourself and your own actions with extreme care. The fault, in the eyes of the parent, always lies with the child or with outside influences.... The true fault is not that of the child itself, but of the parent.* [25]

For a quarter century Hoover was a member of the Alexandria, Virginia, Aerie (chapter) of the Fraternal Order of Eagles. This organization, founded in Seattle, Washington, February 6, 1898, sponsors programs in support of old-age security, cancer research, youth guidance, and inter-faith brotherhood. In 1944 Hoover wrote in the group's *Eagle* magazine:

> *Eagles can do a great deal to combat juvenile delinquency. Eagles are outstanding, experienced, respected men. By working with law enforcement agencies and providing guidance for selected children, Eagles might well direct many coming citizens away from the path of crime. Youth today needs our assistance more than ever before, and we cannot refuse its call.*

It was following the publication of this article that the Fraternal Order of Eagles established the National Eagles Youth Guidance Commission and began a series of local, national, and international youth-serving undertakings.[26]

When Hoover, in the mid-1960's, began to detect signs of the rebellious activity of youngsters, which grew in intensity during the latter part of the decade, he again addressed the responsibility of parents for the actions of their offspring. Thankfully, he said, less than 5% of the young people were becoming involved in serious criminal activities:

> But there can be no doubt that our juvenile crime problem is a most serious one. It is an indictment of our moral standards in both the home and the community in many areas. A drastic decline of parental authority in some segments of our society is one big cause of the rise of juvenile crime. In some respects, a number of our juveniles are victims of a society where discipline has been replaced by indulgence. They have been cheated out of a sense of responsibility and a respect for authority... .
>
> Law-enforcement agencies, schools, churches, and other organizations of society can help, but they are poor substitutes for responsible parents. If we can eliminate parental delinquency, we will virtually wipe out juvenile delinquency at the same time. [27]

During his lifetime, it was often said that J. Edgar Hoover *was* the FBI. Perhaps he felt that way, realizing, as history has shown, that it would not be the same without him. And his dedication to the Bureau and his country, could hardly be challenged. During one of his discussions about Italy with Art Cammarota, he said he had never been outside the United States and, rather wistfully, commented that he had always wanted to visit Davos, Switzerland, the birthplace of his mother, to whom he was very devoted. He explained that he considered that his responsibilities to the United States and to the FBI precluded his foreign travel.[28]

That may account for the fact that he could not seem to divorce himself from that alter ego, the FBI, even when he received highly tempting offers from the world outside the Bureau. The man had numerous opportunities to accept positions that promised much more money or prestige. One was the editorship of *True Detective* magazine at $100,000 a year, a fabulous sum at the time. He declined the position of Head of Race Course Security at a huge salary. Corporate heads frequently courted him, but he repeatedly turned them down. Howard Hughes offered him an executive position and told him to name his own salary; Hoover elected to stay with the FBI. [29]

In the true tradition of an American hero, J. Edgar Hoover, who had served as Director of the FBI for 48 years, remained in his position until the day of his death and died with his boots on May 2, 1972. In a eulogy to him, Chief Justice of the United States Warren E. Burger stated, "He was firm in his demands for excellence but he always demanded more of himself than from others, and his high standards produced the institution that is, in a very real sense, the lengthened shadow of a man." [30]

THE LENGTHENED SHADOW OF A MAN

As this active and outgoing man was honored in life, so were the outpourings of tributes to him heard across the length and breadth of the nation upon his sudden and unexpected demise when he dropped dead in his home. For intensity, they would rival those accorded Princess Diana of England when she died so tragically in an automobile accident.

Sports writer Bob Considine paid tribute to him in his column in the Baltimore *News American* on May 7, 1972:

J. Edgar Hoover's troubles with the political leftists rested, I suspect, on the fact that they were always catching him red-handed, holding high the American flag.

That they didn't particularly like nor understand.

The man was an uncompromising patriot, an increasingly unused word which is still, however, not marked archaic in Webster's Collegiate Dictionary. "One who loves his country and zealously supports its authority and interests."

He was proud to be one. He resolutely opposed organizations and individuals he felt were out to do us in, or fracture the law. It must have been especially cold comfort to him to go after the Berrigans,* for he was basically a deeply religious man. But there was the evidence, delivered by a scoundrelly informant, and Hoover felt he must act... .

For the better part of half a century, Hoover never stopped hammering away with righteous indignation at public enemies (and private foes) ranging from Communists to car thieves, Bundists to baby-snatchers, Black Panthers to Mafia Godfathers. A tough cop isn't in the business to make friends.

Toward the end of a long interview... with President Lyndon Johnson [he was] asked to name the man he considered to be the greatest living American.

The President looked briefly into his Dr. Pepper, rocked his heavy White House rocking chair, and said "J. Edgar Hoover."

We must have looked slightly surprised, for LBJ continued in his best John Wayne manner, "Without Hoover, this country would have gone Communist 30 years ago."... .

John Edgar Hoover, one of the rather rare public figures ever born in Washington, D.C., put in a full day's work, the last day of his life. When he entered what became his FBI it was corrupt enough to employ that ultimate scoundrel, Gaston B. Means. When he left, against his will, it was the world's most towering symbol of law enforcement ... his imperishable monument.[1]

The Considine tribute is representative of many carried in publications across the nation, examples of which are included in Appendix C.

**The World Almanac and Book of Facts, 1974*, p. 981, recorded that the Reverend Philip Berrigan, Josephite order, with his brother the Reverend Daniel Berrigan of the Jesuit order, conducted raids on draft boards, destroying their records. This thrust them into the vanguard of radical Catholic antiwar activists.

On the same day that Hoover passed away, Congressman W. S. (Bill) Stuckey, Jr., of Georgia introduced a concurrent resolution in the House expressing the sense of the Congress that his body should lie in state in the U.S. Capitol Building. Congressman Stuckey said, "I cannot think of a more dedicated man than J. Edgar Hoover. He built the FBI to its stature of today and consequently has made the country a safer one both from within and without."

Both the Senate and the House conducted special sessions to pay tribute to Hoover. A book covering these sessions, including praise by 147 members of Congress, was published pursuant to Senate Concurrent Resolution No. 64. Excerpts are included in Appendix A.

One of the more touching tributes was pronounced by Congressman Frank E Denholm of South Dakota:

> *No one has served with greater dedication. Mr. Hoover was a man of compassion, decency, dignity, and destiny.... This is a sad day in May. J. Edgar Hoover is dead.... There are some that may rejoice but the multitudes shall sorrow — for today he has left in honor to his surest reward.... I join in sorrow, for today a leader of men — a man among men — is no more.* [2]

But how quickly people tend to forget. And the loss of memory was triggered in part by the Church Committee which, assisted by a staff devoted to its objectives, did a hatchet job on Hoover. The hearings were highly politicized and played to the TV cameras which recorded every public session.

After testifying before the Committee and leaving the hearing room, I would observe its chairman, Frank Church, standing in the outside hall basking under a shower of klieg lights, with television cameras grinding, and giving points he wished to make to enhance his then undeclared candidacy for the Democratic Party's nomination for President. On such occasions, the hearings were recessed in time for Senator Church's comments to make the prime-time newscasts. The more outrageous the comments, the more national TV exposure.

Bias and selective highlighting of information were adopted by the committee in publishing the results of its efforts. In effect, it actually served as a milch cow for the printed and electronic media, as well as authors since then who have written about Hoover.

Since his death in 1972, the elite media in the United States have often sifted the facts regarding his stewardship of the FBI through their own ideological sieve and created a climate which has popularized the sport of vilifying him. Many people under 40 years of age, who don't remember him when he was alive, have all too frequently been led by biased reporting to look upon him and the organization he headed for nearly one-fourth of our nation's history as of 1972 as one huge wart, with hardly an outcropping of truth, conscience, or integrity.

If this were so, why was he not fired by one of the eight presidents or 16 attorneys general under whom he served? And why did Congress, upon his death, accord him the ultimate honor reserved for presidents and military heroes? His body lay in state in the Rotunda of the U.S. Capitol on the catafalque on which had rested the coffins of just seven presidents, including Lincoln, Eisenhower, and Kennedy. He was the only civilian in the history of our country to be so honored. Thousands filed past the bier to pay him respect.

As he lay in state, Chief Justice of the Supreme Court Warren E. Burger hailed him as "a man who epitomized the American dream of patriotism, dedication to duty, and successful attainment." He remarked on the fact that when Hoover left his office for the last time, the portrait of Chief Justice Harlan Fiske Stone was the one ornament that dominated his office. He continued:

> He was a man of high principle whose beliefs were based on Christian faith and he was steadfast in his beliefs throughout his entire life. He was a man of great courage who would not sacrifice principle to public clamor... . He was not ashamed to express his patriotism and love of country or his Christian beliefs that guided his life... . I am proud to join in this salute to a great American who served his country so well and earned the admiration of all who believe in ordered liberty. [3]

An overflow crowd gathered at the National Presbyterian Church on May 4 for the funeral service where President Nixon, in a lengthy eulogy to the Director, said,

> J. Edgar Hoover was one of the giants. His long life brimmed over with magnificent achievement and dedicated service to this country which he loved so well... .
>
> He personified integrity; he personified honor; he personified principle; he personified courage; he personified discipline; he personified dedication; he personified loyalty; he personified patriotism... .
>
> The good J. Edgar Hoover has done will not die. The profound principles associated with his name will not fade away... .
>
> Each of us stands forever in his debt. In the years ahead, let us cherish his memory. Let us be true to his legacy. Let us honor him as he would surely want us to do... .
>
> J. Edgar Hoover loved the law of his God. He loved the law of his country and he richly earned peace through all eternity. [4]

In my mind, J. Edgar Hoover, the man I knew well as my boss, deserved these tributes. When I joined the FBI in 1942, I considered him a national hero even then because of his successful battle against crime during the 1930s and the early stages of subversion. Nothing that has happened since has changed my opinion of him, and I had the distinct advantage of knowing the man much better than many who have denigrated him.

Special agents of the Bureau who worked under him hold him in equally high regard. At the gathering of these men at his graveside in Washington's Congressional Cemetery on May 2, 1997, to commemorate the twenty-fifth anniversary of his death, several tributes were paid him. Patrick J. Mullany, President of the Society of Former Special Agents of the FBI, spoke of him in reverent terms and said: "Despite the modern day pundits and would-be historians, we ask of them to fairly look at this man as the world should and not repeat stories that have absolutely nothing to do with the character that we knew for so many years as Director."

One tribute evidencing great devotion was paid by former Special

Agent, now blacksmith, Daniel R. Brainard of Spicewood, Texas. In 1994, when visiting the cemetery, Dan was shocked at the overall deterioration of the grounds and noted that the grave site of the former Director was in very poor condition because of severe budget constraints at the cemetery. The Society took on the task to improve the Hoover grave site and Dan volunteered to design and develop a permanent enclosure for it.

He constructed a hand-forged, wrought-iron fence, consisting of dozens of spindle-topped pickets, each of which he pounded out over a white-hot coke fire. His remarks in describing the process and comparing it to his service under Director Hoover voiced the thoughts in our minds: "You start out with raw steel, not unlike you start out in life, and you beat on it until it takes the shape that you're looking for. When you get through the process, the steel takes a shape precisely like the pride that each and every one of us takes in having served."

Pointing to his fence with a hinged gate bearing the seal of the Federal Bureau of Investigation, Dan continued, "It's going to be there long, long, long after we are gone, just like the pride that we take in having been of various types of service to the Bureau."

Virtues and vices. There are now in the public domain perhaps more vices attributed to J. Edgar Hoover than a normally complex man develops in a lifetime. It is only fair to place his virtues on the other side of the scale that weighs the life and character of a man.

I remember him for his devotion to duty, for his dedication to his country, for his foresight, for his regard for the rights of others, for his humor, for his compassion... for his virtues.

A Nation Honors a Distinguished Citizen - The body of J. Edgar Hoover in the flag-drapped casket lies in the Rotunda of the Nation's Capitol. This picture was taken by a bureau photographer from the dome of the Rotunda.

APPENDIX A

A sampling of tributes paid to J. Edgar Hoover by 63 Democrats and 84 Republicans during special sessions of Congress the day he died, May 2, 1972.

SENATORS

Hubert H. Humphrey (D-Minnesota) "J. Edgar Hoover has been for better than 40 years one of the central figures of our times — a man of unquestioned ability, personal integrity, and professional competence ... Presidents without regard to party have placed their trust and faith in him and the organization that he directed. Inevitably, a man of such strong will and powerful position was subject to controversy. His dedication to the Nation and the law will be living monuments to his illustrious career. In his death the Nation has lost a great patriot and an outstanding servant."

Bob Dole (R-Kansas) "Mr. Hoover's death leaves a void which can never be completely filled. But his career will always stand as a model and an ideal for others who undertake the challenges of serving their country and its people."

Len B. Jordan (R-Idaho) "J. Edgar Hoover was a true patriot. He was true to the best ideals of republican government and to the rights of man. He did more than most to insure the blessings of liberty, of peace, and of freedom from fear and harm for the greatest number. He used the vested power of his office to build a better America. We owe J. Edgar Hoover a profound debt for the dedication of his life for the upbuilding of America. He takes his rightful place among those great Americans whose deeds live on, and his legacy will remain as a constant inspiration."

Robert C. Byrd (D-West Virginia): "J. Edgar Hoover was an American institution.... . I'm glad that he was permitted to remain at the head of the FBI despite his age. Like all unusual men, he was controversial, but I believe he had many more supporters than detractors."

Robert P. Griffin (R-Michigan): "Few men are legends in their own time. J. Edgar Hoover was.... . It is the understatement of ours to say that this man will be very difficult to replace."

James B. Allen (D-Alabama) "Mr. Hoover was not only a fearless and incorruptible law-enforcement officer, but he was also a loyal and dedicated American whose aim in life was to support, defend, and sustain our great Republic in the lofty principles upon which it was founded."

Ernest F. Hollings (D-South Carolina) "I found Mr. Hoover to be a very thorough, very objective, very effective, and very brilliant law-enforcement officer. I realize that in the past several years his competence has come into issue. In fact, it has been suggested on this floor by some who are running for high office that if they were elected to high office their first act would be to discharge Mr. Hoover. This hurt me somewhat."

Herman E. Talmadge (D-Georgia) "J. Edgar Hoover was a tough law-and-order man... . His record will precede him throughout the annals of American history. He is entitled to the respect and appreciation of all law-abiding Americans everywhere."

William V. Roth (R-Delaware) "When Mr. Hoover accepted the post of acting Director of the Bureau in 1924, he faced a formidable task. It is to his credit that the small, poorly organized Bureau became the world-renowned crime-fighting force that it is today."

Henry M. (Scoop) Jackson (D-Washington) "(W)hat J. Edgar Hoover did not do is just as important [as what he did]. He did not let the FBI get involved in politics. He did not let the FBI extend itself into matters better handled by others. And he did not let the FBI be tainted by corruption throughout his long tenure."

Claiborne Pell (D-Rhode Island) "Director Hoover is the very symbol of the FBI that he created and to which he gave his life. His abhorrence of corruption, his high standards of law enforcement and police work, and his personal drive and courage all contributed to the making of his most important memorial—the Federal Bureau of Investigation itself."

William Proxmire (D-Wisconsin) "This nation owes an unusual debt to Mr. Hoover. Ironically that debt is in the very area in which he was most vigorously criticized. He developed a police force

Former Special Agent Dan Brainard speaks during the 25th anniversary of Hoover's death.

consistent with democratic principles. He did this because he insisted on indoctrinating his agents with as zealous a dedication to our civil liberties as to their determination to enforce the law and protect this Nation against its enemies in peace and war."

James L. Buckley (D-New York) "(T)he death of J. Edgar Hoover is a great loss to all who love freedom....Among his most important contributions to our Nation was his forthright and eloquent defense of the principles underlying our national life against the attacks, both open and clandestine, of those who would subvert and ultimately destroy those principles. He early recognized the evil of modern totalitarianism and his superb efforts to thwart both the Nazi and Communist attempts at domestic subversion put all Americans in his debt. Today, perhaps more than ever before, our Nation needs the kind of dedication, integrity, and love of country that marked J. Edgar Hoover's life."

John G. Tower (R-Texas) "FBI Director Hoover was, on many occasions, a most controversial figure, but his devotion to duty and his love of country were unexcelled... . Mr. Hoover was criticized during his lifetime by those who claimed he was overzealous, those who resented his rigid regulations, and those who claimed he was too old to do the job... . How much better to be criticized for zeal and determination than for lethargy which would allow criminals to roam free and which would let scandal flourish."

Howard W. Cannon (D-Nevada) "J. Edgar Hoover molded an institution which has become a bastion in the Nation's fight against crime, communism, and other forms of subversion... . Yet, ever cognizant of the dangers of concentrated power, he consistently opposed every effort to make the Bureau a national police force, and insisted that agents meticulously observe the rights of criminals apprehended." (Senate Document No. 93-68, op. cit., pp. 1-26.)

CONGRESSMEN

M. G. (Gene) Snyder (R-Kentucky) "[Hoover] was, at different times, the idol and the ogre. To a great majority of American citizens he was the permanent embodiment of the patriot. To students of communism, he was the foremost authority on the domestic practice of subversion. To the voter and taxpayer he was the staunchest bulwark against organized crime and the exploitation of the innocent. But to some others — a minority, but a vocal one — he represented the American equivalent of a Gestapo or KGB chief. I join the above-mentioned three categories in rejecting the latter one. I rejected it while he was living and I reject it at his death. History will vindicate me in this judgment — just as history will vindicate the man."

Edward P. Boland (D-Massachusetts) "Within the past few years, of course, Hoover was at sword's point with much of the political world's liberal community. His sulfurous controversies with the New Left are still smoking. Often attackd for his blunt and outspoken manner — even for what his critics charged was a kind of lofty moral dogmatism — Hoover steadfastly refused to surrender his responsibilities. The merits of these disputes... remain debatable.... J. Edgar Hoover's fame in American law enforcement will long outlive the controversies that clouded his declining years."

William G. Bray (R-Indiana) "I am sure he was always proud of the fact that the most dedicated of his enemies, and the most vicious of his detractors, were also the most deadly and unswerving enemies of the American Republic and its citizens.... . I am equally sure he must have counted it a signal honor to be the symbol of the forces that stood between these people and his country."

Bill Nichols (D-Alabama) "America has lost a great patriot in J. Edgar Hoover. This great American was indeed a legend in his own time, and his influence will continue to be felt in our Nation for many years to come."

Richard H. Ichord (D-Missouri) "Few men have been as universally admired or will be missed as greatly.... . His memory will be deeply emblazoned in the hearts and memories of the people of this Nation and shall be a perpetual monument to him."

John H. Rousselot (R-California) "Some in this House have seen fit to be critical and in some cases, actually misrepresent J. Edgar Hoover's record. Even with this unwarranted harassment and sometimes unfair criticism, John Edgar Hoover remained on the highly principled record of the law, good faith, and meritorious performance."

Frank J. Brasco (D-New York) "From bootleggers and Nazi sympathizers to Communists and hijackers, his personal example, men, and organization put the cause of our country first. All America is the better overall for his life's work."

Peter N. Kyros (D-Maine) "Even those who most vigorously disagreed with J. Edgar Hoover saw in him a man whose personal qualities commanded respect. He was a man of extraordinary discipline, unquestioned loyalty, and great personal integrity."

James H. Quillen (R-Tennessee) "To millions of Americans, Mr. Hoover was considered the Dean of Law Enforcement. He did more for the cause of law and order than any other person in the history of this land.... . He was a man of great power and influence who used these qualities in constructive measures for the good of all Americans."

John G. Schmitz (R-California) "(T)wo Americans died this week, John Edgar Hoover and Louis Francis Budenz.... . Both of these men made important contributions to our country's knowledge of the Communist enemy.... . Both men were smeared by the leftist press for daring to expose the full truth about our Communist enemy."

James Harvey (R-Michigan) "He became, as President Johnson so aptly said in 1964, 'a household word, a hero to millions of citizens and an anathema to evil men.' "

Earl B. Ruth (R-North Carolina) "Perhaps his job required controversy and critics. If it did, then he was a remarkable man to have continued to serve his agency and his country in the finest tradition possible."

Chalmers P. Wylie (R-Ohio) "Since his appointment in 1924, he has served every President elected by the American people and they in turn have expressed their total confidence in his ability and integrity.... (H)is record in the service and defense of the Republic in which he so deeply believed and loved will be the ultimate, fitting, historical eulogy for J. Edgar Hoover."

La Mar Baker (R-Tennessee) "The internal security of this country is stronger, because of the vigilance of the FBI under J. Edgar Hoover. Not only we but future generations of Americans, owe him a great debt of gratitude."

C. W. (Bill) Young (R-Florida) "While J. Edgar Hoover was held in contempt by enemies of our country and those who would change America by any means to serve their own ends, he was revered by the vast majority of his fellow citizens, who love their country and are pledged to its continued preservation."

Lawrence J. Hogan (R-Maryland) "It has been a source of deep regret to me that in the past few years, Mr. Hoover and the FBI have been subjected to so much unfair and unjustified criticism.... Because of his unblemished record in service to the country, some of our colleagues, for reasons best known to them, have joined in this cacophony of unwarranted abuse and criticism."

G. V. (Sonny) Montgomery (D-Mississippi) "A man of supreme faith and undaunted courage, J. Edgar Hoover believed passionately in the inherent good of America; he said what he believed and felt no necessity to apologize for it. His faith and devotion to the causes he defended were never doubted by any man, even his most ardent enemies."

Ed Edmondson (D-Oklahoma) "(N)o American has been more hated or more feared by the forces of organized crime and the organizers of internal subversion and revolution.... He was our first line of defense against the enemies of the Republic — both foreign and domestic."

Melvin Price (D-Illinois) "Having served the U.S. Government longer than any man, Director Hoover has earned a special place in American History.... He is clearly a unique individual whom the American people will long remember as a dedicated and loyal public official."

Robert L. F. Sikes (D-Florida) "J. Edgar Hoover stood guard over America through the trials of the twenties, the turmoil of the thirties and the horrors of war in the forties, fifties, and sixties, and until his final breath today, he gave no quarter to those who sought to bring down the America he knew and cherished... . He has done much to maintain for future generations the America he loved."

Harold D. Donohue (D-Massachusetts) "In the midst of constantly changing customs and values J. Edgar Hoover remained a national and world champion of those qualities and virtues that our founders regarded as the enduring strengths of this Nation... . The noble manner in which he carried out his responsibilities will forever be an inspiration to those seeking peace and justice throughout the world."

Thomas G. Abernethy (D-Mississippi) "Mr. Hoover had stability. Occasionally attacked in recent years, particularly by some of those to the left, by Reds and Communists who would overthrow this Government, by just plain radicals, and sometimes by well-intentioned people, he never lost his cool... . I dare say there will never be another to gain the height, the respect, and the prestige gained by J Edgar Hoover as the Director of the Federal Bureau of Investigation."

Gerald R. Ford (R-Michigan) "Mr. Hoover was a veritable rock of strength, a man looked to with a feeling that here was an individual with the greatest integrity. He was incorruptible. He was unswerving in his devotion to duty. I cannot think of any other American, certainly in my lifetime who served his Nation more faithfully or more steadfastly. America's debt to J. Edgar Hoover is great."

Carl Albert (D-Oklahoma) "I do not think there is any doubt in anyone's mind that he was totally dedicated to preserving a law-abiding, orderly way of life in this country. He was first, last, and always a great patriot. He was determined to protect it from its enemies from within and without. Not only in his dedication but in his ability he must be considered one of the greatest officials in the history of our Government."

Hale Boggs (D-Louisiana) "Last year I directed some criticism at some of the policies of the Bureau with which I was in disagreement, but at no time was that criticism directed at the Director. I said it then and I say it now... . There is no man who has served this country with greater dedication, with greater love, and with greater productivity... . [Hoover] leaves a great name, he leaves a country which respects and admires the magnificent contribution that he has made to it and to all of us."

John B. Anderson (R-Illinois) "When J. Edgar Hoover came before the Rooney Subcommittee on Appropriations in early March, he said: 'You are honored by your friends and you are distinguished by your enemies. I have been very distinguished.' It is certainly true that the late Director was distinguished by his enemies, but this sustained tribute here this afternoon bears ample testimony to the fact that he was also distinguished and honored by his friends." (Senate Document No. 93-68, op. cit., pp.29-92.)

APPENDIX B

The following information regarding honorary degrees and awards conferred upon Hoover was contained in a release by the FBI captioned "J. Edgar Hoover" included in a "Press Kit Presented for use of Press, Radio, & TV Newsmen" at the dedication of the J. Edgar Hoover FBI Building on September 30, 1975.

HONORARY DEGREES

- The George Washington University
- Pennsylvania Military College
- New York University
- Kalamazoo College
- Westminster College
- Oklahoma Baptist University
- Georgetown University
- Drake University
- University of the South
- University of Notre Dame
- St. John's University Law School
- Rutgers University
- University of Arkansas
- Holy Cross College
- Seton Hall College
- Marquette University
- Pace College
- Morris Harvey College
- The Catholic University of America

AWARDS

- March 8, 1946: Hoover was presented the Medal for Merit by President Truman.
- November 13, 1954: He was awarded the Cardinal Gibbons Medal by the National Alumni Association of The Catholic University of America for outstanding service to his country.
- May 27, 1955: President Eisenhower presented to him the National Security Medal for his outstanding service in the field of intelligence relating to National Security.
- January 27, 1958: President Eisenhower presented to Hoover the President's Award for Distinguished Federal Civilian Service.
- April 28, 1958: He received the U.S. Chamber of Commerce "Great Living American" award.
- June 16, 1959: He was presented the "American Citizen" award by the Junior Order United American Mechanics.
- August 4, 1961: The U.S. Senate passed a resolution commending Hoover upon his 37 years of "distinguished service to the United States as Director of the FBI."
- December 7, 1961: Hoover received the Mutual of Omaha Criss Award for "his outstanding contribution to the personal security and safety of the American public."
- August 14, 1962: The Order Knights of Pythias conferred its first annual Distinguished Service Award upon Hoover.

- November 9, 1962: The Jewish War Veterans of the USA presented Hoover their highest award, the "Gold Medal of Merit," which was inscribed: "In recognition of outstanding and meritorious service in the battle for civil rights and liberties. His integrity and devotion to justice will be remembered forever."
- November 16, 1963: He received the "Pro Deo et Juventute Award" from the National Catholic Youth Organization Hebrew Congregation "for his unswerving devotion to the betterment of brotherhood among all races, creeds and colors."
- November 24, 1964: He received the "Sword of Loyola Award" because "his life has been one of selfless devotion to country and God."
- December 12, 1964: Hoover received the "Gold Medal" of The Pennsylvania Society "for distinguished achievement."
- October 19, 1965: He was awarded the "Grand Cross of Honour" by the Supreme Council, 33 degree Scottish Rite.

On several occasions Hoover also received the "George Washington Honor Medal" and other awards from the Freedom Foundation at Valley Forge

Appendix C

Deseret News (Salt Lake City, Utah) May 3, 1972.

[An] institution is often defined as the lengthened shadow of the man at the top.

That is the secret of the success of the Federal Bureau of Investigation over the past half-century: It was an extension of the complete honesty and incorruptibility of J. Edgar Hoover....

It was Hoover's iron discipline... [that] was the very foundation upon which he built the FBI into a respected, world-famous organization noted for its integrity... .

It is noteworthy that critics who have differed with Hoover on his handling of problems did not question his good motives. Among these was Senator Edmund Muskie, who once called for Hoover's removal from office. Declared Muskie:

"While some of us may have questioned some of his approaches in recent years, no one could question his loyalty and dedication to his country."

Danville Register (Danville, Virginia) May 5, 1972.

John Edgar Hoover...though he lived in a violent world...was not a violent man. He saw himself as a soldier, fighting for his country in an endless battle against crime and stealth and treason. It was not the battlefield he would have chosen — as a boy he wanted to be a minister — but fate made it his and he marched forward (sans peur et sans reproche).

It was said of... Hoover in his later years that he was the most powerful man in Washington. There was usually a glint of disapprobation in the statement, as if his power derived from secret files and covert blackmail. Those who knew him, his work, and the Federal Bureau of Investigation which he had built... to the world's finest investigative arm, were aware of the injustice and meanness of the allegation, whether implied or explicit.

During his years as the FBI's Director, he never used such powers as he had for personal advancement or to do harm. He had no ideas of advancement from the moment he became head of the FBI. The Bureau was his life, a reflection of his drive and philosophy... . Had he been an ambitious man, the Bureau would, indeed, have become what his enemies attempted to make it out to be — a secret police. His only ambition was to build the FBI into the most efficient and unassailable instrument of the law enforcement process.

J. Edgar Hoover's power was considerable, but it stemmed from his inner qualities. He was criticized for being a harsh disciplinarian, but this he was because he knew that to be effective the FBI had to be like Caesar's wife — not only free of scandal but free of the appearance of scandal. And he insisted on that prescription not only for himself but for the entire Bureau, down to the lowest file clerk... .

What set [him] apart from other men in Washington was the utter sincerity of his belief in the Calvinistic ethic which was the cornerstone of his religion, in the ordinary virtues which are no longer so ordinary, in the patriotism which echoed and re-echoed through his speeches and public statements... . And because he believed in these things so undeviatingly, he prevailed over others whose moral muscle had grown flabby in compromise. This was the secret of his power, however unlikely this may seem to a cynical age.

The people of America, the men and women of the towns and plains, understood this far better than those of inflated intellect who spent their days trying to discover the dirt under his fingernails... .

[I]t is easy to forget that John Edgar Hoover had a warm human side which only a few observed. He loved to play jokes on his friends and to be the target of their banter. He was dedicated to the $2.00 window at the race tracks, and he found relaxation at the ball park. He enjoyed a pre-prandial drink in the evening and those few hours in the week when he could read light fiction or listen to undemanding music. He found satisfaction traversing again and again the words of his favorite writer, Henry Thoreau.

Jackson Sun (Jackson, Tennessee) May 4, 1972
"As much as he loved the bureau, he hated communism. He reduced the Communist party in the United States to a shell, riddling the organization with agents so that members never were sure whom they were talking to."

That fact alone, from a wire service report on the death of... J. Edgar Hoover, is sufficient for the nation to be forever indebted to this dedicated public servant whose record is one long and unbroken progression of competence loyalty and effectiveness... .

Despite... Hoover's enormous contribution of service to this country, he did not, especially near the end of his career, escape the barbs of critics, most of whom used his increasing age as an excuse for their attack.

But the record speaks best. During the years of Hoover's leadership, there never was a known case of scandal inside the FBI, and Hoover's stock remark about his agents was: "They can't be bought."

The nation has been fortunate to have had a J. Edgar Hoover. It could use many, many more like him.

Watertown Public Opinion (Watertown, South Dakota) May 5, 1972.

J. Edgar Hoover [was]... the most indefatigable defender of law and order any nation ever had. Hoover's imprint in the vital field of law enforcement will be all but imperishable.

The bulldog-jawed "No. 1 G Man,"... was far more than a prominent policeman. To a considerable degree, he was the spokesman for all law enforcement, especially in its relationship to the body of statute law which forms the cornerstone of government as Americans know it.

One of Hoover's last messages, the last, in fact, to appear in the monthly FBI Law Enforcement Bulletin, expressed his convictions in an effective nutshell, profiling a great American and his dedication to the ideal by which he lived:

"Our greatest democratic heritage is the rule of law. It is the foundation for and guardian of the rights, liberties and orderly progress we enjoy... .

"The struggle to insure the rights of the individual and his social organization by written decree has roots which reach far back into antiquity. The authors of our Constitution were mindful of this when they drafted that historic document."

It is a tribute to Hoover's dedication and devotion that the organization he led... remains one of the great bulwarks and guardians of freedom.

And certainly well in the forefront of history's most distinguished champions of that freedom must rest the name of J. Edgar Hoover.

Phoenix Gazette (Phoenix, Arizona) May 4, 1972
J. Edgar Hoover is dead.

For almost half a century Americans have slept more soundly at night because he lived.

Enemies of the United States rejoiced at the news. Their agents among us felt safer for it. That strange domestic clique which finds nothing to criticize in Communist aggression and terrorism, but is outraged daily by our own resistance to it, has set about already trying to rewrite the history of J. Edgar Hoover and his times.

They can't make it stick.

When one man has survived so many storms and come to the age of 77 still respected where respect counts and feared where fear is a compliment, still fighting for the security of his country, still true to principles which have made his name a synonym for integrity and honor, rewriting history to tarnish his image would be a task beyond the mean abilities of his detractors.

The total trust placed in Mr. Hoover by eight presidents and 16 attorneys general, not to mention the tough loyalty accorded him by the most and the best of his men, would take more expunging of the Record than is possible in a country where a shred of free speech and free thought remains. Mr. Hoover has written a record that no adjectives can embellish, no attacks diminish... .

J. Edgar Hoover, for all he was and all he did, was an authentic giant of modern times, a man unafraid and incorruptible. The nation will miss him, as such rare patriots are always missed.

Boston Globe, Boston Herald Traveler, Boston Record American (Boston, Massachusetts) May 4, 1972.
J. Edgar Hoover's devotion to the United States was, as President Nixon said, unparalleled. He was a legend in his own time... .

His honesty, integrity and enduring devotion to duty were recognized even by his critics. For most men, that would be tribute enough. But Mr. Hoover was no ordinary_man. He leaves behind more than words of praise, more than memories for those who knew him to recall at their leisure. He leaves us with the example he set... .

For in a world filled with tyrannies both petty and great, a world where anonymous millions endure repression and live in fear of their own governments and police, J. Edgar Hoover wrought no less than a miracle. With his own two hands he molded a force that none except his country's enemies need fear.

Mr. Hoover held an awesome power. He knew it. It did not corrupt him. To his everlasting credit, he used this power to protect, not to oppress... .

Wrongdoers in high places and in low feared Mr. Hoover and his G-Men. He and his men could not be bought. And the wrongdoers knew this well.

It is a reflection of the man.

<u>Florida Times-Union</u> (No city given) May 3, 1972

The FBI... is Hoover's monument. He molded it, shaped it and watched over it... .

He fought powerful politicians to keep politics out of it. He fought the crooks who were in it when he was appointed and he tossed them out.

He fought attempts to give it so much authority that it would become what he always dreaded, "a national police." He fought attempts to emasculate it.

He successfully resisted attempts to relax the strict standards he set for agents.

While he fought, he built. And it wasn't bureaucratic empire-building but rather day by day infusion of the standards of probity and respect for human rights that should characterize good law enforcement.

When Hoover grew up in Washington, he was impressed by the fact that in the game of "cops and robbers," all of his playmates wanted to be the robbers. That was the glamorous role... .

After Hoover succeeded in building something worthwhile — a police agency that has become a model, not only in the United States but in the world — he authorized publicity on the exploits of his agents.

"If there is going to be publicity," he said, "let it be on the side of law and order."

The youngsters of the 1930s were switched from a steady diet of John Dillinger, Machine Gun Kelly and Pretty Boy Floyd, and the exploits of the "G-Men" made it once again respectable in childhood games to play the part of the "cop."

Behind the publicity was, however, a reality with which America could feel comfortable. The agents of the FBI were held to high physical and educational standards, they were superbly trained, they were innovators in scientific law enforcement techniques and Hoover's strict prohibition against the third degree heightened public confidence in the agency.

"The test tube is mightier than the rubber hose," Hoover said, and time and time again, the National Crime Laboratory and the FBI's fingerprint file — both Hoover innovations — bore out the truth of that saying.

<u>Chicago Today</u> (Chicago, Illinois) May 3, 1972. [copied as written, including short forms of words, and typos.]

J. Edgar Hoover's death is like finding part of the landscape suddenly missing. It leaves an emptiness where most of us, thruout our lives, had been aware of a looming figure — comforting to many, threatening to others, but always there.

By governmental standards of permanency, Hoover seemed as everlasting and unchanging as the pyramids... . [H]e and the FBI were synonmys in the public's mind, and his name came to have many others! Strength, permanence, stability, order, security... .

In a government built on checks and balances, separation of powers, the belief that no man is absolutely right, Hoover was an anomaly. He had virtual one-man authority over a powerful arm of government; his policies and administrative decisions over the FBI were not tested against other viewpoints, they were simply obeyed. His determination to keep total authority in his own hands in spite of rising criticism heaped up more fuel for criticism.

And yet this frightening concentration of power was also the greatest proof of Hoover's integrity. For all the temptations and the opportunities for abuse, Hoover did not abuse it... . He took over a small, unimpressively staffed agency shoot thru with politics and patronage, and turned it into an efficient, finely-tuned organization of professionals whose services to this country are beyond calculating. And he dedicated his life totally to keeping it that way... .

With J. Edgar Hoover gone the FBI remains. It is his monument, and no man could ask for more.

Times Union (Albany, New York);
Seattle Post-Intelligencer (Seattle, Washington)
 both May 3, 1972
Item: J. Edgar Hoover, the nation's chief law enforcement officer for 48 years, dies suddenly in Washington at age 77.

To the best of his prodigious ability, J. Edgar Hoover served his country. His devotion to the United States was, as President Nixon said, unparalleled... .

His friends lauded his honesty, integrity and enduring devotion to duty. Even his critics granted him these attributes. For most men that would be tribute enough... .

He leaves the nation a living monument — not to himself, but to the ideals on which the nation is founded — the Federal Bureau of Investigation. In this imperfect world, Mr. Hoover's achievement is outstanding... .

The FBI's total success in dealing with the threat of Nazi sabotage and spying during World War Two, and the amazing complete infiltration of Communist Party cells in the Cold War of the 1950s, provided ample evidence of Mr. Hoover's efficiency... .

President Nixon put it best:

"For millions he was the symbol and embodiment of the values he cherished most: courage, partiotism [sic], dedication to his country and a granite-like honesty and integrity."

Las Vegas Sun (Las Vegas, Nevada) May 4, 1972, Article by Hank Greenspan.

The man who could say "no."

John Edgar Hoover could and did to Presidents and attorneys general, and to members of Congress, as well, whenever attempts were made to use the Federal Bureau of Investigation for what he considered improper purposes.

There were efforts made to turn the FBI into a political investigative arm of the President and the party in power, but the only man to ever head the agency had enough stature to refuse to play the game... .

With all the vast capabilities of the FBI at his command, J. Edgar Hoover could have become a virtual dictator, ruthlessly destroying his enemies and even directing the course of the other branches of government through fear.

Ours is the only nation in history where a man of such potential power rejected these opportunities.

The nation is indebted to him because he chose, instead, to defend our institutions and our system of justice... .

Were there no J. Edgar Hoover, with his dedication and stature, who knows but what we might have awakened some morning and found we had no liberties left at all. (Senate Document No. 93-68, op. cit., pp, 179-272.)

Notes and Sources

Disciplinarian at the Helm

1. William B. Breuer, *J. Edgar Hoover and His G-Men* (Westport, CT/ London: Praeger: 1995), p.11; Don Whitehead, *The FBI Story: A Report to the American People* (New York: Random House, 1956), pp.55-7.

2. Breuer, *J. Edgar Hoover and His G-Men*, pp. 12-3.

3. Whitehead, *The FBI Story*, pp. 70-1.

4. Ibid., Forward.

5. Alan H. Belmont, *As I Recall It: Incidents in the Life of a G-Man*, unpublished manuscript, pp. 129-30.

Early Environment

1. *Encyclopaedia Britannica, Micropaedia,* Vol V, p. 124.

2. W. Cleon Skousen, "J. Edgar Hoover — As I Knew Him," *Behind The Scenes* (Salt Lake City, UT: The Freeman Institute, 1979).

3. Ibid.

4. *The Washington Times*, October 19, 1997, p.2; Darlene Clark Hine, editor, *Black Women in America* (Brooklyn, New York, 1993), p. 794..

Escalating Responsibilities

1. Whitehead, *The FBI Story,* p. 21.

2. Ibid., p. 37.

3. Hearings Before the Senate Select Committee to Study Governmental Operations With Respect to Intelligence Activities, (hereafter referred to as Church Committee), Vol. 6, p. 549.

4. Ibid. Vol. 6, p. 550.

5. Whitehead, *The FBI Story,* pp. 39-40, 46-7.

6. Church Committee, Vol.6, pp. 550-1.

7. Ibid., Vol. 6, p. 555.

8. Ibid., Vol. 6, pp. 555-6.

9. Ibid., Vol. 6, p. 556.

10. Ibid., Vol. 6, pp. 557-8.

11. Ibid., Vol. 6, pp. 558-9.

12. Ibid., Vol. 6, p. 560.

13. Ibid., Vol. 6, pp. 560-62—Memoranda of Hoover's meetings August 24 and 25, 1936, at the White House with FDR and Cordell Hull.

14. Socialist Workers Party et al. v Attorney General of the United States, et al., 73 Civ 3160 (TPG), pp. 7529 et seq., Defendants' Exhibit PC — (hereafter referred to as SWP trial); Church Committee Volume 6, pp. 563-66.

15. Directive of the President of the United States, September 6, 1939. See Statutory Authority for the FBI's Domestic Intelligence Activities: An Analysis Prepared for the Use of the Committee on Internal Security, House of Representatives, dated October 3, 1973, p. 58.

16. Whitehead, *The FBI Story,* pp. 170-1.

17. Ibid., pp. 177-80.

18. William B. Breuer, *Hitler's Undercover War: The Nazi Espionage Invasion of the USA,* (New York: St. Martin's Press, 1989), pp. 241-4, 258.

19. Whitehead, *The FBI Story,* Foreword.

20. Author's conversation with Richard G. Fletcher, Jr., October 4, 1997.

21. Whitehead, *The FBI Story,* Foreword.

22, *The World Almanac and Book of Facts, 1998* (Mahwah, New Jersey: K-III Reference Corporation, 1997), pp. 504, 572.

23. Encyclopaedia Britannica, Volume 19, p. 1011.

24. Robert Louis Benson and Michael Warner, editors, *Venona: Soviet Espionage and the American Response 1939-1957,* (Washington: National Security Agency and Central Intelligence Agency, 1996) pp. 117, 119.

25. From Hoover's Official and Confidential file No. 34. These files, 164 in all, were maintained in Hoover's outer office to restrict access to particularly sensitive information. Hereafter information from them will be referred to as O and C files, followed by the file number and, where appropriate, the serial number or its description.

26. Church Committee Book II, Final Report, p. 74.

27. Loch K. Johnson, *A Season of Inquiry: The Senate Intelligence Investigation* (Lexington, KY: The University Press of Kentucky, 1985), pp. 74, 97.

28. Aleksandr I. Solzhenitsyn, "A World Split Apart" (Washington Ethics and Public Policy Center, 1980) p. 9.

29. W. Mark Felt, *The FBI Pyramid From the Inside,* (New York: G. P. Putnam's Sons, 1979), p. 316.

30. Church Committee, Volume 6, p.283.

31. Report of House Judiciary Subcommittee on Civil and Constitutional Rights regarding the FBI Counterintelligence Programs, dated 11-20-74 and designated Serial No. 55, p. 46 - hereafter referred to as Judiciary Subcommittee Serial 55.

32. Report of the National Commission on Civil Disorders, 1968, Appendix C. p. 297.

33. Judiciary Subcommittee Serial 55, op. cit., pp. 45-6.

34. Jonathan Aiken, *Nixon: A Life,* (Washington: Regnery, 1991), pp. 412-3.

35. SWP trial, Brownell testimony beginning at p.5077.

36. Whitehead, *The FBI Story,* Foreword.

37. FBI Law Enforcement Bulletin, May 1, 1972, pp. 13-4.

HOOVER, WIRETAPS, AND BUGS

1. Olmstead v United States (277 U.S. 438); O and C files 129 serial 1, p.3; 164 serial 30, p.2.

2. O and C file, 164 serial 30, pp. 2-3.

3. Ibid., 129 serial 1, p. 4.

4. Nardone v United States (302 U.S. 379); O and C file 164 serial 30, p.3.

5. O and C file 164 serial 5.

6. Nardone v United States (308 U.S. 338); O and C file 129 serial 1, p.6.

7. O and C file 164 serial 27, Director's statement March 13, 1940.

8. Ibid., 164 serial 27, Department press release March 18, 1940.

9. Ibid., 164 serial 27, Excerpts from Director's address to National Academy March 30, 1940.

10. Ibid., 163 serial 3.

11. Ibid., 129 serial 6, FDR letter to Eliot, February 21, 1941.

12. Ibid., 129 serial 2, p.6.

13. Ibid., 129 serial 9.

14. *The New York Times,* October 9, 1941; O and C file 164 serial 10.

15. O and C file 164 serial 11.

16. Ibid., 164 serial 27, Department press release March 31, 1949.

17. Ibid., 164 serial, FBI press release January 13, 1950.

18. Ibid., 164 serial 30, p. 17.

19. Ibid., 163 serial 2.

20. Ibid., 164 serial 30, p.6.

21. Ibid., 114 serials 3, 6.

22. Ibid., 114 serial 10.

23. Ibid., 164 serial 28, pp.6-7.

24. Ibid., 129 serial 2, p. 9a; serial 29.

25. Ibid., 24 serial 47.

26. Ibid., 129 serial 2, p.10.

27. Church Committee Book II, Final Report, p. 105.

28. Felt, *The FBI Pyramid,* pp. 105-09

29. O and C file 114 serial 50.

30. Ibid., 129 serial 1, p. 9.

31. Ibid., 114 serial 10.

32. Ibid., 114 serials 11, 13.

33. Church Committee Book II, Final Report, pp. 12-3.

34. O and C file 114 serial 17.

35. Ibid., 129 serial 1, pp. 19-20.

36. Ibid., 129 serial 1, pp.12-3.

37. Ibid., 129 serial 1, p. 13.

38. Ibid., 129 serial 2, pp. 48-9.

39. Ibid., 114 serial 37.

40. Ibid., 164 serial 27, Department press release March 18, 1940.

41. Church Committee Book II, Final Report, pp. 24-5.

HUMOR AND PRACTICAL JOKES
1. *Society of Former Special Agents of the FBI,* (Paducah, KY: Turner Publishing Co., 1996), p. 23.

2. Cartha D. "Deke" DeLoach, *Hoover's FBI: The Inside Story by Hoover's trusted Lieutenant* (Washington: Regnery Publishing, Inc. 1995), p. 182.

3. DeLoach, *Hoover's FBI,* pp. 93-5.

4. Felt, *The FBI Pyramid,* pp. 194, 200.

5. Argosy magazine, July 1975, p.13.

6. FBI Director Clarence M. Kelley, speaking at September 30, 1975, dedication of J. Edgar Hoover FBI Building.

7. Belmont, *As I Recall It,* pp. 115-6.

8. DeLoach, *Hoover's FBI,* p. 352.

9. All information regarding the Hoover-Viner relationship was provided the author by Leonard Viner during numerous interviews and conversations since 1979.

10. Author interview with Leonard Viner, March 7, 1991.

11. Author interviews with Leonard Viner, June 9, 1988, and March 7, 1991.

12. Ibid.

COMPASSION

1. John J. Grady's letter to author January 19, 1987.

2. Congressional Record, Volume 128, No. 115, August 19, 1982, pp. H 6708-09

3. Valeria B. Stewart's letter to author December 2, 1997.

4. Author's conversations with Sam Noisette

5. DeLoach, *Hoover's FBI,* p. 92.

6. FBI release on J. Edgar Hoover issued at dedication of J. Edgar Hoover F.B.I. Building September 30, 1975.

7. W. Donald Stewart's letter to author December 2, 1997.

8. Ben Fulton's letter to author April 15, 1997.

9. Author interview with Art Cammarota, July 19, 1997.

10. Felt, *The FBI Pyramid,* p. 193.

11. Robert J. Lamphere and Tom Schactman, *The FBI-KGB War: A Special Agent's Story,* (New York: Random House, 1986), pp. 225-6.

12. Felt, *The FBI Pyramid,* p. 94.

13. *Ashville Citizen & Times,* July 25, 1981, "Hoover Cared About Civil Liberties," by William H. Lawrence.

COINTELPRO

1. Church Committee Book II, Final Report, p.4.

2. Ibid., p. 7.

3. The briefing paper was introduced as Defendants' Exhibit KJ during the 1981 SWP trial.

4. Bureau file—hereafter referred to as Bufile—62-85205 serial 1100.

5. Bufile 62-85205 serial 1115.

6. Ibid., serial 1100.

7. Memo Sullivan to Belmont, "Disruption of the Communist Party, USA, Internal Security-C," July 17, 1956.

8. Bufile 100-3 serial 164.

9. Church Committee Book III, Final Report, pp. 5-6.

10. Attorney general's press release November 18, 1974, re COINTELPRO, p. 10.

11. Defendants' Exhibit QT and author's testimony at pages 7543 to 7547 of transcript, SWP trial supra.

12. David Martin, "Investigating the FBI." (Washington: Heritage Foundation, Fall 1981), Policy Review Reprint 18, pp.121-2.

13. Guide to Subversive Organizations and Publications, May 14, 1951, prepared and released by the House Committee on Un-American Activities.

14. World Communist Movement Selective Chronology, Vol. II, prepared by the Legislative Reference Service, Library of Congress.

15. *The World Almanac, 1974*, (New York: Newspaper Enterprise Association, Inc., 1973), pp. 855-6, 878.

16. Bufile 100-3 serial 104.

17. Hearings before the U.S. Senate Judiciary Subcommittee to Investigate the Administration of the Internal Security Act and Other Internal Security Laws on "Trotsky Terrorist International," July 24, 1975, (94th Congress, 1st Session), pp. 14-15—Hereafter referred to as Senate Sub committee hearings July 24, 1975.

18. Senate Subcommittee hearings July 24, 1975, p.16.

19. Ibid., pp.25, 30-1.

20. Ibid.. pp. 56, 68-9.

21. Ibid., pp. 43, 57, 66.

22. Appendix to Hearings before the Select Committee on Assassinations of the U.S. House of Representatives (95th Congress 2nd Session), Vol. VI, March 1979, p. 181.

23. Bufile 100-436291 serials 1, 4, 16, 259; Attorney general's press release November 18, 1974, op.cit., p. 10.

24. Don Whitehead, *Attack on Terror: The FBI Against the Ku Klux Klan in Mississippi* (New York: Funk & Wagnalls, 1970), pp. 90-1.

25. Church Committee Book II, Final Report, p. 74.

26. Attorney general's press release November 18, 1974, op. cit., p. 10; Whitehead, *Attack on Terror,* p. 302; Bufile 100-00 serial 1518.

27. Policy Review Reprint 18, op. cit., pp. 123-4.

28. Church Committee Vol. 6, pp. 528-30.

29. Bufile 100-00 serial 1518; Attorney general's press release November 18, 1974, op. cit., p. 10.

30. Bufile, 100-499698 serial 1.

31. Weather Underground Organization (WUO) Report of Chicago FBI office dated August 20, 1976, pp. 16, 19, 21 (obtained through a Freedom of Information Act request).

32. WUO Report of Chicago FBI office op.cit., pp. 176-85.

33. Bufile 100-00 serial 1518; Attorney general's press release November 18, 1974, op.cit., p.10.

34. Judiciary Subcommittee Serial 55, op. cit., p. 1.

35. SWP trial transcript, op. cit., pp. 1182-1201.

36. *The New York Times Index*, March 19, 1974.

37. Judiciary Subcommittee Serial 55, op.cit., p.47.

38. *The Washington Star-News*, November 16, 1974, pp. A-1, A-8; *The Washington Post*, November 19, 1974, pp. A 1, A 4.

39. Church Committee Vol. 6, pp. 282-3.

40. Policy Review Reprint 18, op. cit., pp. 116, 130-2.

41. SWP trial, Brownell testimony, pp. 5153-5.

IN RE: MARTIN LUTHER KING, JR.

1. John Barron, *Operation SOLO: The FBI's Man in the Kremlin* (Washington, D.C.: Regnery Publishing, Inc.,1996) p. 263.

2. O and C file 24 serial 54 pp. 4-5.

3. Ibid., serials 70, 90.

4. Ibid., serial 54, p. 4.

5. Church Committee Book III, Final Report, pp. 97-9.

6. Felt, *The FBI Pyramid*, pp. 120-1.

7. O and C file 24 serial 47.

8. Ibid., serials 44, 46, 48.

9. Church Committee Book III, Final Report, pp. 115-6; O and C file 24 serials 39-40; Bufile 100-106670 Serial 251.

10. William C. Sullivan with Bill Brown, *The Bureau: My Thirty Years in Hoover's FBI*, (New York/ London: W. W. Norton & Company, 1979), p. 135.

11. Felt, *The FBI Pyramid,* pp. 119-20.

12. Church Committee Book III, Final Report, pp. 105-8; *Argosy* magazine, July 1975, p. 17.

13. Church Committee Book III, Final Report, pp. 109-10.

14. Church Committee Vol. 6, pp. 65-6.

15. Church Committee Book III, Final Report, p.106.

16. O and C file 24 serials 29 et seq.; Church Committee Book III, Final Report, p. 120.

17. O and C file 24 serial 112; Felt, *The FBI Pyramid,* pp. 124-5 fn.

18. Felt, *The FBI Pyramid,* pp. 125-6.

19. Congressional Record, Vol. 128, No. 115, op. cit., p. H 6704.

20. O and C file 24 serials 83-4, 86; Church Committee Book III, Final Report, p.181.

21. Associated Press release, *The Orlando Sentinel,* October 12, 1989, p. A-3.

22. Article "King's lover's book reveals pre-assassination tryst," *The Washington Times*, January 26, 1995, p. A6.

23. *The Washington Times* "Commentary" Section F, October 23, 1989, pp. 1, 4.

24. David J. Garrow, "How King Borrowed," *The Washington Post,* November 18, 1990, pp. C 1, 5.

25. Felt, *The FBI Pyramid,* p. 121.

26. Church Committee Book III, Final Report, p.156.

27. Felt, *The FBI Pyramid*, p. 121.

28. O and C file 24 serial 7; Church Committee Book II, Final Report, p. 221 fn 67.

29. *Human Events*, October 29, 1983, pp. 4-5.

30. Church Committee Book II, Final Report. p. 220.

31. Church Committee Book III, Final Report, p. 159.

32. DeLoach, *Hoover's FBI,* p. 212.

33. Johnson, *A Season of Inquiry*, pp. 126-7.

34. Church Committee Book III, Final Report. p.158.

35. *The New York Times,* article "Dr. King Accepts Nobel Peace Prize as

Trustee," December 11, 1964, datelined Oslo, Norway, December 10, 1964.

36. Johnson, *A Season of Inquiry,* p. 127.

37. Church Committee Book III, Final Report, pp. 158-61.

38. Ibid., pp. 82, 142.

39. Garrow's November 18, 1990, article, op.cit.

THE HUSTON PLAN

1. Church Committee, Vol. 2, titled "Huston Plan," dated September 23, 24, 25, 1975, pp. 273-6.

2. Felt, *The FBI Pyramid,* p. 113.

3. Church Committee Vol. 2, pp. 1, 4, 60.

4. Ibid., pp. 3, 16-7, 53, 60, 68-9.

5. Church Committee Vol. 2, p.1.

6. Ibid., pp. 171-88.

7. Ibid., pp. 1-2.

8. Felt, *The FBI Pyramid,* p. 116.

9. Submission of Recorded Presidential Conversations to the Committee on the Judiciary of the House of Representatives by President Richard Nixon, April 30, 1974, pp. 122-4 (hereafter referred to as Nixon tapes).

10. Felt, *The FBI Pyramid,* pp. 147-9, 293, 305.

11. Church Committee Vol. 2, pp. 70-1.

DR. KISSINGER'S ROLE IN WIRETAPPING

1. Hearings before the Senate Foreign Relations Committee, 93rd Congress, 2nd Session, on "Dr. Kissinger's Role in Wiretapping" (Washington, Government Printing Office, No. 37-795) pp. 220, 322-4 (hereafter referred to as Kissinger wiretapping hearings).

2. Church Committee Book III, Final Report, p. 324; Kissinger wiretapping hearings, p. 23.

3. Church Committee Book III, Final Report, p. 325.

4. *The Washington Post,* October 18, 1993, p. A 18.

5. Kissinger wiretapping hearings, p. 247.

6. Ibid., pp. 23, 116, 119, 165.

7. Ibid., p. 117.

8. Author interview with Bernard A. Wells, Jr., July 31, 1997.

9. Kissinger wiretapping hearings, pp. 117-8, Sullivan's letter dated July 4, 1974.

10. Ibid., pp. V, VII, 111.

11. Ibid., pp. 24-6, 30.

12. Ibid., pp. 27-8.

13. Ibid., p. 28.

14. Ibid., p. 28-9.

15. Ibid., pp. 29, 34, 63, 95.

16. Church Committee Book III, Final Report, p. 345; Kissinger wiretapping hearings, p. 103.

17. John Ehrlichman, *Witness to Power* (New York: Pocket Books, 1982), pp. 153, 156.

18. Nixon tapes, pp. 95-8, 101.

19. Kissinger wiretapping hearings, pp.40, 87; *The Washington Post,* November 10, 1977, p. C 8; *Argosy* magazine, July 1975, p. 17.

20. Felt, *The FBI Pyramid,* p. 141.

21. Kissinger wiretapping hearings, pp. 42, 75.

22. Felt, *The FBI Pyramid,* p.141.

23. Kissinger wiretapping hearings, pp. 73, 112, 302-3; *The Washington Post,* article "Kissinger vs. Hoover On Wiretap Requests," June 16, 1974.

24. Kissinger wirtapping hearings, pp. 35, 58; *The Washington Post,* November 13, 1992, p. A 4.

25. Charles W. Colson, *Born Again* (Lincoln, Virginia: Chosen Books, 1976), p. 44.

THE PENTAGON PAPERS CASE

1. Neil Sheehan, Hedrick Smith, E. W. Kenworthy, and Fox Butterfield, *The Pentagon Papers* (New York: Bantam Books, Inc., 1971), p. ix.

2. *Encyclopaedia Britannica,* Vol. 18, pp. 994, 997; Neil Sheehan, et al., *The Pentagon Papers,* pp. ix, 3.

3. *The World Almanac and Book of Facts, 1974* (New York: Newspaper Enterprise Association, 1973) p. 1005.

4. Colson, *Born Again,* pp. 37-9.

5. Robert Cushman, *Cases in Constitutional Law, 7th Edition* (Englewood Cliffs, NJ: Prentice Hall, Inc., 1989), p. 410.

6. Colson, *Born Again,* pp. 57-8.

7. Neil Sheehan, et al., *The Pentagon Papers*, p. x.

8. Harrison E. Salisbury, *Without Fear or Favor* (New York: Times Books, 1980), p.200.

9. Colson, *Born Again*, pp. 57-9; DeLoach, *Hoover's FBI*, pp. 271-2.

10. Ehrlichman, *Witness to Power*, p. 234.

11. Colson, *Born Again*, p.59.

12. Colson, *Born Again*, p. 39; Ehrlichman, *Witness to Power*, pp. 144, 272-4; Salisbury, *Without Fear or Favor*, p. 224.

13. Kissinger wiretapping hearings, p. 37; Colson, *Born Again*, pp. 231-2, 249.

14. Colson, *Born Again*, p. 59.

15. Church Committee Book III, Final Report. pp. 305-6.

16. Interview of author December 18, 1974, by attorneys of Watergate Special Prosecutor's Office.

17. Ehrlichman, *Witness to Power*, p. 365; Kissinger wiretapping hearings, p. 174; *The World Almanac & Book of Facts, 1974*, p. 39.

18. Colson, *Born Again*, pp. 60-1.

19. Ibid., pp. 230-1.

20. Kissinger wiretapping hearings, pp. 32, 173-4.

21. Ehrlichman, *Witness to Power*, p. 365; *The World Almanac & Book of Facts, 1974*, p. 1004.

22. *The World Almanac & Book of Facts, 1974*, p. 40.

23. Ehrlichman, *Witness to Power*, p. 367.

24. Ehrlichman, *Witness to Power*, pp. 261, 364, 366-7; *Encyclopaedia Britannica, 1994 Book of the Year*, p. 62.

25. *Facts on File for 1974*, (New York: Facts on File: 1974), p.194.

26. Colson, *Born Again*, pp. 192, 226-7, 243-4; *Facts on File for 1974*, p. 43.

27. *Facts on File for 1974*, p.618.

28. Ehrlichman *Witness to Power*, p. 371.

29. *The World Almanac & Book of Facts, 1994*, pp. 1012-3.

30. *The World Almanac & Book of Facts, 1974*, p. 40; Ehrlichman, *Witness to Power*, pp. 342-3.

31. *The World Almanac & Book of Facts, 1974*, p. 41.

32. *The Watergate Hearings Break-in and Cover-up* as edited by the staff of *The New YorkTimes* (New York: Bantam Books, Inc.: 1973), p. 5.

33. Colson, *Born Again*, pp. 59-60.

34. Felt, *The FBI Pyramid*, p. 131.

35. Ibid., p. 139.

36 Ehrlichman, *Witness to Power*, p. 143.

37. DeLoach, *Hoover's FBI*, p. 411.

38. Ehrlichman, *Witness to Power*, p. 144-6.

THE SLIDE DOWN THE TOTEM POLE
1. Felt, *The FBI Pyramid*, p. 130.

2. Church Committee Book II, Final Report, p. 125, footnote 621.

3. Brochure of the History Book Club advertising Sullivan's book, Winter 1979.

4. Felt, *The FBI Pyramid*, p. 141.

5. *The Washington Post*, November 10, 1977, p. C 8.

6. *The Washington Star* article "Aide Admits FBI Break-in OK Possible," May 18, 1977.

7. *The Washington Post* Bookworld, Anthony Marro's review of Sullivan's "My Thirty Years in Hoover's FBI," September 30, 1979.

8. *The Washington Post*, November 10, 1977, p. C 8.

9. Ibid.

10. *The Washington Star-News*, November 26, 1974, p. A-2.

11. *Law Enforcement News,* October 22, 1979, p. 11.

12. Author interview July 17, 1997, with person requesting confidentiality.

13. Felt, *The FBI Pyramid*, p. 142.

14. Ibid., p. 106.

15. Ibid., p. 142.

HOOVER AND THE KENNEDYS
1. O and C files 149 serial iii; 96 serial 16.

2. O and C file 14 serial 18.

3. Ibid., serial 2.

4. Ibid., serial 21.

5. Ibid., serials 8, 18, 31, 33, 41, 49, 59.

6. Ibid., serial 62.

7. Ibid., serial 64.

8. Ibid., serial 73.

9. Ibid., serials 88-9.

10. Ibid., serials 87, 94-6.

11. O and C file 96 serial 16.

12. Ibid.

13. O and C file 13 serial 140.

14. Ibid., serial 142.

15. Ibid., serials 143-4.

16. Ibid., serial 147.

17. *New York Post*, August 4, 1960, p. 24; O and C file 13 serial 47.

18. O and C file 13 serial 209.

19. UPI release 109, November 10, 1960; O and C file 13 serials 32, 255, 309, 318, 321-1; Bufile 94-37374 serial 122.

20. O and C file 13 serials 204, 210, 218, 221, 223.

21. Ibid., serial 391.

22. Ibid., serial 409.

23. Ibid., serials 434, 436.

24. O and C file 96 serial 5; United States Library of Congress Catalog Card No. 56-10936 (1957).

25. O and C file 96 serial 9.

26. O and C file 13 serial 299; 96 serials 4, 16.

27. O and C file 14 serial 49.

28. Mary McGrory, *The Washington Post*, December 7, 1997.

29. O and C file 13 serial 231.

30. Ibid., serials 359, 364-5.

31. *The Washington Post*, December 16, 1977, p. A 3.

32. O and C file 96 serial 3.

33. *Encyclopaedia Britannica*, Vol 3, p. 281.

34. O and C file 96 serial 3.

35. O and C file 13 serial 361.

36. O and C file 96 serial 16.

37. *New York Herald Tribune*, November 21, 1960, p.22; O and C file 13 serial 17.

38. *Los Angeles Examiner*, Vincent X. Flaherty column, March 3, 1961; O and C. file 14 serial 76.

39. DeLoach, *Hoover's FBI*, p. 59.

40. Felt, *The FBI Pyramid*, p. 62.

41. Anthony Summers, *Official and Confidential: The Secret Life of J. Edgar Hoover*, (New York: G. P. Putnam's Sons, 1993), p. 289.

42. O and C file 129 serial 1, p. 15.

43. Ibid., p. 21.

44. O and C file 129 serials 21, 25.

45. O and C file 114 serial 19.

46. O and C files 129 serial 25; 114 serials 31-3.

47. Felt, *The FBI Pyramid*, pp. 50-1.

48. O and C file 129 serial 1, p. 28.

49. O and C files 129 serial 1, pp. 28-9; 114 serial 47.

50. O and C file 129 serial 1, p. 32.

51. Ibid., p. 33.

52. Ibid., pp. 25-7.

THOSE ALLEGATIONS OF PERVERSION

1. Summers, *Official and Confidential*, pp. 390-1.

2. *The Washington Post* "Parade" magazine, September 10, 1995, p. 2; one-hour documentary "Jack Anderson: The Fall of J. Edgar Hoover," September 15, 1995, on A&E Network.

3. *National Review*, December 2, 1991, p. 47.

4. *Congressional Record*, March 18, 1993.

5. Summers, *Official and Confidential*, p. 22.

6. *Encyclopaedia Britannica*, Vol. 16, p. 968.

7. Summers, *Official and Confidential*, p. 14.

8. Larry King Live, CNN Cable TV presentation, February 12, 1993.

9. *The Washington Post,* Bookworld, February 21, 1993.

10. *Washington City Paper*, March 26-April 1, 1993, p. 40.

11. *The New York Times*, February 15, 1993, p. C 16.

12. *The Washington Times*, February 9, 1993, p. E 4.

13. Summers, *Official and Confidential*, pp. 83, 241, 331.

14. Ibid., p. 95.

15. Ibid., pp. 82-3.

16. Ibid., pp. 241-2.

17. Ibid., p. 391.

18. Ibid., pp. 94, 434-7.

19. Ibid.

20. Ibid., pp. 85-6.

21. Ibid., pp. 75, 80-1, 83-4, 118, 241-2.

22. Peter Maas, "Setting the Record Straight, *Esquire*, May, 1993, p. 57.

23. Summers, *Official and Confidential,* pp. 244-5.

24. *Washington Inquirer*, April 2, 1993, p. 5.

25. Summers, *Official and Confidential,* pp. 253-7.

26. *The Washington Times*, March 4, 1993, p. G 3.

27. Ibid., July 17, 1993, p. C 3.

28. *Esquire*, May 1993, p. 58.

29. DeLoach, *Hoover's FBI*, pp. 63, 65, 88.

30. Felt, *The FBI Pyramid*, p. 201.

31. DeLoach, *Hoover's FBI*, p. 64.

32. Maas, *Esquire*, May 1993, p. 56.

HOOVER AND ORGANIZED CRIME

1. Whitehead, *The FBI Story*, pp. 83-4, 90-1.

2. Ibid., p. 103.

3. Breuer, *J. Edgar Hoover and His G-Men*, pp. 156-63, 172-7.

4. Ibid., p. 157.

5. Ibid., p. 158.

6. Ibid., pp. 159.

7. Ibid., pp.163, 168, 173.

8. Ibid., p.172.

9. Ibid., pp. 173-4

10. Ibid., pp. 176-7

11. Summers, *Official and Confidential*, pp. 226-7.

12. Whitehead, *The FBI Story,* pp. 102, 110; Larry Heim's letter to the editor of *The Oregonian*, Portland, OR, July 11, 1989.

13. Summers, *Official and Confidential*, p. 227.

14. DeLoach, *Hoover's FBI*, pp. 303-5.

15. Summers, *Official and Confidential*, p. 445.

16. DeLoach, *Hoover's FBI*, pp. 297-8, 303-6.

17. Maas, *Esquire*, May 1993, p. 57.

18. Summers, *Official and Confidential*, p. 242.

19. Maas, *Esquire*, May 1993, p. 57.

20. DeLoach, *Hoover's FBI*, pp. 300-1.

21. Summers, *Official and Confidential*, p. 446.

22. Ibid., pp. 225, 241-2.

23. FBI Annual Report for fiscal year 1971.

24. Summers, *Official and Confidential*, p. 309.

25. From the Encyclopaedia Britannica, Micropaedia, Vol. IX, P. 858: The Teapot Dome scandal, also known as the Oil Reserves, or Elk Hills, scandal, concerned a secret lease made on April 7, 1922, by Secretary of the Interior Albert B. Falls granting Harry F. Sinclair of the Mammoth Oil Company exclusive rights to the Teapot Dome (WY) reserves. Fall received more than $200,000 from a source associaated with Sinclair. He also requested a $100,000 "loan" from Edward L. Doheny of Pan American Petroleum Company, and secretly leased portions of Elk Hill and Buena Vista Hills oil reserves in California to Doheny. The leases were declared fraudulent by the Supreme Court. Fall was convicted of accepting a bribe in the Elk Hills negotiations and was imprisoned. Doheny and Sinclair were acquitted of any crime.

THE OFFICIAL AND CONFIDENTIAL FILES

1. George E. Allen, *J. Edgar Hoover Off-Duty*, undated pamphlet received November 3, 1997 from Ambassador James E. Nolan.

2. Felt, *The FBI Pyramid*, pp. 185-8.

3. Ibid., pp. 229-30.

4. Summers, *Official and Confidential*, pp. 12, 107, 111, 423, 428.

5. Summers, *Official and Confidential,* pp. 207-8; Larry King Live TV show, CNN cable network, February 12, 1993.

6. Summers, *Official and Confidential*, pp. 289-90.

7. Ibid., p. 285.

8. Ibid., pp. 269-70.

9. Ibid., pp. 289-90.

10. DeLoach, *Hoover's FBI*, pp. 29-30.

11. Curt Gentry, *J. Edgar Hoover: The Man and the Secrets* (New York, London: W.W. Norton & Company, 1991) p. 689, fn.

12. Author Interview with Leonard Viner, March 7, 1991.

13. Summers, *Official and Confidential*, p. 80.

THE ENIGMATIC DIRECTOR

1. *Congressional Record*, Vol. 128, No. 115, op. cit., pp. H6707-8.

2. Felt, *The FBI Pyramid*, p. 200.

3. Valeria B. Stewart's letter to author December 2, 1997.

4. Felt, *The FBI Pyramid*, p. 200.

5. Summers, *Official and Confidential*, pp. 31-2.

6. Ibid., pp. 88-91.

7. Author interview with Art Cammarota, June 24, 1997.

8. Valeria B. Stewart's letter to author December 2, 1997.

9. DeLoach, *Hoover's FBI*, pp. 320, 322, 324, 330-1, 334-5, 338, 340, 343, 345-6, 348-9.

10. Valeria B. Stewart's letter to author December 2, 1997.

11. DeLoach, *Hoover's FBI*, pp. 338-40.

12. Valeria B. Stewart's letter to author December 2, 1997.

13. Nixon tapes, pp. 87-8.

14. Valeria B. Stewart's letter to author December 2, 1997.

15. Allen, *J. Edgar Hoover Off-Duty*, pamphlet received November 3, 1997.

16. Author interview with Valeria Stewart January 9, 1998.

17. Allen, *J. Edgar Hoover Off-Duty*, pamphlet received November 3, 1997.

18. Senate Document No. 93-68, *Memorial Tributes to J. Edgar Hoover in the Congress of the United States and Various Articles and Editorials Relating to His Life and Work, 93rd Congress, 2nd Session* (Washington: U. S. Government Printing Office, 1974), p. 230.

19. Senate Document No. 93-68 op.cit., p.230.

20. FBI release on J. Edgar Hoover, issued at dedication of J. Edgar Hoover F.B.I. Building September 30, 1975.

21. Ibid.

22. Miranda v Arizona (1966), 384 US 436, 483, 486.

23. Church Committee Volume 2, p. 69.

24. FBI release on J. Edgar Hoover, September 30, 1975.

25. J. Edgar Hoover, *Persons in Hiding* (Boston: Little, Brown and Co., 1938).

26. Senate Document No. 93-68 op. cit., p. 175.

27. *The Christian Science Monitor*, July 3, 1965, p. 2.

28. Author interview with Art Cammarota, June 24, 1997.

29. Author interview with Leonard Viner, June 9, 1988; Felt, *The FBI Pyramid*, p. 195.

30. Senate Document No. 93-68, op. cit., p. XVIII.

THE LENGTHENED SHADOW OF A MAN
1. Senate Document No. 93-68, op. cit., pp. 198-200.

2. Ibid., p. 32.

3. Ibid., pp. XVII-XVIII.

4. Ibid., pp. XXIV-XXVI.

INDEX

Editor's Note: This index does not include the Notes and Sources.

(From the original back cover flap)

His intelligence work has been acknowledged by awards from British and Canadian Intelligence services, CIA, the Emperor of Japan, and the Masonic Lodge of which FBI Director J. Edgar Hoover had been a life-long member. In September, 1992, the Board of Directors of the National Intelligence and Counterintelligence Association extended to him an Honorary Life Membership. He also has life membership with the National Intelligence Study Center as well as the Association of Former Intelligence Officers. Mr. Wannall formerly served as AFIO's Chairman and President. He has also served on the boards of other respected organizations including America's Future, Inc.; The Maulden Institute; The Hale Institute; The American Sentinel; and the Harold P. Ransburg Foundation.

Since retirement, Mr. Wannall has continued as an outspoken advocate for a strong and responsible national intelligence establishment before Congressional committees, and civic and educational groups in 23 States. He is a frequent guest on radio and television shows. His appearances have included NBC national evening news, ABC Nightline and Entertainment Tonight, CBS Nightwatch, Cable News Network and the History Channel.

Also available from
Turner Publishing Company

Society of Former Special
Agents of the FBI, Second Edition

FBI Alumni, Inc.

FBI National Academy

Printed in the USA
CPSIA information can be obtained
at www.ICGtesting.com
JSHW022321140824
68134JS00019B/1215

9 781681 623306